WRITTEN BY SALIM–JAVED

Diptakirti Chaudhuri is a salesman by day and writer by night. This is his fourth book and the third on Hindi cinema. He lives in Bangalore with his wife, a son and a daughter.

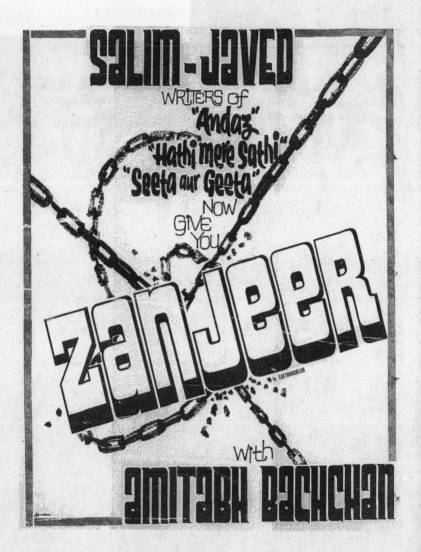

A historic ad, probably the first one to exclusively promote the writers of a film, that announced the emergence of Salim–Javed.

WRITTEN BY SALIM-JAVED

THE STORY OF HINDI CINEMA'S GREATEST SCREENWRITERS

DIPTAKIRTI CHAUDHURI

PENGUIN BOOKS

Na mooh chhupake jiye hum, na sar jhukake jiye
Sitamgaro ki nazar se nazar milake jiye
Ab ek raat agar kam jiye toh hairat kyon
Ki jab talak jiye mashaale jalake jiye . . .

Sahir Ludhianvi

'*Kitnay aadmi thay?*'
'*Sardar, do aadmi thay.*'

From *Sholay*

Contents

PART V: IMPACT AND LEGACY

Introduction:
How My Salim–Javed Story Started
a.k.a. Main Majboor Tha

This story began one evening in the early 1980s.

This was a time when my Hindi film experiences were largely restricted to the Sunday evening fare doled out by Doordarshan. I was just shy of ten years and my taste in movies was dictated by a man called Amitabh Bachchan, and in his absence, I had learned to spot the word 'Action' (or 'Thrills') in the credits. If that existed, then one could look forward to some fisticuffs at the end of three hours of songs and tears—a big incentive for a young boy.

That evening, my mother (the certified movie buff in the family) and I took our positions in front of our black-and-white television set for our weekly Hindi movie fix. My father seldom watched the Sunday film, often preferring to go for a walk instead, but that day he was in the room as well. To my delight, the film—*Majboor*—starred Amitabh Bachchan, which sealed the deal for me. My father, on the other hand, shuffled in his seat and wondered aloud if the film would be worth it. A minute or two into the credits, he got excited and exclaimed, '*Arre*

Salim–Javed, *taholey toh dekhtei hobey!*' ('A Salim–Javed film, have to watch it then!') Apparently, these two gentlemen— Salim–Javed, as I learned then, was not one person, but a team of two—had written the story of the film and also the lines my hero would say.

After the film ended, I thought about this and was quite intrigued that there could be other highlights in a film apart from the actors and the fight director. My father remembered a film called *Deewaar*, which was written by Salim–Javed, and he said it was one of the best that he had watched. I asked him if it had fights and my father mentioned there was just one. I made a mental note to watch *Deewaar* one day but with just one fight, it was not a top priority.

Over the next couple of years, I started noticing this name— Salim–Javed—and was quite delighted to find that they had written many of my favourite films. *Seeta Aur Geeta* was their doing, as was *Yaadon Ki Baaraat*. *Don* had their name too, as did *Haathi Mere Saathi*. And wonder of wonders, my all-time favourite—*Sholay*—was also written by them. Long before I understood what film writing is all about or the difference between the screenplay and the story, I had added Salim–Javed to the list of names to watch out for in a film's credits.

As I read more about writing for the screen, I correlated much of that to the films of Salim–Javed. Satyajit Ray, film writer par excellence, talked about the importance of detailing events, locations and characters in a script. He talked about real dialogues. He talked about backstories of characters, even if they were not shown in the film. Salim–Javed followed many of those principles, without being conscious of them. Watching Salim–Javed's classic films—*Deewaar, Trishul, Kaala Patthar, Shakti*—when I grew older, I realized how good they really were.

When I met Salim sahib for an interview, he said, 'One hit film, two hit films, even three hit films in a row can be a fluke. But ten or eleven hits[1] in a row cannot be a fluke. If a stuntman leaps off a seven-storeyed building and lands on his feet, people would call it a miracle. Second time can also be called a miracle. But if he keeps doing it again and again, you'll have to admit he has a technique.'

But almost in the same breath, he also said that as writers they had no conscious technique. They were not trying to make any social commentary with *Deewaar* and they were not inspired so much by Akira Kurosawa as by Sergio Leone.

That gave me the idea of writing their story in the signature Salim–Javed style—a lot of interesting events that built to a crescendo, a bit of context to make sense, but not much of analysis.

I believe they brought a certain swagger to the profession of writing, long—probably still—considered to be a back-room job. There were more prolific writers, writers who had given a greater number of hits. But none of them had succeeded in changing the dynamics of an industry, notorious for being set in its ways. None of them raised their collars and advertised their success the way Salim–Javed did. They struck me as two extremely humble men personally, who were extremely proud professionally.

Strangely, there aren't too many books on Hindi film writing. Books on Javed Akhtar and Gulzar largely focus on their careers as lyricists (and in Gulzar's case, as a director). Actors, actresses, directors, music directors, lyricists have all got excellent biographies but not the people without whom the industry would have been just a blank sheet of paper.

---

[1] Their first 'low-profile' film was their ninth—*Aakhri Daao*—which released a week before *Sholay*, and their first flop was their eleventh film, *Immaan Dharam*.

Here, then, is the story of two heroes.

A story of a friendship that became a bitter rivalry and finally mellowed down to a cordial relationship. And of the philosophy with which they approached their work. In the process Salim Khan and Javed Akhtar ended up creating two film families that are doing many of the things that they were not able to do themselves.

In a way, my father—who was not a Bollywood fan at all—started this story, and also laid down the benchmark of a good film dialogue. He remembered only one, and when a non-fan remembers something, it is likely to be bloody good. For as long as he lived, any discussion on film dialogues with him began and ended with just one line: '*Main aaj bhi phenke hue paise nahin uthata . . .*'[i]

It is not for nothing *Deewaar* is called the Perfect Hindi Film Screenplay.

Prologue:
The Tale of Two *Zanjeer*s

'Whether it's *Zanjeer, Sholay* or *Seeta Aur Geeta,* the fact that they keep coming back to old scripts proves there's a scarcity of writing. So I am of the opinion that the original writers should be monetarily compensated'—Salim Khan

'Salim sahib's and my contract was with Prakash Mehra Productions (PMP) for our script to be made only in Hindi. The south Indian rights for *Zanjeer* were with us . . . The superhit Hindi films that are made into Telugu get up to Rs 3 crore. So we feel we also deserve a compensation of Rs 3 crore for the Zanjeer remake rights which we hold and have papers to prove it'—Javed Akhtar

When the remake of *Zanjeer* was chosen as Telugu superstar Ram Charan Teja's Hindi film debut, there was considerable curiosity tempered with a fair bit of dismay. Curiosity because this was the film from which Amitabh Bachchan's ascendance to superstardom began. And dismay because every remake in Hindi cinema till now had been very disappointing.

Apart from Ram Charan, the film also marked the debut of Prakash Mehra's son Amit as producer. He 'bought' the rights to the remake *Zanjeer* from his brothers for Rs 4 crore.

When the film was announced in 2012, Salim–Javed contacted Amit Mehra about the monetary compensation they were entitled to as writers of the original. They informed him that the rights resided with them and were not for his family to sell. Initially, they wanted an amicable, out-of-court settlement, and by all reports their demand was not high. Apparently, Amit Mehra tried the schmoozing for which 'old-school' Bollywood was famous. He sweet-talked Javed Akhtar, addressing him as 'uncle' and went to his home with dry fruits. (We are not sure if peanuts were part of his gift!) After this, he chose to ignore their calls and sent them a legal letter stating the remake rights were with him.

Salim–Javed were extremely hurt, and they responded by complaining to the Film Writers' Association (FWA) with documents supporting their claim of rights. This was when they firmed their demand of Rs 3 crore for the Telugu remake rights of *Zanjeer* and added another Rs 3 crore for the Hindi remake rights as well. They argued that the original script was sold to Prakash Mehra Productions for a film starring Amitabh Bachchan, Jaya Bhaduri and Pran. Since the cast had changed, the film was obviously a different one using out of the same script, and the writers ought to be paid for that too. At this point, they refused an out-of-court settlement (which the producers of the new *Zanjeer* offered) because they wanted to set a precedent with the case.

The disputes settlement committee of the Federation of Western India Cine Employees (FWICE) examined the documents presented by both parties and observed that Salim–Javed were indeed the rightful owners of the script, but since the committee did not have the authority to direct a legal settlement, the case went to the courts.

Salim–Javed filed to stay the film's release until they were paid for the rights.

After hearing the arguments, the Bombay High Court, however, did not stay the release on the grounds that Salim–Javed delayed issuing the legal notice and that their actual objective was not to bring a stay, but to be adequately compensated for their work. While reserving judgement on the actual ownership of the rights, the court directed the two parties to arrive at an amicable out-of-court settlement. The lawyers for both the parties requested the matter to be taken in chamber, so the settlement amount would not be divulged to the public.

Insiders believe that the amount was reasonably close to what the duo had asked for originally. Even taking a conservative view, one can safely say that it made Salim–Javed the highest paid writers of Bollywood in 2013 as well.

For the two writers, this is typical of their relationship post their split. While they have been cordial when referring to each other, they have remained distant and are almost never seen together at public events. But whenever their rights have been threatened, they have put up a united front.

This also completes a circle that started in the late 1960s, when the duo first came together, writing brilliant scripts and asking for commensurate compensation. For them, credit was as important as—if not more than—the money. Their desire to be known as the writers of a film is probably best described by a story connected to the original *Zanjeer*.

After a lot of back-and-forth between heroes and producers, *Zanjeer* was eventually sold to Prakash Mehra for Rs 55,000. The sale was on the condition that Salim–Javed would be duly credited in all publicity material of the film. This was of paramount importance to the two, because they had already worked on scripts for three hit films before this and had received little or no credit for them.

As the release date neared, Salim–Javed eagerly waited to see their names on a billboard for the first time but when the posters went up they were heartbroken. Prakash Mehra—caught up in the rigmarole of his first production—had forgotten all about his promise.

What happened after this is indicative of the confidence and chutzpah that differentiated Salim–Javed from their peers. Sometimes, this was as important as their talent in establishing them as the only superstar writers of the Hindi film industry.

When they reminded Prakash Mehra of the deal, he was apologetic but helpless. The posters were already up and there was nothing he could do at that stage. He promised to rectify the oversight in the subsequent rounds of postering. With anybody else, the matter would have ended here but these two writers were on a different kind of mission.

Salim–Javed hired a poster painter. They gave him a stencil that said 'Written by Salim–Javed', and instructed him to paint it on all the posters of *Zanjeer* that he could find. The painter may have been drunk or in a hurry to complete this mammoth task; what he ended up doing was print the line pretty much anywhere on the poster instead of at the bottom, where credits usually appeared. On the morning of the release, Bombay woke up to find all posters of *Zanjeer*—from Juhu to Opera House—stamped with the name 'Salim–Javed'. Be it Amitabh's nose, Pran's beard, or Jaya's face, Salim–Javed was, quite literally, unmissable on the posters of *Zanjeer*.

Both Salim Khan and Javed Akhtar appear a little embarrassed when they recount this incident now. Embarrassed, but not apologetic. Their logic and raison d'être for being here was very clear, and it was not to be anonymous back-room boys. Their work did not end with writing a story. They recommended actors, negotiated distribution deals, participated in the publicity, and even advertised themselves. They had come for the money *and* the fame. And if they did not get it, they were willing to fight for it.

What happened with the poster of the original *Zanjeer* repeated with the contract of the new one. The producers—two generations of them—had hoped to get away from honouring their commitments by sweet-talking the writers. After all, writers were creative types who could be cajoled with some persuasion.

But Salim Khan and Javed Akhtar were a different breed altogether. Their writing talent was matched by their business acumen, their showmanship and their demand for fair credit.

Many things have changed in the forty years since they got together—and then went their separate way—but their belief that content is king is not among them.

This is their story.

Part I:

FLASHBACK

Salim Khan:
A Man on a Filmi Mission

'I had the art of conception but not the art of projection'
—Salim Khan

One of Salim Khan's abiding memories is from when he was four or five years old and had stolen a key-wound motorcycle from a toy cart. When he came home with it and his mother found out, she was livid and made him go back to the cart-owner to return the toy and apologize. When he did so, all his friends laughed. Many decades later, Salim Khan says he still hasn't forgotten the cackle of their laughter. Nor has he forgotten the lessons an upright mother can impart on a child. This theme of honesty above all else would return to many of the films he wrote.

Born on 24 November 1935 in Indore, Salim Khan was the son of a police officer—fifth in a line of Pathans who had migrated from Afghanistan in search of a good education and a better life for their children. His great-great-grandfather Anwar Khan joined the British cavalry and was posted in the Central Provinces (present-day Madhya Pradesh). The family put a premium on education and culture, which led to most of its members joining government service. Salim Khan's father—Abdul Rashid Khan—joined the police force and rose to become the DIG of Indore, the highest position allowed to Indians in British India.

As member of a well-to-do family, Salim's life was quite comfortable until he lost his mother at the age of nine.

She was suffering from tuberculosis, a dreaded disease during that time, and Salim was not allowed to go near her for the last four years of her life. She was in isolation at home and had to go away for long periods to Bhowali, a sanatorium for TB patients. He recalls one particularly traumatic episode, 'One day, she saw me playing and asked the maid who I was because she couldn't recognize me after staying away for so long. When the maid told her that I was her youngest son, Gullu, she called me but did not let me come near her. She made me stand at a distance from her and watched me for quite some time. When I think about this now, I always think how traumatic it must have been for her to not be able to touch her own son. And even now, tears well up in my eyes.'

After his mother's death, Salim grew closer to his father, but he too passed away five years later. 'I was only fourteen,' recalls Salim. 'He passed away in January and I took my matriculation examination in March. As a child, I had a very good life. I had a car, a tonga to ferry me around, and all material comfort but I never got the love of parents.'

He had the idyllic upbringing typical of a small town, growing up with a large group of friends and an extended family. His favourite pastimes were sports and reading. And movies.

He discovered the magic of movies fairly early in his life, even though movie watching wasn't as common or easy as it is now. There were just three cinema halls in Indore that used to show

English films (and another one in the nearby town of Mau), all of which he patronized. A regular at the Saturday matinee shows, his staple fare was, not surprisingly, the action—more specifically, sword-fighting—films made famous by Nadia. He remembers *Hunterwali*, and the several clones it spawned, as fondly as he does Bhagwan Dada, the charismatic comic star. This habit of watching movies carried on well into his teens and even after he left Indore. One of the movies he remembers watching as a teenager was *Garden of Evil*—a Western where two protagonists draw cards to decide who will stay to hold back the advancing Indians.

Blessed with a good memory, he still remembers many details from his childhood, even the name of the barber who used to come home to give his father, him, and all his cousins haircuts at a bulk rate—Hariram Naii.

Salim's father—having been a police officer all over Madhya Pradesh—had extensive experience in handling dacoits of the region and had compelling stories to tell. Many of the more interesting ones stuck. There was a particularly cruel story about a legendary dacoit who cut off the ears and noses of all the policemen he caught. His name was Gabbar Singh.

Salim studied at Indore's St Raphael's School and then at Holkar College. He was quite the 'jock' in college with a 1928 model Jaguar and a Triumph motorcycle that he rode around town. He also played cricket. As the star batsman of the college team, he was extremely popular and his skills were good enough for the college to request him to enrol for an MA in economics in order to keep playing. He practised hard but when he realized he was not able to progress beyond a certain level he got bored of the stagnation.

He tried several other things too. His penchant for war movies led to a fascination for flying and he started training to become a pilot. He even logged the hours required to get a commercial flying license but got bored of that too. Commercial flying is bound by strict rules and regulations, with no scope for showmanship. His dreams of swooping down and zooming back up over a girl's house weren't going to materialize ever, he realized.

But a culture of reading and learning at home ensured that adrenalin-charged activities weren't the only things that interested him. His father insisted that he read books and newspapers regularly, and subscribed to the *Statesman* newspaper from Calcutta (which took three days to arrive).

Salim Khan always had an air of flamboyance about him and a flair for words. In college, he became the 'official' letter writer for all the lover boys in his class, letters that were handed over surreptitiously on the way to college or in a cinema queue. He's quite proud of his letters and says that when he left for Bombay, the quality of his friends' letters dropped so much that their girlfriends went ahead and married other people. '*Sab ke sab Devdas ho gaye*,' he laughs. Incidentally, two of his close friends were called Jai Singh Rao Kalevar and Virender Singh Bias (names which he would soon immortalize).

He also had a doomed love affair when he was in college. 'Boys and girls used to fall in love in college, but the girl's family would marry them off to older boys, who were already working and somewhat settled in life. The same thing happened to me,' he says with detachment.

His good looks and the gift of the gab often led to friendly banter about him being 'hero material'. That banter turned out to be prophetic for he got an offer from Ramesh Saigal—maker of hits like *Samadhi* and *Shaheed*—to act in films, but he turned it down.

The Barjatyas—who would eventually provide a brilliant launch vehicle for Salman Khan—were the ones responsible for Salim Khan's foray into cinema. It was at the wedding of Tarachand Barjatya's son that film director K. Amarnath spotted him and offered him an acting job in Bombay. He offered him Rs 1000 to move to Bombay and a salary while working in his films. The film industry was not a respectable profession then but Salim Khan was a big movie buff and fast getting bored with his life in Indore. He was in the second year of his MA course and had had enough of imitating stars to entertain his friends. When this opportunity presented himself, he jumped at it. '*Dilip Kumar ki dukan band karwa denge . . .*' he told everyone with his customary confidence.

When he was about to leave, his elder brother painted a doomsday picture by saying that Salim would either return very soon or would keep asking for money. Salim Khan vowed that he would do neither.

One of his first films was K. Amarnath's *Baraat* (1960), for which he was hired at a salary of Rs 400 per month. Soon, he got into the Bombay grind of acting in not-so-significant roles in different kinds of films and soliciting work for more of the same.

Probably his most well-noticed role (in hindsight) was the one he played in Vijay Anand's *Teesri Manzil* (a tightly woven murder mystery written and produced by Nasir Husain). He had a role slightly bigger than the hero's friend in the film where he is co-opted by Shammi Kapoor to impersonate him as Rocky the drummer. His entry scene in the film got a very good build-up and his dashing looks and impressive physique meant he could pass off as a hero. Almost.

He played a bit part in yet another Shammi Kapoor starrer, *Professor*, but his bread-and-butter roles seemed to be the swashbuckling, sword-fighting, costume dramas that he had loved during his childhood. Except, audience tastes had changed since and these films were now categorized as B-grade fare. *Kabli Khan* (starring Ajit in the title role), *Darasingh* (starring, well, Dara Singh in the title role), *Raaka* (also starring Dara Singh), *Chhaila Babu* (starring Bhagwan Dada) were some of the quickly shot, quickly forgotten films he acted in. He remembers acting in about twenty-five films though many of them were never released.

He spent about eight years in Bombay struggling to become a hero. By the end of it, conventional employment options were closed for him because he was too old to be eligible for competitive exams for the police, administrative or banking services. However, he did not want to go back to Indore because—thanks to his grand pronouncements before leaving—he was sure he would become the laughing stock of the small town.

A little after he came to Bombay, he met Sushila Charak, a Dogra Rajput girl, who, along with her family, happened to stay in Mahim, the same neighbourhood as Salim. Quite well known in the locality for his good looks and wit, he was often seen holding court at street corners. He caught Sushila's eye then but the first time he spoke to her was when they bumped into each other near Churchgate station and she directed him to an address he was looking for. Their courtship started soon after this meeting and continued for nearly five years during which she refused several marriage alliances brought by her family. Eventually, they got married in 1964, and she changed her name to Salma. Her father, Baldev Singh Charak, was livid with her for marrying a Muslim and that too a film actor, a profession considered quite taboo among the middle classes at the time. About a year after their marriage, Salma and Salim had their first child in December 1965—a son, whom they named Abdul Rashid Salim Salman Khan. Her family cut off all relations with her and maintained no contact till after their third son, Sohail, was born and Salim Khan had built a reputation in the industry.

But before fame found him, Salim Khan's prospects were bleak. His struggles as an actor were becoming increasingly difficult and he was compelled to evaluate other options in the film industry. He zeroed in on writing, having seen Nasir Husain write scripts for his own films—and talk about their importance—when he was acting in *Teesri Manzil*. Salim had participated in the writing process and understood the value of the script in the making of a film. This realization played a major part in his becoming a screenwriter. He says that he figured out that while he knew only a little about writing, most other people knew even less, which gave him a fair shot at success. He started writing a few outlines—some of them based on stories he had heard from his police officer father—and tried peddling them to stars and producers.

One of the big advantages he had compared to others in the film industry of the 1960s was that he was extremely well read and was an avid reader, even when he was busy acting. His favourite haunt was the Victoria Circulating Library in Mahim. In fact, he laughs when he remembers what the owner started saying after a few years, 'I don't have any new books for you. You have read everything here!' Even when Salim bought something that was wrapped in a newspaper, he remembers reading that piece of paper before throwing it away.

His reading habit, along with his academic background, gave him a gravitas that was respected by industry bigwigs like Raj Kapoor and Dilip Kumar and it proved helpful in building an equation with them. Another star he was quite familiar with was Ashok Kumar. He even wrote a script and directly offered it to the actor. In his characteristic fashion, he says, 'I told Dadamoni to listen for just fifteen minutes. "After that you'll tell me to continue."' Ashok Kumar heard the whole script and liked it. Salim was with Dadamoni when producer Brij Sadanah came to sign him for a project and he seized the opportunity to peddle the script to Sadanah as well. Ashok Kumar also endorsed it. At the time, it was common for Hindi film producers to sign on stars without any story or script to base their offer on. The prevalent belief was that they would write something to suit the star.

The script was eventually made into a film called *Do Bhai*, starring Ashok Kumar, Jeetendra and Mala Sinha, which was released in 1969. The story had elements of the popular Salim–Javed formula—an estranged child, an anti-hero, moral dilemmas, and several twists and turns. The film, unfortunately, did not do too well. Salim had decided to cut down on his acting assignments in order to concentrate on writing and though money was hard to come by, he had not lost his flamboyance. In *Do Bhai*, he was credited as Prince Salim.

During this period, he joined Abrar Alvi as a writing assistant. The recommendation was made by actor Ajit, who had worked with Salim in several films and also knew Abrar Alvi quite well. All three of them were working on the Shammi Kapoor-starrer, *Professor*, when this connection happened. As an assistant, Salim spent three-four hours after lunch with the veteran writer. His salary was Rs 500 per month and for that, he would suggest plot ideas, how certain scenes or events would unfold and also be the sounding board for dialogues. He says that he used to suggest ideas he had read in popular novels or seen in Hollywood films.

Once during this stint, he had a very interesting conversation with Abrar Alvi when they were discussing the importance of the writer in films.

Salim said, 'Abrar sahib, there will come a time when writers will be paid the same as stars . . .'

Abrar took a while to comprehend this and asked somewhat incredulously, 'If Dilip Kumar charges twelve lakh for a film today, you think a writer can ever ask for that kind of money?'

Salim replied, 'If the writer can prove that the film ran because of his script, then why not?'

Abrar dismissed this confidence as lunacy and said, 'Miyan, don't repeat this to anyone else. People will think you have gone mad.'

Salim Khan still remembers this conversation as if it happened yesterday.

In the mid-1960s, around the time Salim decided to turn to screenwriting, he was also acting in a film called *Sarhadi Lootera* directed by S.M. Sagar. He was not the hero but had a romantic role in the action film. Those were the days when scenes were written on the sets by anonymous daily-wage writers, who never seemed to be in short supply. Salim, by this time, had started thinking of scripts and scenes as a writer and used to complain bitterly to the director about the poor quality of dialogues. He even offered to write the scenes himself.

The director kept scouting for writers until one day, in desperation, he asked one of his assistants—the clapper boy—to write the day's scenes because the writer hadn't turned up. He liked the boy's work so much that he made him the dialogue writer. The boy was about twenty-one years old.

His name was Javed Akhtar.

Enter Javed Akhtar

When Javed Akhtar was born, his father—poet Jan Nisar Akhtar—a member of the Communist Party, went to the hospital along with some friends directly from the office. Since he was carrying a copy of *The Communist Manifesto*, he decided to change the tradition of reading the Azaan in the newborn child's ears and read from the manifesto instead. This reading was not merely symbolic. Javed's childhood and the atmosphere around him were such that he came to believe deeply in communism and hated the inequalities entrenched in Indian society. And this belief was evident in many of the films he would eventually write.

Born on 17 January 1945 in Gwalior, he got his name from a line his father wrote the day he got married to Safia: '*Lamha lamha kisi jadoo ka fasana hoga . . .*' Jan Nisar Akhtar borrowed a word from it to name his son Jadoo. For a long time, he remained Jadoo and it was only when he was about to be admitted to school that his name was changed to a more formal but similar-sounding Javed.

Jan Nisar Akhtar came from a family of scholars and writers. He was an accomplished poet and he went on to become an acclaimed lyricist for Hindi films as well. His wife, Safia Akhtar, was also very well educated, and taught in a college. She had a keen appreciation of literature and poetry. Since she and her husband spent most of their married life away from each other (due to his status as a 'Wanted' member of the Communist Party), she regularly wrote letters to him. These letters were subsequently published as a collection called *Zer-e-Lab* (*Under the Lip*), which became very popular; that alone was enough for Safia to make a place for herself in the world of Urdu literature.

Javed was extremely close to his mother and she, in turn, had assessed her firstborn's talents very accurately. In a letter to her husband, she described the six-and-a-half-year-old Javed: 'This boy has tremendous control and command over Urdu and is rather hesitant in English. He is extremely talkative but not very practical.' Javed now adds that, 'She described me as someone who makes big plans but doesn't do anything about them. I'm much the same even today.'

When asked about his childhood memories, Javed quotes Woody Allen. The American actor–director, when asked, 'Did you have a happy childhood?' had replied 'No, a normal one.' Javed says the same thing because he managed to get through his childhood with a wealth of memories and influences despite some traumatic experiences.

Javed lost his mother exactly one day after his eighth birthday. He remembers vividly the moment when his aunt took him and his younger brother Salman close to their mother's body for a last glimpse and asked them both to promise Safia that they 'would do something in life, become something in life'. When Javed went through a terrible phase of struggle during his early days in Bombay, this promise was always at the back of his mind.

Jan Nisar Akhtar had already moved to the city at this time as he had to go underground became of his links to the Communist Party. Javed Akhtar says, 'It can be shocking for a

child of that age to lose both parents—one to life and another
to death.' For a long time in his childhood, Javed dreamed
of a white shroud—similar to the one his mother's body was
wrapped in after her death—which traumatized him.

As is evident, these elements of his childhood—an idealized
vision of the mother, an estranged father and a recurring
nightmare—reappeared in his films. Even when his father tried
to reach out to him, he repelled these attempts. 'I can remember
times when he spoke about poetry or literature or writing,
and that definitely did leave an impression on me. I suppose
I wanted to pretend that I didn't care; perhaps I used that as
a kind of defence mechanism because if I had accepted that I
cared, it might have hurt more,' he says.

Born to parents who were both poets, in a family where
four generations before him had been acclaimed poets, Javed's
literary credentials were coded into his genes from birth. He
was an avid reader, indiscriminately poring over books and
magazines from an early age. Be it the poetry of Faiz, the short
stories of Saadat Hassan Manto or Krishan Chander, the novels
of Ismat Chughtai, he read it all. Javed Akhtar says he was most
influenced by Krishan Chander and admired him a lot. His
reading habit was so varied that in his early teens, he was reading
both Maxim Gorky's *Mother* and the detective thrillers (*Jasoosi
Duniya*) of Ibn-e-Safi. The detective thrillers—be it Indian
or American pulp fiction—were a big favourite for their fast
action, tight plots and economies of expression. He remembers
the novels of Ibn-e-Safi for their fascinating characters with
memorable names. 'Ibn-e-Safi was a master at naming his
characters. All of us who read him remember those names . . .
There was a Chinese villain, his name was Sing Hi. There was
a Portuguese villain called Garson . . . an Englishman who had
come to India and was into yoga . . . was called Gerald Shastri.'

This technique of giving catchy names to characters would stay with him. The wide range of reading not only gave him the sensitivity with which progressive writers approached their subjects but also a very good sense of plot and speaking styles. Here, it would be apt to quote a paragraph from Ibn-e-Safi's detective novel, *House of Fear*—featuring his eccentric detective, Imran. The conversation takes place just outside a nightclub:

'So, young man. So now you have also starred frequenting these places?'

'Yes. I often come by to pay Flush,' Imran said respectfully.

'Flush! Oh, so now you play Flush . . .'

'Yes, yes. I feel like it when I am a bit drunk . . .'

'Oh! So you have also started drinking?'

'What can I say? I swear I've never drunk alone. Frequently I find hookers who do not agree to anything without a drink . . .'

This scene would find a real-life parallel as well as a fictional one in Javed's life later.

Javed's memory, like Salim Khan's, is incredible, for he remembers snatches of songs from *Aarzoo*, a film he was taken to see when he was about five years old. '*Aye dil mujhe aisi jagah le chal jahan koi na ho . . .*' is the Talat Mahmood hit he remembers, though he has no recollection of who he went with.

His first fully formed memory of a film was Mehmoob Khan's *Aan*, which he saw the day he was enrolled is Class I of St Mary's School in Lucknow. He had heard of someone called Dilip Kumar and saw him for the first time in Lucknow's Basant Talkies, thoroughly enjoying the star's acting and the film's action. After that, he saw and liked a slew of films, some of which are still acknowledged as all-time classics. Films like *Shree 420, Munimji, Do Bigha Zameen*. He appreciated *Jagriti* for the large cast of children and *Mother India* for the rebel character of Birju—who, he believes, was an early version of the Angry Young Man. His fascination with the negative character, the anti-hero, started with Dev Anand in *Jaal*, a film he watched while in college. One particular film had a deep impact on him, because its maker and actor, Guru Dutt, seemed to exude a rare mix of creative flair and artistic melancholy—*Pyaasa*.

After his mother's death, Javed lived with his maternal grandparents in Lucknow for some time before moving to Aligarh with an aunt while his younger brother Salman remained in Lucknow because 'one family could not be burdened with two orphans'.

It was at his aunt's place in Aligarh that he started watching movies and reading books incessantly. He did his matriculation from there before his father brought him back to Bhopal, where he spent four years, living off friends and in hostels. His charm and obvious erudition made him hugely popular among his friends and helped him earn a living. As a student, he often did not know where his next meal would come from but he managed. He was a proficient debater who often represented his university in college festivals. He also put his phenomenal memory to good use by reading and remembering thousands of Urdu poems (which he still hasn't forgotten).

His deep interest in literature and fascination with cinema had existed long enough for him to analyse what film direction and writing was all about. His interest in writing peaked with films like *Waqt* and *Kanoon*, which had excellent dialogues (by Akhtar-ul-Imaan). He even conjured up a grand plan to use Akhtar-ul-Imaan as his writer if he ever made a film. Obviously, he hadn't decided to become a writer then; but he wanted to learn film-making by becoming an assistant in Bombay. And he wanted to do it with Guru Dutt.

Thus, with a dream of meeting—and maybe working with—Guru Dutt, Javed reached Bombay on 4 October 1964. Tragically, Guru Dutt committed suicide less than a week later (on 10 October) and Javed could never fulfil his dream of working with the maestro.

To start earning money, he started doing odd jobs in the film industry—as an assistant to directors or as a clapper boy. During this time, he also wrote dialogues for scenes in films that were eventually credited to well-known screenwriters.

He was employed by Kamal Amrohi as a clapper boy for Rs 50 per month. This was a period of intense struggle for young Javed, who had to really rough it out—literally in the elements. In various interviews, Javed remembers the first five years of his stay in Bombay as riddled with problems. He had no fixed address, and often had no idea in the afternoon where he would sleep that night. He had exactly three sets of clothes, which he rotated between wearing and laundering. In fact, he changed clothes at the laundry itself. He had no place to stay and frequently spent the nights on the studio premises. A few times, he was allowed to stay in a storeroom at Kamalistan, Amrohi's studio, and one night, found three of Meena Kumari's Filmfare Award trophies in a shoe cupboard. He recalls holding the trophy reverentially every night and pretending that he was receiving the award himself, rehearsing speeches even. This was good practise, which came in handy umpteen times later in his career. One thing that he did not give up even during this tough period was reading. By befriending a second-hand bookseller near Andheri station, he read late into the night in the dim light of the studio compound where he stayed. Just as another man was reading up everything he could lay his hands on in a Mahim lending library.

After Kamalistan Studio was disbanded, Javed even spent a few days in a cave with some friends. The cave was infested with mosquitoes and Javed says they were so big that he could feel them 'mounting him' even before they bit! This did not continue for long as he moved into a flat that was rented at a princely sum of Rs 120 per month with a friend. When his friend moved out, Javed had a tough time finding a flatmate capable of bringing in Rs 60 every month. One of his drinking buddies offered to share the flat with him, but Javed turned him down because he wasn't sure he would be able to earn enough to pay the monthly rent. This friend's name was Shatrughan Sinha.

Despite the fact that Jan Nisar Akhtar was in Bombay and had made a name as a lyricist and poet in the film fraternity, Javed faced these hard times by himself. His father had remarried and Javed found the situation extremely uncomfortable. He had initially moved in with his father but left the house after just a few days because he could not get along with his stepmother. He also never sought work using his father's name or connections.

He had, however, become very friendly with one of his father's friends, Sahir Ludhianvi. The senior poet became very fond of the impetuous but prodigiously talented Javed. Sahir often acted as a buffer between father and son as he knew both their natures very well. He even supported Javed financially during this period but never made it look like a favour.[2]

As the struggles became grimmer, Javed got an offer—of Rs 600 per month—from a famous and successful writer to ghostwrite for him, a job that could last a lifetime. After three days of thought, Javed rejected the offer, deciding that credit was as important to him as the money.

---

[2] Gulzar wrote an excellent short story—*Sahir Aur Jaadu*—which is a fictionalized account of Javed's relationship with Sahir Ludhianvi.

After working with Amrohi and on odd jobs for about a year, he got a job at Rs 100 per month with director S.M. Sagar who was about to start his career with a stunt film called *Sarhadi Lootera*. He was taken on as an assistant director and clapper boy for the film. His primary role was to read out the day's dialogues to the stars and help them rehearse. The dialogue writer hired for the film had left abruptly and a desperate Sagar entrusted Javed with the job temporarily. He did a good enough job for the first couple of scenes to be formally made the dialogue writer. The film's second hero, interested in screenplays and dialogues himself, liked what Javed wrote. His name was Salim Khan.

The Start of a Dream Team

'As a writer, he had the courage and I had the intricacy'
—Javed Akhtar

Although *Sarhadi Lootera* collapsed at the box office, it is remembered for creating a collaboration like no other. The film introduced the two men, but their formal partnership was still some time away. In fact, the thought of a partnership had not struck either of them at this point.

Salim and Javed found common interests to bond over and kept in touch even after the film was completed. Javed used to stay in Andheri (which was pretty much a wilderness in the late 1960s) but moved to Bandra in 1968, where Salim stayed. They often got together in the evenings, watched movies, talked about their favourites and discussed story ideas.

Javed wrote[3] the dialogues for a film that boasted of pretty major stars—Dharmendra and Sharmila Tagore. *Yakeen* was a spy thriller where Dharmendra is a scientist in a top-secret government research project that is being targeted by foreign powers. They replace him with a lookalike who fools

---

[3] He was actually the co-writer of dialogues, along with Deven Verma.

everybody, except the real Dharmendra's dog. Like *Sarhadi Lootera*, this film did not do too well either. Interestingly, it has a small scene in which Dharmendra—who has no best friend in the movie—has to approach his girlfriend's mother himself to ask for her hand in marriage. In the scene, he speaks highly of his government job, salary, perquisites and his good habits (including teetotalism). In hindsight, it is fascinating to see how, a few years later, a tongue-in-cheek reversal of this scene plays out in what is Hindi cinema's most memorable film when Dharmendra's best friend goes to cook his goose in front of the girl's mausi!

But apart from the flops, they had their fair share of heartbreaks at the pitching stage itself—even some funny ones. Javed Akhtar recounted the story of his first ever script narration. He had gone to a producer—Baboobhai Bhanji[4]—after pulling a lot of strings and the man had listened to the script without interruption. After finishing, a nervous Javed Akhtar respectfully enquired what the producer thought of the scene. To young Javed, the producer explained the perils of being original in Bollywood: 'Darling, your story is good but there is a big risk involved . . . this hasn't been used in any film yet.' Javed half-jokingly adds a moral to the story, 'I never wrote a story that has not come before.' Indeed, Salim–Javed's forte became giving an unprecedented spin to stories that 'had come before'.

They were still jobless when S.M. Sagar came to their rescue—or something like it—and asked them to develop a short story into a screenplay. They had no plans to become a team but agreed to do it for the money. They took about twelve days to write the screenplay and the film became *Adhikar*—starring Ashok Kumar, Deb Mukherji and Nanda. The story

---

[4] Baboobhai Bhanji directed only one film in his career—*Tarzan Aur Jadui Chirag*. This is a perfect example of an original story that had come before!

was credited to R.S. Verma, who seemed to have written for a creative writing competition called the Madhuri Film Story Contest and the 'shooting scripts, dialogues & lyrics' were credited to Ramesh Pant. There was no mention of Salim–Javed anywhere in the credits, though they were paid Rs 5000 for developing the screenplay.

The story was a complicated love triangle. Boy meets Girl 1, falls in love and impregnates her. Boy marries Girl 2, following a misunderstanding. Girl 2 finds out about Girl 1 and brings the child from that relationship home, claiming it is hers.

The story was completely different from the standard-issue Bollywood unwed-mother love triangle and the screenplay was good enough to impress Sagar's assistant director, Sudhir Wahi. He suggested that the two youngsters try their luck at Sippy Films.

Sippy Films was the banner of G.P. Sippy, who had strayed into film-making from a variety of jobs including import-export and construction. He had started off with B-grade thrillers but eventually made it big with two successive hits featuring two of the industry's stars—the Shammi Kapoor starrer *Brahmchari* in 1968 and *Bandhan* featuring the hit pairing of Rajesh Khanna and Mumtaz in 1969.

With two massive hits, G.P. Sippy had gained confidence and was joined in the film business by his son, Ramesh, who had dropped out from the London School of Economics and had spent the last seven years doing lowly jobs in different units. Ramesh had new-fangled notions and often talked about changing how the movie business worked. In an industry working on the same stories since time immemorial and shooting scenes written on the sets, he wanted to create a strong story department. Though that wasn't new to the film industry, the way Ramesh Sippy envisaged the department certainly was.

Salim and Javed—still not a team formally—landed up at the Sippy Films office at Khar. They offered to narrate a script with a dialogue straight out of a film: 'You may not necessarily do it but we assure you that you will want to hear it to the end.'

Ramesh Sippy was completely taken aback by their cockiness. He recounts: 'I was tired and was lying down as they began to narrate. And midway I found myself sitting up and towards the end I was leaning forward, listening intently to everything they said . . . That was the first time I could see the whole film, smoothly flowing scene to scene in my head.'

After this session, Ramesh Sippy called his production controller, Narinder Bedi, and directed him to hire the two youngsters. Salim and Javed asked for a monthly salary of Rs 1000 each but were offered Rs 750 instead, with a promise of an increment if their work was satisfactory. 'The salary never increased. It remained Rs 750 for many years . . .' Javed laughs but admits they looked at the money as a memento of sorts and did not want it to be stopped.

Thus, Salim Khan and Javed Akhtar joined the story department of Sippy Films.

They started work on a very unusual story about a widow and widower, which was being sniggered at in filmi circles as box-office suicide because heart-throb Rajesh Khanna would die within a few reels of the film. The film was *Andaz*.

Part II:

THE PARTNERSHIP

Andaz

'Rajesh Khanna witnessed unbelievable popularity, such that no one had ever seen or imagined. In fact from 1969 to 1973, it was a one-horse race. It would be said of those days, that before any Indian child could say mama and papa, he would say Rajesh Khanna'
—Javed Akhtar, speaking after Rajesh Khanna's death

After making two successful films with Shammi Kapoor and Rajesh Khanna individually, G.P. Sippy pulled off a coup by signing them both for *Andaz*. Given the unusual story of the film, it is a wonder both stars agreed to be a part of it—thanks in no small measure to Sippy Films' growing clout in the industry.

Rajesh Khanna was becoming bigger with every release and was probably a bigger star than even Shammi Kapoor in 1971, when *Andaz* was being made. This would have been fertile ground for ego tussles, with both stars needing substantial handling and assurances on their respective roles. It is therefore remarkable that these issues didn't crop up, or at least did not become a hindrance, considering this was the director's first film.

The writing credits for *Andaz* were shared between five different people. The story and screenplay were credited to

Sachin Bhowmick, veteran screenwriter who had written some of Rajesh Khanna and Shammi Kapoor's biggest hits, such as *Aradhana, Aan Milo Sajna, An Evening In Paris, Brahmchari* and *Janwar*. The dialogues were credited to Gulzar, who was fast gaining acceptance in the industry as a lyricist and writer. He too had written dialogues for major hits like *Khamoshi, Ashirwad* and *Shagird*. Additional script work was credited to Satish Bhatnagar, Salim Khan and Javed Akhtar of the Sippy Films Story Department.

Sachin Bhowmick had suggested remaking a French film— *Un Homme et une Femme* (*A Man and a Woman*)—which had won the top prize at the 1966 Cannes Film Festival. Ramesh Sippy liked the story. 'People had made films about widows earlier but I wanted to tell this story in a commercial format. It was never my desire to make very arty films or things that defined a different space. I wanted to make good commercial cinema, with an edge. I saw *Andaz* as an entertaining film, but with characters carrying some baggage. And I felt Shammi Kapoor had reached a point in career where he needed to do more mature roles,' he says.

He approached the 'dancing star' and told him, 'I've decided I'm going to make a film with you. And I'm not going to make the kind of film you've been doing all the time.' This attitude of his was important, because this cockiness and chutzpah were things he had in common with Salim–Javed.

Salim remembers that the story and cast had been decided— they had even recorded and picturized a song, and had signed on Gulzar to write the dialogues, but the screenplay was not ready. Salim–Javed came in and wrote the complete screenplay of *Andaz*.

With two veteran writers (Bhowmick and Gulzar had been around for nearly a decade by then) involved, it is easy to dismiss the story department's contribution as patchwork, which was mainly doing on-set additions and changes to suit the exact requirements of the day's shooting. But it is interesting to note that Rajesh Khanna interacted with Salim–Javed enough (and was impressed enough) to request them to write his next film (*Haathi Mere Saathi*). Even Hema Malini remembers that towards the end of *Andaz*'s shooting, Ramesh Sippy was almost always huddled with the young writers (whose names she did not know then). Clearly, their contribution and promise were much more than the subsidiary credit they got.

Andaz is the story of a widower Ravi (Shammi Kapoor) living in a sprawling estate with his daughter, Munni, and mother. He is a dutiful family man who is very concerned about his younger brother Badal (Roopesh Kumar), a bit of a wastrel, studying in the city. Ravi is actually an orphan adopted by the family.

A single mother, Sheetal (Hema Malini), comes to the town with a son, Deepu, and starts teaching at the local convent. Ravi and Sheetal bond over their single-parent status and start developing feelings for each other.

A flashback reveals Sheetal's relationship with Raj (Rajesh Khanna), who impregnated her and died in an accident, and whose father refused to acknowledge Sheetal. A second flashback reveals that Ravi was married to Mona (Simi Garewal) who died because she concealed a fatal risk during her pregnancy to fulfil Ravi's dream of having a child.

When Ravi and Sheetal are about to take their relationship further, Badal returns home and tries to break them up by revealing Sheetal's past as an unwed mother. But this ploy fails when it is revealed that Ravi wasn't picked off the streets but is actually his mother's biological son born out of wedlock.

Badal then rapes and murders a domestic help Mahua (Aruna Irani), and tries to frame Ravi. But Ravi manages to clear his name and in the climax, Badal is arrested after a fight and Sheetal is accepted into Ravi's family.

Though they received credit only for 'Additional Script Work' (and were completely missing from the publicity material), there were some elements in the script that were very similar to their soon-to-be-developed signature style. These could be their own contributions or influences they picked up from lead writer Gulzar. He had a penchant for writing natural dialogue and while working with him, they ensured all the characters spoke in a different dialect or style. Mahua, for example, speaks in an unusual accent, which is common to people in the hills. Badal has a sleazy, lilting way of talking. This difference in talking styles of characters is something Salim–Javed would do throughout their career.

Gulzar has very fond memories of working with the duo and the many evenings he spent with them.

Andaz came in a long list of jubilee hits that Rajesh Khanna delivered from 1969 onwards, which cemented his superstar status, and created a hysterical fan following and unprecedented box-office clout. The film was promoted with him at the centre, even though his was a 'special appearance'.

A few weeks after *Andaz*'s release, Sippy Films took out an advertisement in the trade magazine *Screen*: 'The Million Rupee Week – Ever since the movies began, no movie has grossed over a million rupees in its first week in Bombay as *Andaz* has done! Never before, perhaps never again!'

This ad appeared the day *Haathi Mere Saathi* was released in Bombay. The film went on to become an even bigger hit than *Andaz*. As it turned out, not only Rajesh Khanna, but even Sippy Films broke *Andaz*'s record soon after.

And Salim–Javed played a major role in both.

Haathi Mere Saathi

Haathi Mere Saathi came to Salim–Javed purely on the basis of the rapport they had built up with superstar Rajesh Khanna during the shooting of *Andaz*. While the actor's role in the film had been a very short one, it was enough for him to gauge the flow and flair these two young writers brought to the script—even though they received no official credit for it. Salim says, 'Rajesh Khanna thought his guest role in *Andaz* was the best guest role ever written.' During the shooting and after the success of that first film, the duo had struck up a friendship with the superstar and were regularly invited to his place for drinks.

At one of these sessions, Rajesh Khanna told Salim of a predicament that was typical of a film star's success in the 1970s. The superstar was in the process of purchasing a bungalow (which he named Aashirwad after he had bought it) on Carter Road in Bombay from actor Rajendra Kumar. To fund the purchase, he had taken a substantial signing amount from the producer—'Sandow' M.M.A. Chinnappa Devar—for acting in the remake of a south Indian hit. The signing amount of Rs 5 lakh—a suitcase full of cash—was something unheard of in those days, even by Rajesh Khanna's standards. He seemed clueless even about the original movie's language (Tamil) but knew that it was a terrible script.

'I need the money to buy the house but I cannot act in the film the way it stands . . . *Tum log kuch kar sakte ho?*'

He assured them that he would negotiate with the producer to get them both money and credit. At the time, Salim and Javed were not officially a team as they were still employees of the Sippy Films Story Department. When they agreed to the proposal, *Haathi Mere Saathi* became the first film where the duo got joint credit.

The somewhat fairy-tale-ish plot of the original film in Tamil and the profusion of animals in a circus-like setting had made Salim–Javed quite apprehensive about the reaction of the Hindi film audience. When they discussed this with Rajesh Khanna, he told them that they could change everything and write a fresh script. 'You can make as many changes but keep just five characters the same . . . the four elephants and me,' he warned them. Producer Devar came up with a similar but funnier claim, 'I make film with Murugan [a popular deity in Tamil Nadu], Rajesh Khanna and Elephant.'

When they began work, the flow was quite smooth and they had a first draft ready in just twenty days. This would become a hallmark of most of their landmark projects, where the basic screenplay would be completed in one short burst of creativity.

Rajesh Khanna had taken it upon himself to get the screenplay approved by the producer and the director (who happened to be the producer's brother). While Salim and Javed were working on the script, the actor used his rapport with Laxmikant–Pyarelal and Anand Bakshi and recorded the title song. For the final presentation of the script, he called Salim–Javed, the director and the producer to his house and orchestrated a complete show. The narration started and at the right moment in the script, Rajesh Khanna pressed the Play button on his tape recorder and the sounds of '*Chal chal chal mere saathi o mere haathi*' filled the room—creating a rousing atmosphere that floored the producer.

The latter had only one objection—to a scene in which the hero got drunk. He shouted 'Hero, no *sharaafi*' (meaning 'the hero cannot be a *sharaabi*') because a drunk man cannot perform on the trapeze. The writers duly afflicted the hero with a fever instead!

The detailed narration took place in Chennai a few days later with the help of an interpreter for the benefit of the predominantly Tamil unit. Javed says, 'I recall we were often speaking so loudly that Mr Surinder Kapoor, Anil Kapoor's father, once knocked at our door and asked if everything was okay. He was staying in the same hotel and shooting his own film in the city!'

The story combined two popular Hindi film plots—the rich-girl-poor-boy romance and the love triangle—presented as a carnival of music and animals.

As a child, Raju (Rajesh Khanna) is saved by four elephants, and as his father lies dying, he instructs Raju to take care of them.[5] Though Raju is heir to a massive fortune, his preoccupation with his elephants costs him his entire inheritance and his lady love, Tanu (Tanuja), whose father (Madan Puri) is opposed to their relationship. Eventually, Raju wins back Tanu, rebuilds his fortune with the help of his four elephants and starts a zoo called Pyar Ki Duniya.[6] Raju's continued preoccupation with his elephants makes Tanu feel neglected and, after the birth of

---

[5] His last words were '*Yeh haathi tere saathi . . .*' [ii]

[6] The film was originally called *Pyar Ki Duniya,* before Laxmikant–Pyarelal's hit song prompted them to change the title.

her son, extremely apprehensive of his safety. When the lead elephant—Ramu—realizes they are the cause of the couple's estrangement, he brings them together and sacrifices his life to save his master from the bullets of a rival circus owner (K.N. Singh).

As is obvious, the story was particularly suited for children and family audiences. The film's appeal was somewhat like a Disney film. It was a fable-like story with strong moral values, which did not degenerate into sermonizing but managed to keep the viewers—especially children, who loved it—hooked with its fast pace, stunts and music.

The entire film was full of pretty clever stunts by the elephants, many of which were improvised on the sets. The producer, Devar, was an expert animal trainer himself and commandeered his elephant troupe like a ringmaster. The end result was a movie with action centred on the animals, making it look like a circus unfolding on screen. The Society for Prevention of Cruelty to Animals (SPCA) gave a special award to the film for spreading awareness about their cause. Laxmikant–Pyarelal's music too was very well received and smashed several records.

There were certain touches to the script that would become part of Salim–Javed's signature in the coming years. Despite having Rajesh Khanna—the king of romance—as the hero, he is not overtly romantic. In fact, there is a humorous touch to his wooing, like the scene in which he proposes to Tanuja.

There was a distinct message of socialism in a few scenes as well, where the cavalier attitude of the rich towards the poor is mentioned. Quite surprisingly, these lines were said by Tanuja's character, who could well have conformed to the Hindi-film stereotype of the rich heroine and remained vacuous. Maybe it was the writers—with their social roots—speaking.

However, *Haathi Mere Saathi* did not have any major 'repeat-value' dialogues which became Salim–Javed's forte in the coming years.

The reviews of the film ranged from moderate to positive. The writers were not identified by name but some of the reviews mentioned the script in passing. *Hindustan Times* said, 'This is a Madras production and as can be expected, the producer is not content to rest on the laurels of the elephants' performance alone and has woven a workable script around them.'

Haathi Mere Saathi turned out to be a stunner at the box office. Even by Rajesh Khanna's reputation for delivering blockbusters, it was a massive one. Not only was it the biggest hit of 1971 (which saw box-office biggies like *Mera Gaon Mera Desh*, *Andaz*, *Caravan* and *Amar Prem*), it also went on to become the highest-grossing Hindi film ever of the time, a record it maintained for a while. Until then *Johny Mera Naam* had been the highest grosser (having collected Rs 50 lakh in each of the film territories) but *Haathi Mere Saathi* raced ahead with collections in excess of Rs 1 crore per territory. The impact of the film—and the power of the revised script—is best described by fact that the producer remade it in Tamil, which turned out to be an even bigger hit than the original Tamil film on which *Haathi Mere Saathi* was based.

The experience was not all milk and honey for Salim–Javed, though.

For such a successful, record-smashing film, they were paid a paltry sum of Rs 10,000 and requests for a bonus were summarily turned down. Contrast this to the payment made to the music directors, Laxmikant–Pyarelal. Pyarelal recalls the producer coming to their houses with Rs 1 lakh each placed on a silver plate when they signed the film. 'He repeated this when the work was completed!' he smiles.

Even the credit—partly negotiated by Rajesh Khanna himself—was given rather grudgingly, if one tracks the mentions in the trade advertisements. There was no mention of the screenwriters in any of the pre-release ads; the story was credited to the producer. The double-spread ad on the day of the film's release (in *Screen,* dated 14 May 1971) credited 'Saleem-Javeeth' (sic) for the screenplay, but this was also removed after the third week. Well-known writer Inder Raj Anand was credited for the dialogues though Salim–Javed wrote nearly all the lines as well. In a later interview, the producer claimed that he had not signed them for the screenplay but merely for 'story discussions' on Rajesh Khanna's request. He claimed that their contribution was merely a few action-scene suggestions.

As a result of the producer's refusal to acknowledge their contribution, Salim–Javed never worked with him again. Later, two major stars (Dharmendra and Rishi Kapoor), on being offered films by Devar, asked the producer to get the scripts written by Salim–Javed but the writers didn't budge. In fact, their relationship with Rajesh Khanna also soured after this, because despite his promise to negotiate on their behalf, nothing had come of it. This was quite symptomatic of the situation writers faced in 1960s, as remuneration and recognition were not given as a matter of course.

Interestingly, producer Devar and director Thirumugham repeated the 'animal' formula in their next Hindi venture, *Gaai Aur Gori*. Starring Jaya Bhaduri and Shatrughan Sinha, the film told the story of a cow who 'averts a train accident', 'fights a dog which attacks her mistress' and 'unites an estranged husband and wife'.

Gaai Aur Gori released in 1973 and (needless to say) sank at the box office. That was the year Salim–Javed wrote *Zanjeer*.

Salim–Javed thus ended 1971 with two films in the year's top ten grossers—*Andaz* and *Haathi Mere Saathi*. While Rajesh

Khanna's charisma and both the directors' deft handling of the scripts contributed substantially to the success of the films, the two writers' efforts played an undeniable part as well.

But as two cocky youngsters in an industry which placed a premium on grey hair, there was hardly any buzz about them. They were, of course, valued members of the Sippy Films Story Department and some of the script ideas they were peddling seemed to have serious potential. In fact, one of the script ideas was something quite unthinkable in the male-dominated Hindi film industry for it had the heroine playing a double role as the prime mover of the film. It was called *Seeta Aur Geeta*.

Seeta Aur Geeta

'If the word "romp" didn't exist before *Seeta Aur Geeta,* it would have been coined to describe this fun, cute film'
—Carla Miriam Levy aka @filmigeek, Bollywood fan and blogger

Salim–Javed—in their second pairing (though not officially so)—did what they would soon develop into an art form. They took an extremely popular theme and gave it a distinctive twist to make it completely their own. In fact, after they were done with the script, the original was hardly remembered.

They took the plot of *The Prince and the Pauper*—a story of two identical characters whose personalities and circumstances were completely dissimilar. This plot had already been used to great effect in the superhit *Ram Aur Shyam*, with the legendary Dilip Kumar essaying the two roles. Made just five years ago, the film was absolutely fresh in viewers' minds but that did not stop Salim–Javed from giving it a distaff twist.

Docile Seeta (Hema Malini) is brought up in a mansion by a cruel aunt (Manorama) who steals her monthly allowance (from her trust fund) and plans to control her inheritance by marrying her off to someone of her choice. Geeta (Hema Malini, again) is a flamboyant gypsy girl who performs roadside acrobatics for a living. When they accidentally switch places, Geeta falls in love with a doctor Ravi (Sanjeev Kumar) and takes the fight to Seeta's aunt. Seeta, meanwhile, falls in love with Geeta's street-performing partner, Raaka (Dharmendra), and helps him overcome his bad habits. Seeta's aunt's brother, Ranjeet (Roopesh Kumar), finds out about the switch and kidnaps Seeta. Geeta's mother reveals that the two girls are twins and she—being childless—had taken away one. And justice is served to the villains in a rousing climax.

Seeta Aur Geeta was the script with which Salim–Javed came into their own. It is obvious from each scene in the film that everybody associated with it was having lots of fun and that brought an infectious energy to every frame. Their trademark touches—which would get stronger in the coming years—were visible throughout; you can almost hear them chuckle as you watch some of the scenes.

Whistle-inducing dialogues—both comic and emotional— crackled through the film and exploded at regular intervals.

When Geeta (thought to be Seeta) is caught by the police and brought to the station, she wreaks mayhem and is perched atop the ceiling fan when her uncle and aunt arrive. When the aunt says '*Neeche aa jao, beti*', Geeta responds with '*Upar aa jao, moti*'.[iii] It was an incredibly popular line, which drew hysterical laughter when it was first uttered on-screen and had—what the film industry calls—tremendous repeat value. Not only this line, but each one of Hema Malini and Manorama's interactions had a manic sense of humour. For example, '*Hum tere chacha aur chachi lagte hain*', was parried with '*Soorat se toh chamcha aur chamchi lagte ho*',[iv] and '*Kahan chali gayi thi, Seeta meri beti?*' was met with '*Mahabaleshwar gayi thi, haathi mere saathi.*'[v]

It was critical to have these interactions because Manorama as the Chachi—for all practical purposes—was the main villain.

After watching her torturing Seeta, seeing the Chachi suffer at Geeta's hands in a series of entertaining scenes is almost cathartic for the audience.

And it wasn't only with Manorama. Hema Malini had fantastic lines throughout the movie, which even top heroes would have killed for. Whether it was a comic situation where she brushes off her borrowed clothes with a droll '*Main maange ke kapdon mein hamesha achhi lagti hoon,*'[vi] or a fiery assurance to her grandmother—'*Jab tak tumhare aankhon mein aansoo hai, jab tak tumhare dil mein dard hai, jab tak iss ghar mein zulm hai, main yahan se nahin jaoongi*'[vii]—Hema's lines were mind-blowing.

It helped that the director was completely in sync with the writers and Hema's scenes were filmed in a way that brought maximum impact to the lines. When she confronts Roopesh Kumar about his misdemeanours, she keeps on bouncing a ping-pong ball on a racket while delivering her lines, making Roopesh squirm. It was a brilliant touch that brought out the character's cool aggression perfectly.

Another notable aspect of the script was the different styles of speech that distinguished each character.

Foreign-returned doctor Ravi's dialogues were sprinkled with throwaway lines in English. The street performer Raaka had lots of local Bombay slang like *laafa*, *khunnas*, *halkat*, *bhankas* and *bindaas*.[7] Geeta's speech was like Raaka's while Seeta had halting, almost incomplete sentences. Even a minor

---

[7] In one scene from *Seeta Aur Geeta*, Raaka gets angry with Geeta and says, '*Jis din yeh teen kilo ka haath padh gaya na toh fillum ke poster ki tarah deewaar pe chipka doonga.*' [viii] Nearly thirty years later, his son—acting in *Damini*—would make this line famous but in deference to his father, he would assert a lower weight for his arm: '*Dhaai kilo ka haath*'! This is actually a strange coincidence, since the dialogue writer for *Damini*—Dilip Shukla—had no recollection of the original line from *Seeta Aur Geeta*.

character like Seeta's cousin, Sheila (played by Honey Irani) had a distinctive style—with a smattering of English words, the way modern young girls spoke in those days.

Seeta Aur Geeta's box-office performance was again stupendous, and it became the top-grossing film of 1972. Hema Malini was the second choice for the role and was taken only because the Sippys could not afford the fee Mumtaz wanted. However, after this film, Hema Malini became the undisputed No. 1 heroine of the industry.

But what *Seeta Aur Geeta* did went beyond mere numbers and ranks. It changed the way women characters behaved and were perceived by the film industry. Suddenly, women doing action became the rage. In *Gehri Chaal*, Hema Malini was asked to fight the villains while male stars like Jeetendra and Amitabh Bachchan watched from the sidelines. Something similar happened in Salim–Javed's own film too. Prakash Mehra insisted on Jaya Bhaduri featuring in the fight scene of *Zanjeer* because of *Seeta Aur Geeta*. Hema's powerhouse performance— and the script—was the pivot for this change.

After *Seeta Aur Geeta*, the similar storyline was rehashed in a slew of remakes over the next two years, one in Hindi the very next year starring Jeetendra (*Jaise Ko Taisa*), another in Telugu (*Ganga Manga*) and a third in Tamil (*Vani Rani*). The durability of this formula carried well into the 1990s, with hits like *Chaalbaaz* (starring Sridevi) and *Kishen Kanhaiya* (with Anil Kapoor in the title roles).

Despite such success, Salim–Javed were miffed with the Sippys for giving credit for 'their' film to the Sippy Films Story Department. By this time, they were rapidly gaining acceptance among producers and had already sold a couple of story ideas for films. Their annoyance was recognized by the Sippys as much as their talent. G.P. Sippy was on a roll and wanted to make a

major multi-starrer. He very clearly understood that this would
only be possible if they had a kick-ass script, which would be
Salim–Javed's and theirs only, he promised. And the next film
would make history, he predicted.

But before box-office history could be rewritten, Salim–
Javed had already written a character which would rewrite
several careers and the history of the Hindi film industry. The
character was Inspector Vijay Khanna of *Zanjeer*.

Zanjeer

'*Arre, baap re baap*'—A member of the audience during the scene where Inspector Vijay Khanna loses his temper with Sher Khan in the police station

In hindsight, it is easy to say that *Zanjeer* was an idea whose time had come.

On the one hand, people were fed up with government inaction, apathy and corruption. There was rampant unemployment across classes and a thriving crime scene (often in connivance with the system). *Zanjeer* was able to tap into these rumblings of discontent and give them a cinematic voice in the fiery figure of the Angry Young Man[8], an iconic character brilliantly conceived by Salim–Javed—and one that spawned a whole new breed of films. On the other hand, the most common form of entertainment—Hindi cinema—had moved far away from reality; its brand of fantasy and romance did not cut the mustard any more. After a dream run that lasted till 1971 (when he had six out of the year's top ten grossers), Rajesh Khanna had delivered several flops in 1972. People—in a way—were sick

---

[8] See the chapter on the Angry Young Man in Part IV of this book.

of the saccharine-sweet romance and the dancing-around-trees routine.

And yet, not one major star of the day was ready to act in the film.

According to Salim Khan, he had decided upon a treatment of *Zanjeer* even before he teamed up with Javed. The inspiration had come from his father's stories of dutiful police officers fighting in the ravines of Chambal. However, this was more of a concept and not a full script, and was first sold to Dharmendra (for a princely sum of Rs 2500). He was to be the main lead, Prakash Mehra would direct and Dharmendra's brother, Ajit, would be a partner in the production. However, the partnership between Ajit and Prakash Mehra did not work out and Dharmendra dropped out of the film after his brother's exit.

The script was then offered to Dilip Kumar, who thought it would make a very good film but felt the lead character was too one-dimensional and did not allow enough scope for 'performance'. Much later in his career—during the shooting of *Shakti*—Dilip Kumar told Salim Khan that there were three films he regretted not doing in his career: *Pyaasa*, *Baiju Bawra* and *Zanjeer*.

The first actor who was signed for the film was Pran—for the role of Sher Khan. There must have been something in Salim–Javed's narration for as soon as Prakash Mehra heard the script he could envision no other actor in the role.

Once Pran was on board, he—being the good soul that he was—fixed up a meeting with Dev Anand. Salim–Javed felt it would be a case of horrible miscasting and their apprehensions were proved correct when Dev Anand asked for a couple of songs to be picturized on him. (Take a moment to imagine Dev Anand—God bless his soul and swagger—twirling a police baton and singing a romantic duet in *Zanjeer*. Now thank God and proceed.)

Prakash Mehra had such confidence in the script that he refused Dev Anand—one of the biggest stars of the day. It then went to Raaj Kumar's durbar. He too loved the script, probably because he had been an inspector before joining films, and agreed to do the role, but—and this was a big but—he wanted the film to be shot in Madras. One apocryphal story goes that he did not like the smell of Prakash Mehra's hair oil and made this preposterous demand to wriggle out of having to work with him. You might wonder whether the script really was all that path-breaking if an actor could find it wanting when weighed against the smell of hair oil. But that's what Raaj Kumar was all about.

Salim–Javed, in the meantime, were completely sold on a new actor who seemed to have earned a reputation for delivering flop after flop. Every time a hero rejected *Zanjeer*, they pestered Prakash Mehra to take on this new hero. Mehra was more than a little surprised at their recommendation because the industry couldn't stop making fun of 'lambooji'. Javed Akhtar says, 'I don't know why the industry could not see what we thought was absolutely obvious—that Amitabh Bachchan was an exceptionally good actor!' They had seen Amitabh Bachchan's films—some more than once—and were convinced of the actor's ability to portray the role of the angry police officer.

During this time, Pran's son was working in Madras and staying with a certain Ajitabh Bachchan, who took him to watch a film called *Bombay To Goa*, which starred his brother, Amitabh. Pran's son liked the film so much that he heartily recommended the hero to his father, who passed on the recommendation to Prakash Mehra. Pran's word added weight to what Salim–Javed had been saying all along and Mehra finally agreed to meet this new actor. Salim remembers that they introduced Prakash

Mehra to Amitabh Bachchan at Rajkamal Studios, where the latter was shooting for *Pyar Ki Kahaani*.

Partly out of desperation and partly out of respect for Salim–Javed, and Pran, Prakash Mehra signed Amitabh Bachchan for *Zanjeer* reportedly for a sum of Rs 60,000. It was probably the first time in the history of Hindi cinema that writers had expressed such strong opinions about the casting and even got their way, the confidence in their vision overshadowing commercial considerations. Left to himself, Prakash Mehra would have certainly chosen a more saleable hero.

Salim–Javed's mission to make *Zanjeer* a big, impactful film did not end here. They approached Jaya Bhaduri—a top star at that time—and narrated the story. She was hesitant since there was not much of a role for her. Salim recalls telling her frankly that there was no reason for her to act in *Zanjeer* except one—Amitabh Bachchan, with whom she was in a serious relationship then. She agreed, again thanks to the writers' persuasive powers.

This degree of passion and involvement to make a project viable and marketable was absolutely unique to Salim–Javed. During the making of *Zanjeer*, their ambition and desire to be noticed probably pushed them to deploy all their efforts towards ensuring its success. But they maintained this level of involvement in their projects even after they became major stars.

In *Zanjeer*, young Vijay sees his parents gunned down by a faceless killer on the night of Diwali. He only sees a bracelet with a horse on the hand that fires the gun.[9] He is adopted by a police officer's family and grows up to be one too. He is,

---

[9] The scene of the parents' murders—where only the killer's bracelet is seen by a hiding Vijay—is somewhat inspired by the Western, *Death Rides a Horse*. In that film, there are several killers and the child hero notices one identifying mark on each e.g. a locket, a scar on the forehead, a tattoo etc.

however, traumatized by recurring nightmares of the horse and his career is affected by his violent reactions to crime. In his twelfth posting, he meets Sher Khan (Pran) who runs gambling dens in Vijay's area. He challenges Sher Khan to a fight and his daredevilry impresses the Pathan so much enough that he shuts down his illegal network. Vijay keeps getting tip-offs from an anonymous caller (Om Prakash) about smuggling activities and he starts capturing these consignments. This puts him in direct conflict with smuggling kingpin Teja (Ajit), whose public face is that of a respected businessman. In the course of one such investigation, Vijay meets a roadside knife sharpener, Mala (Jaya Bhadhuri), who witnessed a crime related to the case. Due to the risks to Mala's life, Vijay brings her home and eventually falls in love with her. Soon after Teja frames Vijay in a corruption case and has him jailed for six months. When Vijay is released, he vows to destroy Teja. He has a brief change of heart (due to Mala's insistence that he refrain from violence), but ultimately, he—along with Sher Khan—attacks Teja in his mansion. This is where he finds out that Teja was the one who murdered his parents and proceeds to kill him—on the night of Diwali.

'*Jab tak baithne ko na kaha jaye, sharafat se khade raho. Yeh police station hai, tumhare baap ka ghar nahin.*' [ix] If one must specify the moment when the Angry Young Man entered our collective consciousness, this would be it.

And *Zanjeer* was full of such lines—in different styles to suit each character. Inspector Vijay Khanna's lines were simple and he delivered them in an understated manner. Sher Khan's lines were more bombastic: '*Aaj zindagi mein pehli baar Sher Khan ki sher se takkar hui hai.*' [x] And don Teja's lines were as dapper as his suits. When his moll asks about the new inspector's raids on his activities, he deadpans, '*Kabir keh raha tha ek inspector ko paise ki zaroorat hai . . .*' [xi]

Such dialogues—with a breathtaking economy of expression—were not what the Hindi film audience had ever heard. A Hindi film heroine had never—okay, probably just once before[10]—used words like *laafa, bhankas* and *halkat*. But since Mala was a roadside vendor, this was the language that was natural to her character.

Apart from the realistic dialogues and their suitability to the characters, the setting of the film was contemporary and mirrored the prevailing sentiment perfectly.

The film was set at a time when the nation was growing up and coming to terms with terrible realities. Adulterated medicine killed children, illicit hooch flooded the markets, goons could be hired for a pittance and honest people were always cornered.

When offered Rs 50,000 to kill Vijay, Sher Khan says, '*Ek inspector ki jaan ki keemat pachaas hazaar rupiyah? Maloom hota hai bada hi imaandar insaan hai.*'[xii] It was a succinct yet devastating comment on the times.

Salim–Javed's socialist inclinations came to the fore when they addressed the middle-class apathy towards initiating social change with a brilliant monologue spoken by Vijay. When Mala requests him to not risk his life and focus on setting up their home, Vijay bursts out, '*Hum apne ghar mein aise hi khubsoorat parde lagwayenge aur main yeh jaanne ki koshish bhi nahin karoonga ki in pardon ki doosri taraf duniya mein kya ho raha hai . . .*'[xiii] This one scene—though not the best known—exemplifies how good Salim–Javed were at their craft and how Amitabh Bachchan was the perfect voice for their words. In short, *Zanjeer* was that perfect balance of situation and talent—both writing and acting.

However, *Zanjeer* faced the issue that projects without stars face even today. It did not sell. No distributor was willing to

---

[10] In their previous film, *Seeta Aur Geeta.*

bet on a seemingly uncharismatic hero and an untested, violent plot.

Salim–Javed swung into action once again. They worked their charm with the Sippys and held a special preview of *Zanjeer* for G.P. and Ramesh Sippy. Since the duo was writing *Sholay* for the Sippys and the cast was being decided, the pretext was to showcase Amitabh Bachchan for the role of Jai. Salim–Javed paid Rs 1000 out of their pockets to book the Blaze preview theatre and got the Sippys to attend. That swung the tide. When Amitabh Bachchan—a rank newcomer—was signed on for *Sholay* for Rs 1 lakh, it sent a message to the entire industry that this new actor was hot enough for the Sippys. That alone gave potential distributors of *Zanjeer* a lot of confidence.[11]

Salim–Javed were paid Rs 55,000 for *Zanjeer*'s script but given the value they added to the film—apart from the script—this seems like a pittance. They had a finger in pretty much every pie, from casting to distribution. And yet when the posters were printed they were forgotten, and so they had to get some improvised poster-painting done as well!

Salim-Javed's stunt of getting their names painted on the posters paid off.

Zanjeer's was the first poster that writer–director Vinay Shukla remembers seeing which had the names of the writers on it. 'Who is this Salim–Javed?' he had wondered when he saw the poster somewhere near Opera House, initially thinking they were one person.

---

[11] Amitabh was desperate to get the role in *Sholay* and he had also requested Dharmendra to put in a word with the Sippys. When Dharmendra did so and Amitabh got the role, he was very grateful. He repeatedly mentioned this in many interviews and speeches, thus upsetting Salim. Salim maintained Dharmendra's efforts were more out of courtesy and certainly not based on any conviction about Amitabh's talent. Later, Amitabh apologized to Salim and acknowledged his and Javed's efforts warmly.

Director–writer Sriram Raghavan remembers the radio spots for *Zanjeer*, which promised listeners that it would be '*Yaadon ki zanjeer mein lipta hua inteqam ka shola*'.[xiv] As a ten-year old, he remembers being very excited by this line and, during a family movie outing, he was the only one rooting for *Zanjeer* while the rest wanted to go for *Anamika* (which had released just two weeks after *Zanjeer*).

The trade publicity of *Zanjeer* was mounted around Pran and his run-in with Amitabh Bachchan. The first ads said 'Friendship between the man of law and the outlaw'. There was no mention of the revenge plot, with the ad pitting Pran and Amitabh Bachchan as two adversaries, their faces dominating the page.

Salim–Javed paid money out of their own pockets to release an ad on the day *Zanjeer* opened. It featured on a premium position—*Screen*'s inside back cover—and said: 'Writers of *Andaz, Hathi Mere Sathi, Seeta Aur Geeta* now give you *Zanjeer* with Amitabh Bachchan'. (The same issue of *Screen* had a pre-shooting ad of Prakash Mehra's next film—*Hera Pheri*—but without any mention of that movie's writers.)

This ad is very interesting because, probably for the first time in the industry, writers had got an exclusive ad in a trade magazine. And also because none of these films was exclusively or directly credited to them when they were released. In one fell swoop, Salim–Javed wrested the credit for writing these hits and announced it to the industry in style: they were the writers of not only *Zanjeer* but three major hits of the recent past as well. In short, they went from being rank newcomers to hot property in a single day. Their savvy in marketing themselves came to the fore, and it would aid them for the rest of their careers.

Though *Zanjeer* is probably not among Salim–Javed's best scripts, the impact of the violence, the dialogues and the seething anger in the hero was quite unprecedented. Javed watched *Zanjeer* several times in theatres and found the audience reaction to be unlike anything he had ever seen. 'The reaction was very unusual. People didn't clap or whistle in the theatre; they watched the film in total silence and awe.' Referring to the audience reaction of '*Arre baap re baap*', he says, 'This is something I had never heard before, and have never heard since. By the time the audience saw *Deewaar*, they were already familiar with that kind of anger. In *Zanjeer*, it was a totally new experience for them.'

Salim–Javed had a fair bit of disagreement with Prakash Mehra during the making of the film because the director made some changes unilaterally, ostensibly due to 'commercial considerations'.

'*Zanjeer* would have been ten times better if he had followed the script faithfully,' the writers said later.

But despite those changes, the impact of *Zanjeer* was instantaneous. One week after its release, *Screen* carried a picture of Amitabh Bachchan and Pran on the front page, calling them 'Thespian Duo'. The caption of the photograph also mentioned the contribution of Salim–Javed's script to their performance. The front page also carried a news item with the headline: 'G.P. Sippy's next is star-studded venture'. Amitabh Bachchan had well and truly arrived.

Screen's review called *Zanjeer* a 'Well-made crime thriller with effective acting, visuals.' The review in the *Times of India* said, '*Zanjeer* comes up with an unusual hero for the Hindi screen . . . Salim–Javed provide one of the cleverest scripts encountered in some time—a script which respects a clipping pace, keeps those inevitable inessentials down to the minimum, and springs a good many plausible surprises efficiently.'

The biggest beneficiary was undoubtedly Amitabh Bachchan, who would appear in similar roles for nearly two decades after

Zanjeer. And his characters' anger became a template for several heroes of his generation and those who came after him. Ten years later, when *Ardh Satya* was released—in which Om Puri delivered a brilliant performance as an upright cop—it was called 'the art-house *Zanjeer*'. And more than forty years later, producers were still paying top dollar—albeit unwillingly—for the rights of the film.

Zanjeer was Salim–Javed's first hit of 1973. But it was not the only script they wrote that had a revenge motive. The duo had already managed to sell an almost identical story to one of India's canniest producers and that film released towards the end of 1973. It was called *Yaadon Ki Baaraat*.

Yaadon Ki Baaraat

A son sees his parents being shot by a killer whose face he cannot see but he does notice an identifying mark on him. He grows up tormented and is always looking for the killer . . . Wait, isn't that the story of *Zanjeer*?

Well, yes.

In an interview published posthumously, Nasir Husain had said, 'It was too late when I realized that Salim–Javed had palmed off the same basic plot to me and Prakash Mehra. But our characters and treatment were completely different, and so both *Zanjeer* and my film were major hits in the same year!'

While agreeing that both stories had revenge as the main angle and the hero was the strong silent sort, it would be doing Salim–Javed a disservice to say that both the scripts were the same. In fact, Salim Khan disagrees with the veteran producer. 'The films weren't really similar. Only the vendetta angle is common between *Zanjeer* and *Yaadon Ki Baaraat*, which was there in *Sholay* also. Ajit's character made the two films look similar. We had told Nasir Husain about it but he said nobody else was willing to play the role.'

They added a complex lost-and-found angle involving three brothers—which had earlier been seen in Yash Chopra's

Waqt in 1965—thus creating the template for this genre that Manmohan Desai would make famous in the coming years.

The young writers and the producer first connected during the making of Husain's *Teesri Manzil*, in which Salim Khan not only played a small role but also participated in the writing of the script. Evidently, he must have impressed Nasir Husain enough for the film-maker to test writers for the first time, and outsource the project to him and his partner.

Husain's son, director Mansoor Khan, says, 'The plot of *Yaadon Ki Baaraat* was a little complex and he needed people to bounce ideas with. The screenplay was written by brainstorming, which would enrich each scene. The basic plot and characters as well as their key characteristics were defined by him.'

This is contradicted somewhat by Salim Khan, who claims that they wrote the complete screenplay and even a bit of the dialogues, since you can hardly write a script without indicating how the characters will speak to advance the action. Nasir Husain would take their basic lines and polish them for better impact, sometimes during shooting. Mansoor Khan recalls, 'My father would always write the final scenes himself, putting pen to paper. He used a particular brand of a 300-page notebook to write in. He would then dictate it to an assistant, who would transcribe it in Hindi and get the script pages photocopied for the actors and the shooting.'

A lot of the juice in the script did emerge from the brainstorming and bouncing of ideas. There is an apocryphal story that when searching for a suitably grand name for the villain, the two writers and the director heard someone in the Nasir Husain Films' office call out the publicity in-charge's name—'*Arre Shakhaal saab . . .*' And G.P. Shakhaal's name became immortalized as the villain's in not one but two Salim–Javed films!

In *Yaadon Ki Baaraat*, a painter[12] sees the killer Shaakaal (Ajit) fleeing from the scene of a murder. To prevent him from becoming a police witness, Shaakaal kills him and his wife but his three sons manage to escape without seeing the killer face. However, in the ensuing confusion, they get separated while boarding a train on the tracks next to their home. Shaakaal's accomplice Jack (Satyen Kappu) is framed for the murder and jailed.

The eldest brother, Shankar (Dharmendra), grows up to be a thief. The middle brother, Vijay (Vijay Arora), grows up to be a normal, fun-loving guy who is just out of college. The youngest, Ratan (Tariq), becomes a musician who plays under the alias, Monto, along with his band, Monto and His Avengers. Shankar is constantly on the lookout for Shaakaal but unwittingly works for him on heists. Vijay falls in love with Sonia (Zeenat Aman), a millionaire's daughter. When Shankar finally gets through to Jack, he learns that Shaakaal's unique feature is his differently sized feet, because of which he wears a size-8 shoe on one foot and a size-9 shoe on the other.

In a triple-barrelled pre-climax development, Shankar kidnaps Sonia to force her father to part with priceless antique jewellery. He also realizes that Shaakaal, whom he has been working for all this while, is his parents' killer. And the three brothers discover each other when Ratan/Monto sings their family song. In the climax, the three brothers save Sonia, keep the jewellery from being smuggled and kill Shaakaal on the same railway track that once separated them.

For a film like *Yaadon Ki Baaraat*, where the story hurtles through on pure adrenaline, a mere plot description does not sufficiently reflect the impact of the film. Lost-and-found sagas

---

[12] The painter's name in the film is Gulzar. He is seen wearing short kurtas and dark-framed spectacles, much like the real-life Gulzar.

depend on how well the gears mesh and how one scene brings about the next. Director Sriram Raghavan says, 'I was a kid then and I got a complete narration of *Yaadon Ki Baaraat* from my mom. We weren't allowed too many movies then. But my parents had just seen the movie. I asked her to at least tell me the story. And she did—scene by scene! How the boys separated, how their paths crossed often but they kept missing the chance to realize they were brothers, and how they ultimately met and how the villain got his foot stuck in the railway tracks and was run down by a train. I was a kid, but I too could see the whole film in my head.'

This lost-and-found template reached its pinnacle in *Amar Akbar Anthony*, which had many of the distinctive features that Salim–Javed fine-tuned in *Yaadon Ki Baaraat*, *Haath Ki Safai* and *Chacha Bhatija*, lost-and-found films written over a span of four years. All these films had:

- Dramatic separation, usually during a family crisis— connected by unique memento
- Multiple meetings of family members as adults, without knowing each other
- Fortuitous reunion, just in time for the climax

If you think about it, these elements have found repeated usage in such films. *Yaadon Ki Baaraat* is one of the best in this genre with typical Salim–Javed twists added into the age-old formula. For example, the 'memento', which connects the family, is a song instead of something physical like a locket, letter or tattoo. A song known to only three people in the world is a very cool concept and presents a more dramatic opportunity of reconnecting the brothers than a physical memento. Incidentally, there is a prevalent belief among Hindi film fans that Ratan, the youngest brother (played by a very young Aamir Khan), asks for the song to be completed because he went to the loo during the antara (*Badle na apna yeh aalam kabhi, jeevan mein bichhdenge na hum kabhi . . .*) and didn't hear the full song. Actually, this is not true because Ratan returns in time for the repeat of the antara. Also, as a family song, it would have been sung several times and hence it is unlikely that one brother would not know the complete song.

Salim–Javed had a special gift for orchestrating the events that bring the separated family members together—unknown to each other. Shankar, Vijay and Ratan meet several times in the film—unwittingly embracing, praising and helping each other without knowing their relationship. Consequently, when the connection is finally established, it becomes an extremely emotional, applause-inducing climax.

What is interesting in the promotion material of *Yaadon Ki Baaraat* is Salim–Javed's increasing prominence. This was only their second film with exclusive credit but with *Zanjeer*, they had made a strong statement by staking a claim to the success of their previous three films as well. Before the release of *Yaadon Ki Baaraat*, they got third billing on the posters—after the music director (R.D. Burman) and the lyricist (Majrooh Sultanpuri), both of whom were huge stars. Indeed the biggest draw of this film—as with all Nasir Husain productions—was the fantastic music. But by the time the film released, Salim–Javed had overtaken Majrooh and were placed right after RD in the credits. This is probably indicative of their respective contributions to the film's success. This is interesting because it was quite uncommon to give certain members of a film's crew greater prominence as the promotions progressed.

The reviews of *Yaadon Ki Baaraat* were not gushing. *Screen* called it a 'crime thriller of familiar sort' and went on to say 'its main handicap is the close resemblance . . . to the current hit *Zanjeer* in the matter of story idea and development which in any case have their debt to foreign sources'.

The impact of *Yaadon Ki Baaraat*, however, goes beyond the lukewarm reviews or the box-office success. (It was the fifth-highest grosser of 1973.) Film scholar Kaushik Bhaumik calls it 'the first masala classic as well as the first Bollywood film'. It is a perfect mixture of all the elements that make a typical Hindi film—crackling storyline embellished with whistle-inducing dialogues, rocking music, stars performing the antics expected of them, multiple tracks adding layers to the enjoyment, eye-catching fashion and locations, and a happily-ever-after resolution of all the problems in the climax.

The result is a very durable storyline that has remained a big favourite of Hindi film audiences for a long time. At the party to celebrate the bumper success of *3 Idiots*, Aamir Khan was asked if a remake of any old film had the power of breaking the blockbuster's record. Aamir Khan speculated that as a story, *Yaadon Ki Baaraat* probably had a good chance. Since he half-jokingly also suggested Mansoor Khan should direct the remake, the Bollywood press breathlessly reported one to be almost on the floors! Mansoor Khan rubbishes the possibility of a remake but agrees that the 'formula' still works.

Salim–Javed had just started perfecting this formula. They would soon reunite with Prakash Mehra to create yet another tale of lost-and-found brothers, this time with both siblings on the wrong side of the law. That film was *Haath Ki Safai*.

Haath Ki Safai

Salim–Javed signed *Haath Ki Safai* with Prakash Mehra when—in their own words—'[they] were not in a position to dictate'. Their experience with the director during *Zanjeer* hadn't been great and they never worked with him after this.

Haath Ki Safai is definitely not one of Salim–Javed's more successful or celebrated films. Though it was a decent hit when it released in 1974, the movie certainly did not set the box office ablaze (like *Seeta Aur Geeta* had earlier) nor did it become a massive turning point for Hindi cinema (like *Zanjeer* the previous year). Yet it is interesting to see how much zest the writers gave to a familiar tale with social context, cool situations and really rocking lines.

While a lot can be made out of Nasir Husain's comment that *Zanjeer* and *Yaadon Ki Baaraat* were both the same story really, we should consider the following 'equations':

- *Zanjeer* = revenge drama (by identifying the killer through a unique symbol)
- *Yaadon Ki Baaraat* = revenge drama (by identifying the killer through a unique symbol) + lost-and-found saga of brothers
- *Haath Ki Safai* = lost-and-found saga of brothers

Basically, they took formulae A and B and managed to pull three different scripts out of them. You might diss this almost slavish adherence to the established formula—which they exhibited throughout their career—but you have to admire their flair for the spoken word and ability to spin a yarn that made the final products completely different.

In *Haath Ki Safai*, two brothers—Shankar and Raju—who live in a small town with their mother, leave for Bombay when she passes away, but get separated on the way. The younger one, Raju, is picked up by a pickpocket trainer, Usmanbhai (Satyen Kappu), and is trained to become an ace pickpocket, known as Raju Tardeo (Randhir Kapoor), so named because of his area of operation. His elder brother Shankar grows up to become a smuggler known as Kumar (Vinod Khanna), who is married to Roma (Simi Garewal). Shankar is constantly on the lookout for his younger brother and always carries their childhood photo in his wallet. Raju meets Kamini (Hema Malini), who seems to be a rich woman, and plans to swindle her. When Kamini runs away from home to escape her cruel uncle both Shankar and Raju try to catch her. Due to a misunderstanding, a pregnant Roma leaves Shankar's home in anger and is given shelter by Raju, while Kamini is in Shankar's house. The villains, who find out about this, use that information to cause a major rift between the two men but Shankar and Raju find out that they are brothers and join hands for the climax.

The mind-boggling complications of the second half have been glossed over in a word or two (like 'misunderstanding' and 'discover') but the chain of events and their pace would have done Manmohan Desai proud.

What stands out in the film is the dialogue—clever and punchy: '*Bachche, tum jis school mein padhte ho, hum uske headmaster reh chuke hain . . .*' xv

As far as versatility of dialogue goes, this line is right up there with the best. Considering that none of the other elements of *Haath Ki Safai*—acting, music, story—have really endured, the durability of this one line is quite amazing. There are several things going for it. Vinod Khanna's character (and indeed the star himself) has an easy charisma, which comes across nicely through this line. Add to that the standard lost-and-found ploy of creating near-misses of the siblings meeting unwittingly and you have some solid contextual weight behind the line. It still pops up quite regularly on Internet forums about the best dialogues of Hindi cinema. And it got a new lease of life when one Salman Khan (with more than a passing acquaintance with one of the creators of the line) deadpanned in his blockbuster *Wanted*: '*Jis school mein tune yeh sab seekha hai na, uska headmaster aaj bhi mujhse tuition leta hai.*'[xvi] Make what you want to of the subtexts!

Apart from the punchlines, all the characters spoke differently and in keeping with their backgrounds. This was a hallmark of all Salim–Javed films and *Haath Ki Safai* was no exception.

Another Salim–Javed trick, of giving a catchphrase to some of the major characters, is evident in the line that Raju keeps saying throughout the film: '*Kyun, kya khayal hai?*' [xvii]

There were other clever ploys too. In one scene, Raju explains his acting prowess by saying, '*Acting toh hamari khoon mein hai. Baap dada bhi yehi kaam karte aaye hain.*'[xviii]—an obvious reference to the Kapoors. In a scene where he is portraying Devdas in a play, he ad-libs, '*Chandramukhi ho ya Paro, ki farq painda, yaaro?*' [xix]—a quip which was later used by writer–director Sujoy Ghosh in *Jhankaar Beats*.

Apart from these, there were some set pieces that seemed to be a part of many of their films. For example, a montage to show a child growing up—a young Shankar hides in an aeroplane model in a park, and it transforms into a real plane in which the adult Shankar is travelling.

The writers' message of socialism comes through in the scene where the two brothers are shown at a medicine shop. They are short of Rs 2.50 to buy the medicines that can save their mother, when a rich lady walks in to buy dog biscuits at Rs 15 a pack. This kind of message—which found resonance in the country's situation then—had been seen in their earlier films and would be repeated in many of their later works as well.

By this time, Salim–Javed had delivered five hits in a row, with two of their films being the top grossers of the years in which they were released. Their success guaranteed them top billing and in the advertisements for *Haath Ki Safai*, their names were right beside the composers' (Kalyanji–Anandji).

Their growing reputation would have been something *Screen* paid heed to when they reviewed that '*Haath Ki Safai* provides fast-paced fare', though it was clearly not among the most successful movies of the year.

One reason for the film's not-so-stellar performance could be the spate of 'thief films' that were released in 1974. When *Haath Ki Safai* opened there was *Chor Chor* (which was releasing simultaneously), *Chor Machaye Shor* (which was in its twentieth week) and *Pocket Maar* (about to release).

Instead of going for novelty of plot, Salim–Javed always went for tried and tested formulae from all kinds of sources and gave those a distinctly Indian twist. From the Bollywood formula of lost-and-found and revenge, the duo now moved to a completely different plot—with more twists and suspense— with their favourite actor. The film was *Majboor*.

Majboor

'Fight of a helpless man with odds and ends of life'—
From the publicity material of the film

In 1970, George Kennedy (of not-so-great fame) and Eli Wallach (of *The Good, the Bad and the Ugly* fame) starred in a thriller called *Zig Zag* in which a dying insurance executive (Kennedy) frames himself for the murder of a tycoon and creates an elaborate smokescreen so that his wife and daughter get the reward money. On death row, he discovers that he was wrongly diagnosed and isn't dying after all. He then escapes from prison to find the real killer and clear his name.

By all accounts, the film was nothing memorable and critics pointed out many plot holes, finding fault with the improbable ending and a slightly confusing shift between past and present.

However, Salim–Javed felt inspired enough to take the story and punch in a lot of shudh desi emotion by giving the protagonist a widowed mother, a kid brother and a disabled sister. By making his family's dependence on the hero abundantly clear through a mix of sentimental scenes and throw away lines, the writers invested the motive with a lot of Indian sensibility.

Ravi Khanna (Amitabh Bachchan) is an executive at a
travel agency and is equally dutiful at work and at home.
He is questioned by the police (Iftekhar and Jagdish Raj) in
connection with the murder of a tycoon (Rehman) who was last
seen at Ravi's agency, but nothing comes of it. Around the same
time, Ravi starts experiencing tremendous pain in his head and
he's diagnosed with a brain tumour. The course of treatment
involves extremely risky surgery that might render him blind
or paralysed. Given his sole breadwinner status, Ravi chooses
to ignore the surgery route and frames himself for the tycoon's
murder—ensuring that his mother gets the reward money
through a decoy created by his lawyer. Ravi is jailed, where he gets
another attack of pain, severe enough to warrant hospitalization
and an operation. The surgery is successful and Ravi now has a
full life ahead of him. He escapes from the hospital with the help
of his girlfriend Neela (Parveen Babi) and starts investigating
the murder. In the course of his investigation, he meets a thief
Michael (Pran) who gives a vital clue that identifies the killer as
the tycoon's brother (Satyen Kappu).

Majboor is probably Salim–Javed's tightest script, with
hardly any subplots or comedy tracks to distract from the main
story as it spirals rapidly towards the climax. Even the romantic
subplot is wrapped up in the first half and by the second half,
Neela is an associate in Ravi's quest to prove his innocence.

The tautness of the script appealed to Ramesh Sippy when
it was first presented to him in early 1973. It was a ready script
which could be completed very quickly and it seemed like a
strong commercial proposition. But after the huge success of
Seeta Aur Geeta, Ramesh's father, G.P. Sippy, wanted to make
a 'badi film'—a multi-starrer on a big scale. He liked another
idea the writers narrated that had a lot of scope for high-octane
action, special effects and 'bigness'. *Majboor,* in comparison,

was a good script but not a great one. Sippy offered Rs 1.5 lakh to Salim–Javed for developing the other script and letting *Majboor* go.

The duo offered the script to Premji, who had produced superhits like *Mera Saaya* (a haunting musical starring Sunil Dutt and Sadhna), *Dushmun* (a Rajesh Khanna-starrer in his golden year, 1971) and *Dost* (which he was making then, starring Dharmendra and Hema Malini). With full faith in Salim–Javed's box-office credentials, Premji bought the script for Rs 2 lakh—much more than what the Sippys were willing to pay for it anyway.

Director Ravi Tandon recalls the narration of the script being very detailed, including the scene were Ravi escapes from the hospital.[13] He also found it interesting that the hero suffered from a brain tumour, which was not a commonly used disease in Hindi films then. He says, 'The problem was how to show it to the audience in a way that they could understand the ailment's severity.'

The film unfolded like a Hollywood thriller with every scene pushing the action forward, and a host of pithy lines, often delivered with deadpan humour. While criminal procedure has never been Hindi cinema's forte, the scenes in which Ravi frames himself are quite believable and they brought credibility to the plot without sacrificing the pace.

Majboor is a rather underrated script as none of the dialogues really endured, but all the situations were very real, with everyday conversations building up mood, character and plot. All the devices of the crime thriller—both as book and film—were ticked off. In a skilfully written scene, when police

---

[13] Incidentally, the hospital scenes of *Don* (where the crime syndicate smuggles Vijay away, thinking him to be Don) were filmed on the sets that were created for *Majboor*.

officers come to interrogate Ravi about the murder, the fact that the victim's body has just been discovered is revealed only at the end of the conversation.

When Ravi meets Michael (Pran), a potential informer who is also a thief, he repeats a dialogue that was also used in *Yaadon Ki Baaraat*: '*Suna hai choron ke bhi kuch usool hote hain.*' The informer—a vital cog in the mystery—replies, '*Tum ne theek hi suna hai. Choron ke hi to usool hote hain.*'[xx]

Pran, as the informer, was the biggest scene-stealer of the film. Salim–Javed always wrote great lines for him because he was a powerful actor. Together, Amitabh Bachchan and Pran made a formidable pair in *Zanjeer, Majboor* and (the then forthcoming) *Don*. They always played honourable men who clashed before forming a partnership.

In *Majboor*, Pran was Michael D'Souza—drunkard and thief but with a heart of gold—who appeared in the last one-third of the film and performed a flamboyant role. He had the film's most popular track: *Daaru ki botal mein kahe paani bharta hai, phir na kehna Michael daaru pee kar danga karta hai*, and a cool habit of circling his fingers around his eyes to get a closer look. Pran borrowed this gimmick from director Ravi Tandon who used to frame his shots like that.

In hindsight, *Majboor* wasn't that big a hit, nor did it come anywhere to being among the highest grossers of the year. In fact, Premji's other release of the year, *Dost,* written by veteran writer Sachin Bhowmick, was a much bigger hit. Despite that, there was something about Salim–Javed's projections about their contributions and their success which made them appear larger than they actually were. They seemed to show a grand vision through their narration, involvement and film sense. This, coupled with the fact that they were pitching themselves as 'end-to-end writers' who provided a complete script, swung the balance in their favour when it came to choosing writers for Premji's forthcoming film, since Sachin Bhowmick—being a Bengali—did not write dialogues in Hindi.

Majboor released in December 1974 and did reasonably well, recovering costs. Two weeks after the film's release, Premji was so happy with Salim–Javed's script that he released a gushing ad in *Screen*, announcing his next venture—and giving top billing to the two writers. The ad said: 'After the thundering success of *Majboor*, Premji announces Suchitra's Production No. 6 written by Salim–Javed, Music Laxmikant Pyarelal, Lyric Anand Bakshi, Directed by Desh Mukerji'. (This film went on to become *Immaan Dharam*.)

Premji's decision to retain Salim–Javed for his next production was more than validated by a film that released a month after *Majboor* and not only rewrote box-office history, but raised the standards of Hindi film scripting as well. The film was *Deewaar*.

Deewaar

'As far as the script is concerned, *Deewaar* is better than
Sholay . . . That was the one script and screenplay where
you didn't have to delete anything after making, it was
such a perfect script'—Yash Chopra

If there is one story that exemplifies the sheer talent and the
confidence Salim–Javed possessed, it is that of how they
narrated the script of *Deewaar* to the cast and crew. Amitabh
Bachchan recalls, 'I remember while narrating the script,
Salim–Javed stopped after five-ten minutes and said *Deewar*
would run for at least ten-fifteen weeks. After half an hour,
they stopped again and said it would run for at least twenty-
five weeks. And after they completed the narration, they said
it would run for at least fifty to seventy-five weeks . . . all in
jest of course.'

For once, the duo were wrong. *Deewaar* went on to run
for more than one hundred weeks in many centres, with daily
showings even three years after its release.

The screenplay—almost unanimously regarded as their
best—was written in a breathless burst of eighteen days, an
unheard-of pace at a time when the slow marination of scripts

was prevalent in the industry. (The dialogues took another twenty-five days or so, again an incredible feat.)

It is another sign of their confidence that they first took the script to Amitabh Bachchan. The actor says, 'We had started another film—*Gardish*—with Neetu Singh and Parveen Babi. Yashji's editor, Pran Mehra, was directing. We were well into its shooting when Salim–Javed narrated the script of *Deewaar* to me. Deservedly, *Deewaar* is rated as the best screenplay of Hindi cinema, with excellent dialogue to boot. It's flawless.'

In early 1974, Amitabh Bachchan had done only *Zanjeer* and was shooting for *Majboor*. His saleability as a lead actor had still not been established firmly. And yet, Salim–Javed went to him instead of any director or producer. While they had not written the script with Amitabh in mind, they felt he would be the right person for it when it was completed. It says a lot about their conviction about what would work best to make their script a success as well as their understanding of how to get a project on the road.

After the actor got excited about the role, the three of them decided to take it to Yash Chopra who seemed best suited to direct it. Yash Chopra had just completed the Dev Anand-starrer *Joshila*, which had not done well. Chopra had not been very happy with the script but he did the film out of an obligation to Gulshan Rai (who had financed his debut production, *Daag*). Now, he was on the lookout for a strong story and a complete script for his next film.

After they gave the director the outline, Salim–Javed gave a full narration to a small group comprising producer Gulshan Rai, Yash Chopra, his long-time editor Pran Mehra and assistant director Ramesh Talwar. This was when the duo predicted the seventy-five-week run for the film.

Once the script was accepted, the first casting discussed between Yash Chopra and Rai had Rajesh Khanna playing

Vijay's role. Rai nominated Khanna for the role because he had already paid the actor a signing amount and wanted him to be in his next film. Salim–Javed suggested that Amitabh would be perfect as Vijay, and convinced Rai that Rajesh Khanna would not be suitable for any role in this film. With their customary confidence, they even offered to write another script more suited to Rajesh Khanna, if Gulshan sahib so desired. They endorsed Amitabh Bachchan so strongly over the reigning superstar that Yash Chopra jokingly asked, 'Does Amitabh pay you commission to recommend him so much?'

After it was agreed that Bachchan would be Vijay, Salim–Javed took the script to Shashi Kapoor and convinced him to play the younger brother. They sold him the role by highlighting the lines that would become famous, and predicted that 'even though the length is short, you are going to get a Filmfare Award, for sure . . .' Shashi Kapoor—being a seasoned star—figured out that although he would not be the prime mover in the film, his role was a strong one and his character had several performance-heavy scenes which would get him noticed. He not only agreed but even cut his hair short to suit the character of a police officer and allotted forty days at a stretch to shoot the film. He performed brilliantly and, sure enough, won the Filmfare Award for best supporting actor that year.

Post the debate over the casting, the only concession Gulshan Rai asked for was the insertion of three songs—not really relevant to the script—ostensibly to please distributors. Javed Akhtar says, 'There was hardly any scope for music in the film. It was meant to be a film about a person who rebels against the establishment.' But the songs were included and they did serve to heighten the suspense at key points in the plot. Film critic Khalid Mohammad differs though. '*Deewar* had bothered me even when I'd seen it as a college student. The Shashi

Kapoor–Neetu Singh song straight after the interval. What was that?' he asks angrily.

As is known by almost anyone with even a passing knowledge of Hindi cinema, *Deewaar* is the story of two brothers, Vijay (Amitabh Bachchan) and Ravi (Shashi Kapoor). As children, they start their lives in a mining town where their father, Anand babu (Satyen Kappu), is a respected union leader. The mine owners kidnap Anand babu's family and coerce him to sign an unfair agreement on behalf of the miners, thus angering them. In a fit of fury, the miners tattoo the words '*Mera baap chor hai*'[xxi] on a young Vijay's arm. Anand babu abandons his family and the two boys are taken away by their mother (Nirupa Roy) to Bombay. Vijay grows up to become a dock worker, while the more educated Ravi looks for jobs. Vijay, the rebellious one, picks a fight with a gang of extortionists at the docks and demolishes them. Impressed with the young man, a smuggler Davar (Iftekhar) recruits Vijay into his gang. Armed with his intelligence, appetite for risk-taking and luck, Vijay soon rises to the top of the underworld. Meanwhile, Ravi becomes a police officer and is charged with investigating Vijay's gang, and that's when he learns about his brother's illegal activities. When Vijay refuses Ravi's request to surrender, the latter leaves his house along with their mother. Eventually, Vijay decides to give himself up when his girlfriend Sunita (Parveen Babi) announces she is pregnant. Before he can, however, his enemies kill her and in a fit of rage, Vijay kills them all. When he tries to escape the police dragnet to go and meet his mother, Vijay is shot dead by Ravi.

What is obviously missing in this plot description is the power of the film's best scenes that distinguished it from the sources from where the basic plot ideas were taken. This is key to Salim–Javed's style. Taking the germ of a story (much borrowed from earlier classics), they studded the bare narrative with an absolutely stunning sequence of words and emotions that went way beyond the original.

The raison d'être of Vijay's anger was that tattoo on his arm—*Mera baap chor hai*. It became the symbol of the fatherless, support-less angry young man. This act of tattooing was something completely unimaginable, even in the hyperbolic world of Hindi cinema. I would say that *this* is the most 'violent' part of *Deewaar*. The film actually had very little physical violence, relying instead on psychological trauma to create impact.

When they narrated this scene for the first time to the film-making team, Ramesh Talwar—Yash Chopra's assistant director—started clapping. He says of the narration, 'I was thrilled as a cine-goer. I was the youngest in the group and closest to the emotions portrayed in the script. When they described the scene, I started clapping . . .' This spontaneous reaction from someone who was closest in age to the intended audience boosted the team's morale. This was critical because Yash Chopra himself was low on confidence after the *Joshila* debacle. He wanted to gauge the others' reactions before forming his own views. And this iconic scene was probably the best antidote to his lack of conviction.

Several of *Deewaar*'s scenes have passed into filmi folklore. Even the minor scenes—where labour leader Anand babu addresses workers at a factory gate or Inspector Ravi Verma accepts a prize—are just terrific.

When Vijay meets Sunita for the first time in the bar, the audience knows he is about to put himself in mortal danger but the suspense built up during their conversation and the long walk to the car is done extremely well. It is the format in which you know the hero is going to survive but you are never sure how that is going to happen—whether he has a plan or just wants to test fate.

Director Sriram Raghavan says, 'The scene where Shashi Kapoor goes to meet A.K. Hangal is one of my favourite scenes. He is obviously guilty of injuring Hangal's son and goes to apologize but the message he gets out of the meeting is completely unexpected. In one way, it is very obvious that you get the moral message but the scene is so true and moving that is stands apart.'

One can enumerate many other such powerful scenes from the film . . . Young Vijay refusing to pick up a coin thrown at him and that same sequence being repeated when he is an adult. His challenge to the dockyard goons. His first heist where he accosts, hoodwinks and makes an enemy out of Samant (Madan Puri). His angry entreaty to God. His first confrontation with his mother and brother.

And of course, the iconic scene where Vijay and Ravi clash over their ideals under a bridge is a sure-shot entry in the list of Hindi cinema's best scenes. '*Mera paas maa hai*'[xxii] is a line which has gone from spoofs to sentimental outpourings, from Amitabh Bachchan's many stage shows to the biggest platform for film awards. When A.R. Rehman won an Oscar (incidentally, for a film based on two estranged brothers), he celebrated his victory with this line written by Salim–Javed.

But *Deewaar*—to its eternal credit—goes way beyond just explosive lines. Once you look past the dialogues, which have survived generations, you realize the whole movie was filmed exactly as it was written, and Salim–Javed's stamp is as evident as the director's—probably more so. Yash Chopra had said that *Deewaar* was the first script he read that had every scene and every shot clearly marked out.

Deewaar's screenplay is a series of dialogue-linked cuts. The opening scene—where Ravi wins a police award—ends with applause and that cheering cleverly transitions to the applause that Anand babu got for his speeches many years back. When he wonders if his voice is reaching the mine owners—'*Agar is waqt meri awaaz un malikon tak pahunch rahi hai . . .*')—the scene cuts to the owners' drawing room where they are listening to his words on a tape recorder. The factory owner talks about finding a possible weakness of the leader ('*Anand babu ki aisi kaun si kamzori hai?*'[xxiii]) and the scene cuts to his wife Sumitra. The most telling cut is probably when a smuggler, impressed with young Vijay's potential, says, '*Ek din yeh ladka kuch banega,*' and the scene changes to a school teacher praising Ravi with the same words, thus delineating the career arcs of the two brothers with finesse and without fuss.

These cuts appear throughout the film and continuously highlight the completeness of the script, which resulted in its being shot almost as is, and explain why Salim–Javed resented any suggestions to change anything in the film.

After the film was ready, a trial showing was organized for Mangesh Desai. Easily the industry's busiest sound technician, Desai saw every major film for re-recording purposes and was considered to be an expert on what works in movies. He felt *Deewaar* was too 'dry' despite being very good.[14] Predicting a long run, he said, 'A couple of songs would add many weeks to this film's run . . .' Gulshan Rai (who had already inserted three songs in an originally songless script) took Desai's feedback quite seriously and briefly considered adding more songs but Salim–Javed put their feet down, and they were supported by the younger members of the crew. Yash Chopra also agreed that too much music would spoil the sombre mood of the film. 'We don't want the film to fall between two stools . . .' Ramesh Talwar cautioned and eventually Rai came around.

---

[14] During this discussion, Salim–Javed suggested changing the title to 'Geeli Deewaar'. 'The dryness will go,' they observed wryly in the face of conventional wisdom on what works in Hindi films.

Deewaar's influences are as rich as they are varied. Director Sriram Raghavan writes, 'If Salim–Javed took one idea and made two movies, they were to also do a total opposite. They took classics of Hindi Cinema—*Gunga Jumna* and *Mother India*—and wonder of wonders, through their amalgamation, created a third classic, *Deewaar*!' Javed Akhtar explains it further, 'Both Salim sahib and I really loved *Mother India* and *Gunga Jumna* . . . but as we developed *Deewaar*'s script, it ceased to be either of these films. While it resembled them in plot, *Deewaar*'s sensibility was totally different. We introduced a certain modernity in the setting of the film, its accent, tempo and language. Its cinematic language also changed from the language in *Gunga Jumna*. It was much more urban, much more contemporary, and the kind of moral dilemmas that it posed were very much of its own era.'

With this combination of two classic films came the story of Bombay underworld don Haji Mastan's early life. The similarities were slim even though rumours expanded them manifold.[15] What was common was Mastan's initial days as a coolie in the Mazgaon docks of Bombay where he rebelled against an extorting Pathan gang and beat them up, thus gaining tremendous clout among the coolie community. However—unlike Vijay Verma—Mastan

---

[15] *Once Upon A Time In Mumbaai* (a film sued by Haji Mastan's family) had a line which directly alludes to the filmic quality of Mastan's life. Kangana Ranaut tells Ajay Devgn (ostensibly playing Mastan), '*Tumhare upar ek film banni chahiye. Banne se pehle hi superhit hai . . . Acting kisi aur se karwa lenge. Woh naya ladka hai na—Amit? Naya superstar? Bahut suit karega. Uski aankhen bhi tumhari tarah hai. Bahut bolti hain . . .*' ('A film on your life will be a superhit from the word go . . . We will get someone intense to play you. You know the new star—Amit? He'll suit the role. His eyes are like yours, they speak a lot . . .') While moving court for *OUATIM*, Haji Mastan's daughter said, 'My father had seen *Deewaar* and did not exactly find Amitabh Bachchan's character modelled on him!'

did not do it all alone. He got together a gang of toughs armed with rods to do it. In fact, Salim Khan turns the rumours around when he says, 'It probably suited Mastan to build his own aura by claiming the film was based on his life.'

Coming back to the filmi influences, the battle between right and wrong—with two brothers on opposite sides of the law and a mother weighing in on the side of good—was not new, but the setting was and so was the power. Salim–Javed updated the dacoits-in-villages setting to a modern, urban backdrop and made it absolutely real. The frustrations of the job-seeking youth, the unfairness of extortion gangs, and the glamour and contrasting ruthlessness of smugglers were brought out with amazing realism.

Javed Akhtar calls *Deewaar* their 'most moral film'. In the end, all the efforts of the 'bad brother' are proven wrong and emphatically so. In the climax, Inspector Ravi Verma need not kill his brother. He can simply shoot him in the legs to disable him (just the way he does to a thief he is chasing in an earlier scene). But he does kill his brother, with the blessing of their mother who says, '*Bhagwaan kare goli chalate waqt tere haath na kaanpe.*'[xxiv] If there was a message about the nation being above all else, it was never more strongly delivered.

When *Deewaar* opened in January of 1975, the initial reviews were far from gushing.

Screen headlined their review as a 'Meaningful drama of conflict between brothers' but felt 'its main handicap is that it has not chosen to do it with an entirely fresh conception of story and character relationships, which could have put it on a different level', while reserving a few words for 'skilful scripting, which creates many unusual situations of conflicts invested with some hard-hitting dialogue, off-beat and consistent characterisations'.

In *Hindustan Times*, film critic K.M. Amladi spent most of his review dwelling upon the Haji Mastan influence, and dismissed Salim–Javed's contribution to the second half by saying, 'Since they have to justify their existence, one finds the post-interval happenings more as a figment of their imagination than as an imitation of Mastan's life pattern.'

In *Filmfare*, a critic gave the film one star in a review that I could not make any sense of!

The reviewers did not catch the contemporary context that Salim–Javed brought to *Deewaar*. Writer-director Vinay Shukla says, 'It was the first Hindi film made with a modern, urban sensibility. Traces of feudalism gone. All the characters, be it Amitabh's, Shashi Kapoor's, Nirupa Roy's, Parveen Babi's, were products of an industrial society.'

Like countless people, the characters migrated to Bombay from a north Indian town. Both brothers faced the rampant unemployment and poverty prevalent in the country then, each choosing to tackle it in a different way. The menace of smuggling was an ever-increasing problem, which was the backdrop of the story. Even Parveen Babi's character was a prostitute without any moral justification. She had no ill mother or paralysed brother to take care of and yet she sold her body. For the first time commercial cinema had characters that were *real*, characters the audience recognized as one of their own. And this is a major reason for *Deewaar*'s success.

Deewaar, featuring the ultimate Angry Young Man, was helped—in no small measure—by the political events that were unfolding at that exact moment. People were already angry and there were leaders who were mobilizing this anger. After getting a great response in his home state of Bihar (during the latter half of 1974) and the rejection of his call to dissolve state assemblies, Jayprakash Narayan travelled across India in January and February of 1975 to garner support. Some commentators have called the JP movement 'India's second freedom struggle'. Despite the ban on entering Delhi and a near-curfew around the Parliament, JP led a procession of 7,50,000 people—all of whom were raising slogans against a 'weak government' and demanding action against the corrupt—into the city. While lakhs of discontented marched and crores seethed, they were presented with a 'hero' who was forced by the 'system' to a life of crime, which he eventually gives up for his mother.

Deewaar's position in the Indian cultural consciousness has burgeoned into something gigantic over the years. It has far exceeded its inspirations in the projection of The Mother Figure of Hindi cinema. The mere recounting of '*Mere paas maa hai*'—as a line without context—doesn't even begin to explain the mesmerising hold it has had over Hindi film audiences all these years. However, the film's biggest impact was on Amitabh Bachchan's career, unequivocally establishing his stardom for more than a decade. It also firmly cemented the partnership of the star with Salim–Javed, what became a symbiotic relationship of producing some of the most memorable roles of Indian cinema. The mandir scene with Amitabh's monologue 'berating' God for his mother's illness is an excellent example of how well they worked together. Javed Akhtar recalls having a discussion with the actor before shooting the scene, which they felt had too harsh and defiant a tone. 'But Amitabh was quite convinced and said, "If I start the dialogue on a low note, then somewhere in-between I'll have to raise my tone. So instead, I'm going to start the delivery of dialogue from a very strong stance and work my way down."' Never before had an actor assimilated the writer's vision so well and never before had a writer–actor team created so much impact at the box office.

At the Filmfare Awards that year, *Deewaar* pretty much swept the evening, winning seven out of nine nominations.

The two awards it did not win were—ironically—for best actor (where *Aandhi*'s Sanjeev Kumar beat Amitabh Bachchan) and best supporting actress (where *Julie*'s Nadira beat Nirupa Roy). Salim–Javed became the first writers to win all the three writing categories—story, screenplay and dialogues—in one year. Their three-in-one record stood till *3 Idiots* equalled it in 2009. Imagine, thirty-five years.

Deewaar—after conquering the box office—formally anointed Salim–Javed as the newest kings of the Hindi film industry. I don't use the word 'king' metaphorically; the producers of *Deewaar* sponsored an ad in *Screen* that carried the picture of two crowns and the line 'Story Kings Salim–Javed'. Forget composers and writers, even Amitabh Bachchan at his peak did not receive such an endorsement from adulating producers.

In all the publicity material for *Deewaar*, the writers' names were right below the director's, and the actors, director and producer openly acknowledged their contribution. (Just to present a counterpoint, in the ads for *Zameer*—which released around the same time—the story and dialogue credits were tucked at the bottom of the page.)

Coincidentally or not, *Screen* ran a front-page article less than a week after *Deewaar*'s release that talked about 'The changing film scene: Seventies bring big improvement in form, content', and went on to say that 'Today the writer is a dominant factor in films – almost next only to the director (sic).'

After the mega-success of *Deewaar*, if somebody had said that its records would be broken before the year was out, people would have laughed in disbelief. But when *Deewaar* was nearing its thirtieth week in Bombay, two Salim–Javed films released in successive weeks. One of them was the 'greatest story ever told'. The other was a low-key production called *Aakhri Daao*.

Aakhri Daao

*A*akhri Daao is Salim–Javed's least-known film. In all the books, articles, monographs, interviews and reviews about them and their films, there is hardly any mention of this film. Even on the usually reliable imdb.com, the film was credited only to Javed Akhtar for the longest time.

Probably the biggest reason for this ignorance is the timing of its release. *Aakhri Daao* was released on 8 August 1975, a week before the supernova called *Sholay*, which annihilated all the box-office records that stood then. The easiest casualties were the other films released around the time. Despite reasonable reviews and a bankable star cast, *Aakhri Daao* managed neither business nor memory space.

In the O'Henry short story *A Retrieved Reformation*, safe-cracker Jimmy Valentine—after carrying off a few heists—falls in love and decides to reform. He is at a bank with his lady love when a little girl gets accidentally locked in a safe. Jimmy has two choices—open the safe and save the girl from suffocation, thus exposing himself to a police officer on his trail, or remain undercover and let the girl die.

The heroes of O'Henry short stories have one thing in common with Salim–Javed's heroes—even if they are thieves, they are men of honour. Or to put it in their words, '*Choron ke bhi ussool hote hain.*'

As had become their modus operandi, Salim–Javed took this dilemma of a thief and created the character of Ravi, who advises safe-building firms by day and then breaks into safes by night, ostensibly to save damsels in distress from blackmailers. And then must return from his reformation for one last heist.

Ravi (Jeetendra), a reformed safe-cracker, is tricked into opening a rich man's safe by two thieves—Saawan (Danny Denzongpa) and Julie (Padma Khanna). They frame him for theft and murder. On the run from the police, Ravi reaches a hill estate owned by Mr Kaul (Satyen Kappu) and gets a job there. He also befriends Kaul's daughter Reena (Saira Banu) and is soon accepted as a brave and honest estate manager. His safe-cracking skills are witnessed by the entire community— including DSP Khurana (Iftekhar)—when he rescues a little girl stuck in a safe. Soon, Saawan and Julie arrive at the estate with a safe—full of antique jewellery—which they have stolen but are unable to open. By blackmailing Ravi with threats of exposing his past, they install themselves at the estate as his friends and compel him to break the safe. Despite Ravi's attempts to avoid them, he is cornered. Finally, he ends up breaking open the safe but manages to inform the police. Julie, in a dying statement, absolves Ravi of the previous allegations and Ravi starts a new life with Reena at the estate.

Aakhri Daao certainly isn't among Salim–Javed's better scripts. When I say this, I am not comparing the film to their classics, but to the duo's less successful but still competent ones. For example, the songs clearly hampered the pace of the film—a thriller—and seemed forced, unlike in, say, *Deewaar*. Salim Khan says, '*Aakhri Daao* got engulfed in the *Sholay* frenzy. It was somewhat like *Shaan*, which also fell short when compared to *Sholay*.'

What is interesting in *Aakhri Daao* is the fair amount of similarity it has to other films—most notably *Sholay*. The bigger film obviously occupied Salim–Javed's mindspace almost entirely and *Aakhri Daao*'s writing time was probably a subset of *Sholay*'s.

Like in *Sholay*, a lady driver (Reena) receives a guest (Ravi) at the station and drives him (in a car, not a tonga) to his destination. A servant shows Ravi to his cottage, just like Ramlal shows Jai and Viru to theirs. Reena is shown shooting in an orchard when Ravi arrives and goes one better than her, a scene reminiscent of the more famous orchard shooting sequence.

The similarities were not just limited to *Sholay*. Just as Davar questions Vijay in *Deewaar* and finds his confidence to be sky-high, Kaul questions Ravi's ability to manage his estate and hires him on the basis of his confidence. '*Tum iss ilake ko nahin jante*,' says Kaul. '*Aap mujhe nahin jaante*,'[xxv] replies Ravi. When two people are escaping after committing a crime, a police vehicle catches up with them and—after a few tense moments—it transpires that it is a false alarm and the police are after someone else. This scene from *Aakhri Daao* was repeated in *Shaan* (where Amitabh Bachchan and Parveen Babi are escaping after stealing a necklace). And the most curious example is a line that appears in a later film as well. Commenting on Ravi's presence in the vicinity of a stolen safe, DSP Khurana says, '*Agar yeh ittefaq hai to bahut dilchasp ittefaq hai . . .*'[xxvi]—exactly what tycoon R.K. Gupta would say in *Trishul* several years hence.

One of the reasons for the film's pre-release buzz was that the plot was similar to a James Hadley Chase novel—*Come Easy, Go Easy*—where the anti-hero gets caught during a safe-breaking heist but doesn't reform completely. Given the dark theme of Chase's novel, the similarity with *Aakhri Daao* is more on the thematic level.

Director Sriram Raghavan remembers being quite excited about this before the film released: 'I was a big fan of James Hadley Chase and was very thrilled that they made a Chase novel. I have not seen a Chase film working. When you are reading a Chase novel, you see it as a movie unfolding and the real thing ends up being disappointing. I did not dislike it when I saw it at the time it came out. It was a theek hai kind of film, though not in the league of their other films.'

This opinion was echoed by the reviews of *Aakhri Daao*, which weren't bad but there was no praise for the script. *Screen* called it a 'well-shot crime drama' and said 'The film has also been very well handled on the cinematic level by the director, who has employed a number of imaginative techniques for picturising the scenes. But it is a pity that the main content points, the scripting and the narration do not go to make a convincing crime drama.' They wondered if a technical felicity could be attributed to the writers: 'Jump cuts have been put to excellent use with a subtle link acting as a bridge. These could have been scripted or edited but are worth admiring.' *Trade Guide* magazine reported: 'Aakhri Daao does excellent in 1st week in Delhi, UP; distributor's share [Rs] 3,22,000 despite heavy rains.'

The choice of writers and the cast ensured the film opened well, but it immediately got caught under the juggernaut of the most successful film in the history of Indian cinema. And so *Aakhri Daao* became a forgotten interlude between two record-breaking, history-altering scripts. Though 1975 was the best year Salim–Javed would ever have, it was not because of this film. They had reached what appeared to be their zenith with *Deewaar*. They would surpass that with *Sholay*.

Sholay

'The Greatest Star Cast Ever Assembled! The Greatest Story Ever Told!'—Announcement of *Sholay* before release

An army officer's family is massacred. He remembers two junior officers who were court martialled. They were rascals but also brave. The retired officer decides to enlist them in his mission for revenge.

Salim–Javed had originally sold this four-line idea—and only this four-line idea, without any treatment—to producer Baldev Pushkarna for Rs 20,000. Pushkarna had just produced a hit— *Roop Tera Mastana*, starring Jeetendra and Mumtaz—and had signed on Manmohan Desai to direct his next film. Manmohan Desai, fresh off hits like *Sachaa Jhutha* and *Rampur Ka Lakshman*, found the subject too grim and too different from his forte of breezy comedies. Salim–Javed ended up selling him the concept of a lost-and-found comedy, *Chacha Bhatija*. Prakash Mehra, who was making *Zanjeer* then, also passed on the idea.

That was when Salim–Javed went back to their first employers—the Sippys. After the towering success of *Seeta Aur Geeta*, G.P. Sippy was sniffing around to make a blockbuster and was therefore on the lookout for a suitably grand story. His son, Ramesh, had promised Salim–Javed credit and publicity when they wrote a film for him (as they hadn't been credited for the work they did for *Seeta Aur Geeta*). In any case, Ramesh's modern sensibilities were more in sync with these two maverick writers than with the older, diligent writers of the industry.

The Sippys bought the four-line plot for Rs 1,50,000 and told the writers to develop the script for a 'badi film'.

Salim–Javed started writing *Sholay* in March 1973, in a small room in the Sippy Films' office. Bouncing ideas off Ramesh Sippy, reliving childhood memories, digging into long-forgotten books and movies, they came up with the first treatment in fifteen days.

The story was hardly original. Apart from illustrious foreign predecessors like Kurosawa's *Seven Samurai* and John Sturges' *The Magnificent Seven*, several desi plots were also done in the same vein. Raj Khosla directed *Mera Gaon Mera Desh* in 1971, taking Vinod Khanna to negative role stardom as daku Jabbar Singh. While *Sholay* was still being made, *Khote Sikkay,* in which an avenger (Feroz Khan) hires five petty criminals to help him catch dacoit Jhanga (Ajit) was released in 1974.

Producer–director–actor of cult B-grade films, Joginder also entered the fray—officially—by suing Ramesh Sippy and Salim–Javed for stealing the idea of *Sholay* from his 1972 film *Bindiya Aur Bandook*.[16] Salim–Javed themselves acknowledged the influence of Sergio Leone and admitted that the massacre of Thakur's family was inspired by a similar scene in *Once Upon a Time in the West*. The inspiration for Viru's famous tank scene came from a movie called *The Secret of Santa Vittoria* featuring Anthony Quinn.

---

[16] *Bindiya Aur Bandook* had the trademark Joginder line—'Ranga khush'— which went on to become the title of another cult film that released in 1975.

What Salim–Javed did in *Sholay* was take all these bits and pieces and shape them into a massive structure of drama, action, emotion and tragedy. Encouraged by the confidence Ramesh Sippy showed in them, they were actually able to understand each other's visions and 'see' the film as they wrote the scenes.

In her book *Sholay: The Making of a Classic*, well-known film critic Anupama Chopra says, 'Ideas were tossed back and forth, scenes written and rejected, characters created and killed. Mostly they just hurtled on. The characters kept coming through. It was as if the story was writing itself. "There was a wave of creativity," says Salim, "like a sea at high tide."'

Javed Akhtar describes Gabbar Singh as 'one of the few [characters] I enjoyed writing . . . I remember very clearly that while writing *Sholay*, I would get very excited and relish the prospect that once I completed two scenes, the next would have Gabbar in it.' Writing Gabbar was so much fun because they developed an entirely new vocabulary for this iconic villain that made the character even more menacing.

Not surprisingly, both Sanjeev Kumar and Amitabh Bachchan wanted to play Gabbar. The role had such an aura that two of the leading men of the times were willing to give up their 'heroic' image to play the villain, something unprecedented in the convention-bound Hindi film industry. It is said that Sanjeev Kumar offered to do all kinds of things—like shave off his hair, blacken his teeth and develop some mannerisms—to bring an interesting dimension to the character.

The process of finding the actor who would do justice to this edgy character was trickier. It is a well-known fact that Danny Denzongpa—originally signed to play Gabbar—dropped out because of an earlier commitment made to Feroz Khan's *Dharmatma*.

Fortunately, Javed Akhtar remembered seeing an actor called Amjad Khan in a play called *Ae Mere Watan Ke Logon* performed at a youth festival in Delhi way back in 1963. Amjad's performance as an army officer had made such an impact that he had mentioned it to Salim several times during their partnership. Salim, in turn, had worked in a few films with Amjad's father, Jayant, and knew of the young actor too. In a coincidence of epic proportions, Salim bumped into Amjad at Bandra Bandstand one day. He immediately offered to take him to Ramesh Sippy, saying that the finest role in the biggest film in recent times could be his. Salim's suggestion was endorsed by Satyen Kappu (who had worked with Amjad in theatre) and Amjad was taken on. The connect was so strong that, several years later, Ramesh Sippy admitted, 'The writers brought him and the moment he entered the room, I knew we had our man.' Thus after Amitabh Bachchan as Jai[17], Amjad Khan as Gabbar was the second major casting decision that was made on the basis of Salim–Javed's recommendation.

Ironically, Salim–Javed never worked with Amjad Khan again because of a major misunderstanding during the filming. Amjad Khan's unconventional voice was seen by many as a major dampener, and with so much riding on the character of Gabbar, there was a lot of negative buzz around the casting. It is a testimony to Salim–Javed's ownership of the project that they told Ramesh Sippy to replace Amjad, since they didn't want their recommendation to spoil the chances of the film. When Amjad found out about this, he was extremely upset. He never forgave the writers for what he considered a severe blow to his nascent career.

---

[17] Salim–Javed's role in Jai's casting has been described in the chapter on *Zanjeer*.

As writers, Salim–Javed need not have concerned themselves with a potential error in casting. After all, it was the director who always took the final call on the cast. But just as they never shied away from taking credit where it was due, neither did they back away from their responsibility of making a film successful. Although Ramesh Sippy was clearly the captain of the ship, he was greatly aided by Salim–Javed's vision of the film and their involvement in the process of filming.

When Hema Malini struggled with the pages and pages of dialogues that Basanti was supposed to deliver, Javed Akhtar—present at the shoot—enacted the scene for her and Hema Malini finally 'got' Basanti tangewali. To explain the jailor's role to Asrani, Salim–Javed got hold of a book on World War II and showed the actor pictures of Adolf Hitler, and information on the man, which became the basis of the jailor's get-up and his high-pitched speech. Salim and Javed had met Jagdeep during the shooting of *Sarhadi Lootera*. At the time, Javed mimicked the speaking style of Bhopali women and Jagdeep picked it up. With his guidance, Jagdeep made the character his own without ever having been to Bhopal in his life.

Salim–Javed's influence on *Sholay* extended way beyond the written pages of the script. They attended the shooting in Bangalore regularly and often fine-tuned dialogues and scenes during filming. How Javed wrote the lines of Viru's most memorable scene—the drunken monologue atop the tank—makes for an interesting story. He kept postponing it till it was time for him to return to Bombay from Bangalore. He started writing on his drive to the airport and continued while an assistant went inside to take care of the check-in formalities. He placed the sheets of paper on the hood of his car and kept writing right till the boarding call. He just about managed to catch his flight! Despite the tearing hurry in which they were written the lines went on to catch the imagination of generations of cine-goers.

In addition to their involvement in the shooting process, the writers exhibited tremendous skill in adding depth and nuance to the script, especially to some of the supporting characters: Ramlal, Radha, Mausi, Imam sahib, Ahmed, Kaalia, Sambha, Thakur's family, Ramgarh's residents. Even Gulzarilal the postman, who appears in just one scene, and Gabbar Singh's father Hari Singh, whom we never see, have a longevity that goes far beyond what an ensemble cast in a hit film normally has. In fact, no other film has been able to create such a long list of minor characters who have lived on for so long. Every character was painstakingly created and each scene lovingly crafted. G.P. Sippy too did not spare any expense in funding the film to ensure it was made exactly the way Ramesh Sippy visualized it, despite massively overshooting the budget.

Even in the promotions, *Sholay* was way ahead of the pack. From 30 May till the release on 15 August, each (weekly) issue of the trade magazines had one ad dedicated to one of the main characters, ending with one showcasing the entire ensemble cast. It really is a tribute to the writers when the supporting cast of a major film is featured in a pre-release ad.

There was an unprecedented pre-release buzz around the film. But trade magazines—barometers of a film's business—were divided in their assessment of the film. The feeling was that *Sholay* would not be able to recoup the massive investments made to produce it. The day the film released, *Screen* carried a front-page report with the headline: 'Big crowds for advance booking of *Sholay*' and it went on to say 'Unprecedented crowds were witnessed at all the theatres in Bombay city and suburbs wherever the advance booking opened on Monday. The police had a hard time controlling thousands of cine-goers . . .' Citing the mega-starcast and Salim–Javed's script as major draws, it reported that cinemas had increased ticket prices by 15–20 per cent and they hadn't seen a bigger rush since *Mughal-e-Azam* some two decades ago. This was not a poor opening by any stretch of the imagination.

However, one week after the release, the other major trade magazine—*Trade Guide*—predicted that '*Sholay* will be a sad experience for distributors . . .' They directly criticized the writers for the tragic ending and said, 'It is surprising how Salim–Javed could commit such an error. Tragedy can be conceived in a classic, but not in a mass-action entertainer.' They went one step further and prescribed an alternate ending, '. . . if the end is changed and Amitabh is kept alive and one reel is devoted to the Amitabh–Jaya romance leading to wedlock.' This radical prescription was accompanied by a detailed analysis of the first week's business, and the conclusion: 'We are of the opinion that *Sholay* will do a business of hardly 40 lakhs per major territory . . .'

In the same issue, which carried such a confidently damning report on the first page, the writers of *Sholay* sponsored a full-page ad on the last page that said, 'This is a prediction by Salim–Javed . . . *Sholay* . . . will be a grosser of Rupees One Crore in each major territory of India.'

This was such an audacious show of confidence that the industry did not know how to react. It was always the producers who fought for their films and expressed confidence in their potential. Here, it was the writers who were boldly making an outrageous prediction and were actually putting their money where their mouth was.

Despite this confidence from the writers, what weighed on the makers' minds was the massive bill of Rs 3 crore, making it the most expensive film made in India until then. To put this in perspective, the Sippys had spent only Rs 40 lakh on *Seeta*

Aur Geeta while *Sholay* had been conceived with a budget of Rs 1 crore. The ballooning bill meant that every half-criticism and negative rumour gnawed on Ramesh Sippy's mind.

His insecurity led to him to call a meeting at Amitabh Bachchan's residence with Salim–Javed to figure out how to 'salvage' the film. The suggestion on the table was not to kill Amitabh Bachchan, who was now too big a star (and fresh off a cinematic death in *Deewaar*). Salim–Javed were dead against this change and felt the slight ache at the end was part of the film's charm, but there was too much at stake for the Sippys. They wanted to reshoot the end and re-release it as a happy ending when the film opened in other parts of the country. (This was possible because films had staggered releases in those days.)

This discussion took place on the first weekend after the film's release with hardly a couple of days' reaction to go by. Salim–Javed managed to convince Ramesh Sippy to hold on till Tuesday and take the plunge if the audience reaction didn't change by then. On Tuesday, Ramesh Sippy met the manager of a theatre called Geeta, in Bombay's Worli area. He pointed out the impact of the film was tremendous because the sales of his snacks and cold drinks had come down. Huh? Well, people were so stunned by the never-seen-before images and especially the twist in the story just before the interval, they did not come out of the hall. This was the first time Ramesh Sippy relaxed a little and felt that he may be on to something really big.

Then, the reviews started trickling in.

Screen magazine called it a 'Strong drama of conflicts with a big canvas, powerful performances', while the popular tabloid *Blitz* simply called it 'the best film ever made in India'. While pointing out that the story was not original (and the 'greatest story ever told' claims may not hold), they did agree that *Sholay* was indeed the 'greatest star-cast ever assembled'.

But it was not all positive. In *Filmfare*, Bikram Singh gave the film just '2 Stars' and panned it quite badly. 'Writers Salim and Javed churn out the rehash which needs a good memory more than imagination . . . A major trouble is the unsuccessful transplantation it attempts – grafting a Western on the Indian milieu . . . The film could have gone easy on the depiction of violence.' Other reviewers also raised eyebrows at the 'uncensored violence' (K.M. Amladi in the *Hindustan Times*).

The initial trade reports—for the first week or so—were subdued as word-of-mouth reactions from the viewers took time to pick up but once they did, there was no stopping the *Sholay* juggernaut.

In its first run, Ramesh Sippy estimates *Sholay* made a staggering Rs 25 crore. To put this in perspective, it made more than *eight* times the production cost—which was the highest ever at that time. As per economic estimates, inflation occurred eighteen times in the last four decades, which would put just the *domestic* gross collection of *Sholay* at Rs 450 crores. Till September 2015, only a handful of films—*PK, Bajrangi Bhaijaan, Dhoom 3, Chennai Express*—have crossed Rs 400 crore globally. Adjusted to inflation, *Sholay* did that kind of business in India alone.

More than pure numbers, *Sholay* is the ultimate classic of Indian cinema. It is no longer a mere film but more of a historical event, much like the Emergency or Partition.

Anupama Chopra likens watching *Sholay* to a karaoke experience where everybody has heard the dialogues so many times before that the whole theatre mouths them along with the stars. And this is where the magic of Salim–Javed kicks in. That magic is best explained by one aspect of the film's business that they—and only they—impacted.

In a music market ruled by HMV, *Sholay*'s music rights were bought by Polydor, a new entrant owned by Ramesh's then brother-in-law, Shashi Patel. In an unprecedented deal, Polydor paid an advance of Rs 5 lakh to buy the rights to the film's soundtrack. This meant that they would have to sell 1,00,000 records to break even in a market where top-end musicals sold 25,000 units. When the film released, the records just did not sell—despite heavy promotion—and there was major panic because of the investments involved. And that's when the Polydor marketing team realized the true strength of *Sholay*'s 'soundtrack'—its dialogues. It released a 58-minute record of the film's famous dialogues and hit the jackpot. As the records vanished from stores, Polydor ended up releasing fifteen different records of popular segments from the film—like 'Viru ki shaadi', 'Soorma Bhopali', 'Radha ki kahaani', 'Gabbar Singh'—and each one became a hit. Altogether, Polydor sold a mind-boggling 5,00,000 records—*five* times their break-even target. It was the first time that the music industry had clocked such numbers and that too for dialogues, which had never been featured in records before *Sholay*.

Come to think of it, Salim–Javed overshadowed even R.D. Burman, then the industry's hottest composer, in terms of impact on audio sales. And that was a very, very massive thing to have happened.

The entire advertising campaign of *Sholay*—a majorly lavish one—was designed around its stars and writers. Two weeks before the release date, a full-page ad in trade magazines reiterated the claim of the 'The Greatest Story Ever Told' with pictures of Salim–Javed and the caption 'Only they could have written it'. (The same ad also has R.D. Burman and Anand Bakshi being complimented for 'The finest music ever created'.)

Salim–Javed were deeply involved in all the elements that went into the making of *Sholay*. Right from influencing casting decisions to fighting for the climax to be left untouched, they were almost as much part of *Sholay* as Ramesh Sippy was.

During the entire filming period of two years, they travelled to locations, tightened the script, polished the dialogues and crafted *Sholay* into the gem it eventually became.

When the film was written off by trade pundits, the duo paid money out of their own pockets to run ads in trade magazines—predicting super success for the film. Writers paying money to advertise their film was something the industry had neither heard of nor could imagine. But then, Salim–Javed were not about what could be imagined. Their success went way beyond that.

Salim–Javed's first film—*Andaz*—had released just four years ago. Since then they had written three films that had become the top grossers of their respective years, created a character that would become the most durable of Hindi film icons and penned what would be called the 'most perfect Hindi film script'.

And now they were about to go more than seventeen months without a release.

Immaan Dharam

After the euphoria of *Sholay*, there was a gap of nearly eighteen months before Salim–Javed's next film hit the screens. Announced right after *Majboor* by producer Premji, *Immaan Dharam* was probably the most awaited film in Salim–Javed's career. They had delivered nine superhits before this and, moreover, the film starred Amitabh Bachchan who had become a huge star (riding on the wave of *Adalat*, *Kabhi Kabhie*, *Hera Pheri* and *Do Anjaane* in the previous year). With other major stars like Shashi Kapoor, Rekha and Sanjeev Kumar also in the project, *Immaan Dharam* was expected to be a sure-fire winner.

Veteran technician Desh Mukerji made his directorial debut with this film. He was probably the best-known art director in Bombay at that point, and regularly worked with Yash Chopra and Manoj Kumar (for whom he put together a mammoth fortress in *Kranti*). His work in *Deewaar* was appreciated by Satyajit Ray and for good reason too. The famous '*Mere paas maa hai*' scene was shot in a studio, where Mukerji recreated the bridge. Producer Premji was one of his closest friends and roped him in to direct the film.

Salim–Javed's spell over the industry was probably at its peak around this time and the pre-release publicity of *Immaan*

Dharam—despite the presence of major stars—centred on them. The very first ad (appearing about a month before the release date) had nothing but 'Story by Salim Javed' written just below the title.[18] Subsequent ads had the same layout, but now the stars' faces had been added below the writers' names. All this focus on them raised expectations immensely; it seemed as though the audience was more eager for a Salim–Javed script than an Amitabh Bachchan performance.

The script had its share of twists and turns, with several strong peripheral characters, but the basic plot was quite simple. Ahmed (Amitabh Bachchan) and Mohan (Shashi Kapoor) are professional witnesses who appear in court and lie under oath for money. They are very fond of a blind girl, Shyamlee (Aparna Sen), who lives in their neighbourhood. Shyamlee is in love with Kabir (Sanjeev Kumar), a business tycoon's pious son who is opposed to his father's illicit businesses. When Kabir's father decides to close his shady businesses, his partners kill him and frame Kabir for the murder. Mohan and Ahmed give false testimony that sends Kabir to death row. When they realize he is Shyamlee's fiancé, they start investigating the crime and manage to expose the real criminals, who go into hiding. But the two of them find the hideout and demolish it.

There are several other prominent characters who are not integral to the main plot but add to the film. Durga (Rekha) is a Tamil labourer at a construction site and also Mohan's love interest. Govind Anna (Shreeram Lagoo) plays a labour leader torn between his principles and the hardships his labourers face. Jenny Francis (Helen) is a single mother who 'hires' Ahmed to play her husband in front of her daughter. In an interesting

---

[18] Incidentally, the very next page of *Screen* carried an advertisement for a film where the lead credit was given to another successful writer: '*Shatranj Ke Khiladi* from the short story by Munshi Premchand'.

cameo, Utpal Dutt plays Balbir Singh—an ex-army man with a prosthetic leg—who is Kabir's associate in charitable endeavours and supports the leading duo's attempts to finish off the criminals.

Immaan Dharam did not have the finesse of a Salim–Javed script. Several instances of symbolism—which are very popular in Hindi cinema—became heavy-handed, almost caricature-ish. Film critic Sukanya Verma describes it in one word: 'Excessive!'

With a Hindu and a Muslim as the two leading men, and a Sikh in the supporting role, secularism was the central message of the film. Each character was highly deferential towards other religions. In fact, this was taken to almost comic levels by showing Mohan risking his life to deliver a Quran home and Ahmed reading the Bhagvad Gita with exaggerated respect. These situations were not new to the cinema of those times but they had become clichés. Even the repeated portrayal of Ahmed and Mohan lying on the stand after swearing oaths on their holy books jars after a point.

Sanjeev Kumar's character—presumably called Kabir for his secular, saintly ways—is too sanctimonious to be believable. Since Christianity is the only religion not represented, Kabir makes up for it by spouting lines like 'Forgive them for they know not . . .' and, in the climax, he is even tied up to look as though he's been crucified.

Salim–Javed's strength had always been their ability to drive home a message in entertaining formats, characterized by their trademark fluidity. This was sorely lacking in *Immaan Dharam*.

Secularism in popular Hindi cinema has always been a little exaggerated, often relying on obvious symbolism to make the message clear to the masses. Manmohan Desai, who always packed his films with representatives from different religions, managed to do so with a certain lightness of touch, a nuance completely missing from *Immaan Dharam*.

This view, however, is not shared by two of the film's actors—acknowledged to be among Indian cinema's best. Both felt the film gave them ample scope to perform.

When asked about compromising artistic integrity in accepting some of the tritest roles possible, Utpal Dutt defended his choice of roles in commercial cinema by using *Immaan Dharam* as an example. 'I'm doing *Immaan Dharam* written by Salim–Javed and I'm enjoying every single minute of it as an artiste.'

Amitabh Bachchan is even more effusive about the script. He says, 'It didn't click though I feel it's one of Salim–Javed's finest scripts. An equal amount of work went into my performances in *Immaan Dharam*, *Deewaar* and *Trishul*. Perhaps the film went wrong because it had too many different strands of stories which didn't knit themselves into a tapestry. There were the stories of Shashi Kapoor–Amitabh Bachchan, Shashi Kapoor–Rekha, Amitabh–Helen, Sanjeev Kumar, Aparna Sen and Shreeram Lagoo. Each one of the stories was apt and interesting but somehow they couldn't be interlinked. If the focus had been kept on just one of the stories, I'm certain *Immaan Dharam* would have met with public approval.'

Immaan Dharam opened to tremendous hype in January 1977 and, thanks to the pre-release publicity, ran to packed houses for a couple of weeks. Quite surprisingly, some of the reviews—probably in deference to the star cast—were not too negative. In fact, *Screen* felt the film had 'Entertainment-cum-messages'. But this helped sustain the momentum only for a short while. *Trade Guide* said, 'The film contains a big dosage of preaching, making it unpalatable like a Films Division documentary. The story has been developed in patches and the screenplay has forcibly linked them together, making the film move in jerks . . . the dialogues are good, but again in patches, in some places they are so long and monotonous that the impact is lost.'

The film tanked soon enough. In the 1970s, a film needed to run for twenty-odd weeks to make serious money. *Immaan Dharam* did not even come close to that. With a host of expensive stars, and writers, the film could not recover its costs; it became Salim–Javed's only major flop.

This was a major emotional setback for the duo because their confident—bordering on brash—attitude and their impatience with the established Holy Cows of the industry had made them a fair number of enemies. In an industry where heroes are made or unmade every Friday, this was a dicey position to be in because people were waiting to pull them down.

This angst was visible in a very curious ad Salim–Javed took out the day *Immaan Dharam* released. The full-page ad had just one line: '*Immaan Dharam* is the answer for all criticism' and it carried a small footnote: 'Issued by Salim–Javed, Bandstand, Bandra'. This was their trademark show of confidence, cocking a snook at their rivals. The dismal performance of *Immaan Dharam* in the wake of this smug ad must have made Salim–Javed's disappointment even more unbearable. Salim Khan says, 'We were very proud and confident of our work in *Immaan Dharam*, which is why we announced it with much fanfare with the ad in *Screen*. But it did not run as per our expectations.'

Salim–Javed's story was far from over, though. Their next release was with a director who was finding his mettle with multi-starrers and zany comedies. And after the intensity of *Zanjeer*, *Majboor*, *Deewaar* and *Sholay*, Salim–Javed finally got a chance to show their funny side, last seen in *Seeta Aur Geeta*. This film too was another double-barrelled title: *Chacha Bhatija*.

Chacha Bhatija

In many ways, 1973 was the turning point for Salim–Javed, Amitabh Bachchan and their partnership. The release and subsequent success of *Zanjeer*—their first film together—convinced Salim–Javed that this lanky, intense actor was the right person for their films, which depended more on anger and action than romance and music. This was also the year when they recommended Amitabh for *Sholay* and unknowingly laid the groundwork for another superhit partnership.

The *Sholay* script bounced around between the Sippys, Manmohan Desai and Prakash Mehra. When Manmohan Desai (and his producer Baldev Pushkarna) refused the script, Salim–Javed sold them the concept of *Chacha Bhatija*. They were writing the film in Juhu's famous Sun 'n' Sand Hotel and during one of the sessions, they praised Amitabh a lot and called him over to introduce him to Manmohan Desai. Apparently, the director was quite aloof during the meeting and Amitabh felt awkward, so he left quickly. After he left, Desai is said to have even made a slightly derogatory comment about the actor. Salim–Javed predicted that, one day, the director would be compelled to work with the talented actor. In fact, Manmohan Desai's first production—*Amar Akbar Anthony*—released a month after *Chacha Bhatija*. And the bond between the producer–director and the actor became so strong in such a short span of time that during the shooting of *Amar Akbar Anthony*, Manmohan Desai promised Amitabh Bachchan that he would never make a film without the star.

Returning to *Chacha Bhatija*, the story of the film is credited to Prayag Raj, long-term associate of Manmohan Desai, while Salim–Javed got the credit for the screenplay and dialogues. In the sentimental world of Hindi cinema, one is never sure who is credited for what exactly and there are several instances of relatives, close friends and associates being credited for what is actually very little work. Given Salim–Javed's stature at the time and the possessiveness they displayed over credit, it is unlikely that Prayag Raj was just a passenger on this one. He most likely came up with yet another lost-and-found story, one that was neither about brothers nor about fathers and sons; it was about an uncle and a nephew.

Seth Ranbir Singh Teja (Rehman) lives happily with wife Seeta (Indrani Mukherjee) and younger brother Shankar. This idyll is disrupted when his manager, Laxmidas (Jeevan), and the manager's cousin, Sonia (Sonia Sahni), cause a massive misunderstanding. Teja throws his wife out of his home, unaware that she is pregnant. Shankar, who is very devoted to his sister-in-law, also runs away from home. Seeta tries to commit suicide but is saved by a good Samaritan, Gul Khan (Anwar Hussain); Shankar is given shelter by a Christian woman (Durga Khote). Seeta gives birth to a son while Teja marries Sonia, who is already pregnant from a previous affair but manages to convince Teja that the child is his.

A grown-up Shankar (Dharmendra) turns out to be a black marketeer but reforms to become a taxi driver. Seeta's son Sundar (Randhir Kapoor) is offered a job by Teja, who meets him at a friend's party. Sundar joins Teja's company in Bombay and meets Shankar. Their initial admiration for each other turns into hostility when Teja's company tries to take over Shankar's slum. When they are each other's throats, Seeta reveals their identities and they join hands to expose the villains around Teja. Shankar and Sundar enter the household as servants. Their plans are thwarted when Laxmidas learns of their ruse and kidnaps Seeta. In a climax involving horses on multi-storeyed buildings, they manage to rescue Seeta, save Teja's property from the villains and reunite the extended family.

The script played the two stars—Randhir Kapoor and Dharmendra—well against each other, something that had become the writers' forte. In a review of *Amar Akbar Anthony*, *Hindustan Times* gave Salim–Javed the credit for 'popularizing' double-hero films. 'The time when a Bombay film could draw crowds with one hero and one heroine is long past. Even the pairing of two heroes and two heroines, popularised by Salim–Javed, seems to be on the wane.'

Chacha Bhatija opened very strongly and an advertisement (about four weeks after its release) called it 'The glorious victory march of the biggest box-office hit of 1977'—though that record was broken by the director's next film.

With three of his films—*Amar Akbar Anthony, Dharam Veer* and *Parvarish*—featuring among the top four of the year, 1977 proved to be a golden year for Manmohan Desai. *Chacha Bhatija* was a relatively lesser success but still seventh in the list of top grossers of the year. All four films were essentially lost-and-found sagas, with only *Parvarish* deviating slightly from the formula of a family breaking up in the first reel and reuniting in the last.

Chacha Bhatija's reviews were lukewarm (as was probably expected) but *Hindustan Times*' reviewer K.M. Amladi assigned credit for the lost-and-found formula to the writers, though in a backhanded manner: 'The scriptwriting team of Salim–Javed is the hottest thing going in Bombay film industry nowadays and, it is said, producers pay through their nose to sign them for their pictures. The secret of their success can be summed up in two words: Lost . . . Found. Their plot structures seem nothing more than a strident variation on these two—the long storyline littered with the strangest of coincidences. Not that the other screenwriters don't indulge in this but what makes Salim–Javed click is the apparent ease with which they construct characters as parts of some jigsaw puzzle, the life-pattern neatly fitting in the end.'

The lost-and-found formula—which Manmohan Desai became synonymous with—was Salim–Javed's forte, with films like *Seeta Aur Geeta*, *Yaadon Ki Baaraat* and *Haath Ki Safai* to their credit before they wrote *Chacha Bhatija*. However, they were not the originators of the formula; both Yash Chopra, who made the ultra-glamorous *Waqt*, and Manmohan Desai, who made *Rampur Ka Lakshman*, had most effectively orchestrated the separation and unification of the characters in their films.

Chacha Bhatija is a case study of scenes with estranged family members meeting multiple times—without knowing their true relationship—and making loaded statements! When Sundar and Shankar clash, the nephew threatens the uncle with an angry reference to their blood ties: '*Itna yaad rakhna, agli baar mile to bataa doonga ki in ragon mein utna hi garam khoon daud raha hai jitna tumhare ragon mein.*'[xxvii] Shankar and his taxi are just in time to receive Sundar at the station but he just misses Seeta, his sister-in-law (and Sundar's mother), when she arrives there. When Seth Teja defends Sundar, his second wife retorts, '*Tarafdari to aap aise kar rahe hain ki Kiran nahin, Sundar aapka beta ho.*'[xix] This goes on and even the climax—the way in which the various strands unravel—is quite complex and, dare I say, intelligent, unlike the facile resolution in Desai's later films. This did not necessarily make the film more successful, for sure, but it showed Salim–Javed's natural penchant for adding a spot of intelligence in 'ghisa-pita' stories. Add to that their overt socialist messaging—where Shankar gives up his illegal business and takes up arms against hoarders—and you have a significantly different treatment.

However, one major complaint against *Chacha Bhatija* is the regressive treatment of women and the promotion of outdated ideas. This is quite a departure from Salim–Javed's sensitive handling of strong, modern female characters. The film depicted a clearly subservient role for women, in which the characters yearned for male children and even rejected the idea of adoption outright—traits that seem way out of sync with Salim–Javed's mature sensibilities.

In the *Times of India*, columnist Haimanti Banerjee compared *Chacha Bhatija*, *Dharam Veer* and *Amar Akbar Anthony* and found these films to be similar in many ways. 'Going by the rules of the game prescribed by Mr Desai, whatever is old and dated, must win . . . Are the masses entertained by something which critically analyses existing values, and, in the process, evolves more progressive and dynamic ones? Or are they entertained by the confirmation of traditional norms and notions, so that they are spared the embarrassing realisation of having held on to outmoded, and therefore, regressive values? Going by the sustained and thunderous success of Mr Desai's trilogy, the obvious answer is that the people, both the elite and the illiterate, have unanimously voted for the second proposition . . . Mr Desai proposes to resolve the inevitable and healthy dialectics between tradition and modernity by clinging to the former, at the cost of the latter.'

While the columnist put the blame at Manmohan Desai's door, it's actually Salim–Javed who ought to take on most of it. After all, they were the star writers, who prided themselves on bound scripts that remain unchanged throughout the shooting.

Chacha Bhatija can, however, be considered an aberration because their next film had a female character quite unparalleled in Hindi cinema till then. Her modernity, her strength and her fierce independence would stand out in a film known for its three heroes. As would the film itself: *Trishul*.

Trishul

After the monumental success of *Deewaar*, which was still running three years after its release, the same producer-writer-director combination came up with *Trishul*. Promoted as the Three Faces of Man, it brought together the two male stars of *Deewaar* along with Sanjeev Kumar. Originally, Sanjeev Kumar's part was written for Dilip Kumar but Sanjeev's performance in the film ensured that audiences did not miss the thespian even a little bit.

Trishul was the first film Salim–Javed wrote keeping Amitabh Bachchan specifically in mind, given the actor's growing marketability and the producers' confidence in him. He was part of the script-narration sessions right from the beginning.

This was Salim–Javed's thirteenth film and it was also the first time they revised a script. Writer–director Sriram Raghavan says, 'They were not writing the scripts the way we do drafts. They got it down pat in one go . . . It is amazing that the first time they wrote a second draft for a film was *Trishul*, which was much later in their careers.'

The fact is quite stupendous in itself and a testimony to their genius in delineating a story completely right from the beginning—and their ability to defend their scripts!

Post the success of *Deewaar* and *Kabhi Kabhie*, Yash Chopra was a far more confident director and shot the film in one schedule in Delhi. He wanted to take the cast away from the distractions in Bombay, and help them get into the characters better. It was a fantastic experience and everyone enjoyed every moment of the shoot in Delhi. Amitabh Bachchan remembers, 'Yashji was so activated during the shooting of *Trishul* that he would keep punching and pummelling the air; he was a threat to the lives of his assistants and cameraman!'

Though the first shooting schedule was wonderful for the actors, the results were not as great. When the core team came out of Rajkamal Studios after seeing the first rushes of *Trishul*, they were very disappointed. The four of them—Yash Chopra, Gulshan Rai, Salim and Javed—were absolutely quiet on the drive back. At last, Gulshan Rai asked, 'Salim sahib, is there any way to salvage this film?' Salim replied with his typical dark humour, 'One way is not to release it at all.' Gulshan Rai was most depressed and called Yash Chopra later that night to complain about the writers' almost cold-blooded indifference. Yash Chopra, who was familiar with Salim–Javed's cocky façade, assured the producer that the writers were extremely concerned about the film as their reputations also hinged on it.

Yash Chopra met with Salim–Javed at the Holiday Inn hotel the very next day and identified different points in the film that needed to be improved. They calculated that the portions would take about fifteen days to reshoot. This was about one-third of the time they had taken to shoot the film already and they felt it would be too much for the producer to digest. Therefore they decided to tell Gulshan Rai in instalments of five days to reduce the overall shock. After the first five days, they would say 'just a wee bit more' and shoot for five more days and then shoot for the final five. Salim Khan laughingly remembers, 'We decided to give him the news in instalments in the same way he used to pay us in instalments.'

The ambulance scenes were inserted in this rewrite and gave the frontbenchers some 'taali-seeti' moments. The rewrite resulted in a much stronger film and the pre-release buzz was very good. The film was launched with a series of ads in trade magazines and as had become the norm by now, Salim–Javed's names were listed right after the director's.

In the film, R.K. Gupta (Sanjeev Kumar) is an ambitious executive in a construction firm, who is in love with Shanti (Waheeda Rehman). But when the firm's owner offers his daughter's hand in marriage to R.K. Gupta along with a partnership in the firm, he falls for it and abandons Shanti, despite knowing she is pregnant with his child. Shanti leaves town and gives birth to a boy, Vijay. When he grows up, Vijay (Amitabh Bachchan) comes to Delhi after Shanti's death to exact revenge on his father. R.K. Gupta is now a construction tycoon running his business along with his son, Ravi (Shashi Kapoor). Vijay starts his business off with the impossible task of recovering a piece of land that R.K. Gupta owns but has been encroached upon by a goon. After that, Vijay uses fair and foul means to take away contracts from his father's company. He is soon a tycoon in his own right and continues to make R.K. Gupta's life hell. When a major construction project comes up, R.K. Gupta bets his entire life's savings to build it but Vijay starts another project that could potentially ruin both of them. Vijay comes to R.K. Gupta and announces their relationship, offering to save him from financial doom, but R.K. Gupta has already hired a contract killer to eliminate Vijay. In the climax, the father manages to save the son but is killed himself. The film ends with the two business families uniting.

This was probably the first Hindi film to be set in a corporate world. While characters in Hindi cinema had always been seen running small businesses, this was first time they were managing large corporations, with references to tenders and board meetings peppering the dialogues. Obviously the real intricacies of the corporate world were simplified to a large extent, but Salim–Javed successfully brought the glamour and mystique of high-stakes business to the masses. In fact, they cleverly incorporated current business terminology into regular conversations. For example, when Ravi (Shashi Kapoor) returns from abroad, he refers to his father's secretary Geeta (Rakhee) as 'Computer'—one of the first times the word was used in a Hindi film—because she 'knew the answer to every question'. When R.K. Gupta reminds Ravi about his potential, he refers to a 'business administration course' he has just completed abroad. There were throwaway lines about 'meetings with auditors' and 'cement quotas' and 'court hearings' as well, concepts common in the world of business at that point of time but not outside it. And of course, there is the adrenaline-charged sequence where Vijay steals a contract from R.K. Gupta by submitting a tender that is lower by just one rupee.

These were very new things that Salim–Javed brought into Hindi cinema and indeed, films on the corporate world are still few and far between. This is not to say that *Trishul* was a very realistic depiction of the business environment but the writers managed to take a very personal battle between a father and son and make it 'business'.

After the regressive stereotypes of *Chacha Bhatija*, *Trishul* set new standards in the depiction of women in Hindi cinema.

About Shanti, Javed Akhtar says, 'We did break new ground in *Trishul*: it's the first film in which the heroine sleeps with the man in her life without feeling guilty.' Shanti was an exceptionally strong, modern, yet dutiful working woman. Her character had very little screen time but effectively directed the course of the film, and is probably Salim–Javed's strongest female character.

And not only Shanti. The film had two other working women—Sheetal (Hema Malini) and Geeta (Rakhee)—both of whom were very real. They were honest, hard-working, well-dressed women, who didn't need to be rescued by the heroes!

The hero of *Trishul*, Vijay, was even more groundbreaking than the leading ladies. Javed Akhtar calls him 'the first "real" illegitimate child on the Hindi screen. His parents are not seen going to some abandoned temple where they exchange malas to show they are married in the eyes of God.' And the anger Salim–Javed invested in Vijay was something else. He was almost like a psychopathic villain, stalking his father's family and doing everything in his capacity to make their lives hell. Usually in Hindi films, the code of honour dictates that the families of the warring heroes are left out of their battles. In *Trishul*, Vijay throws that code to the winds and does things like trying to steal his stepbrother's lover and convince his stepsister to elope.

Right from the first scene where he saunters around a dynamite-laden mine, his anger is so powerful that it almost unnerves you. And that rage permeates Salim–Javed's lines. Every time he has to use it, Vijay almost spits out his father's name—and always his full name, R.K. Gupta. In a pivotal scene towards the end, he introduces himself and calls R.K. Gupta his '*naajayaz baap*' (illegitimate father). This is an interesting twist to the standard lingo where it is always the child who is referred to as illegitimate.

The motivation behind Vijay's bitterness is established even before his birth and, quite unusually, through a song. The song continues as Shanti is shown bringing up Vijay and Sahir's lyrics underline her own anger—'*Main tujhe rehem ke saaye mein na palne doongi . . . Taaki tap tap ke tu faulaad bane, maa ki aulaad bane . . . Main doodh na bakshungi tujhe yeh yaad rahe.*'[xxviii] Yash Chopra was great friends with Sahir and he personally briefed the poet on the plot and song situations, which is why there is a perfect sync between the songs and dialogues.

It is to Yash Chopra and Salim–Javed's credit that a bitter character like Vijay, with unscrupulous dealings in most things, manages to remain heroic till the very end. His noble motivation—honour and respect for his mother—balances his ignoble methods very well, never allowing the audience to withdraw their sympathy.

Generating sympathy for a man out to destroy his own father was clearly a triumph of the script that could never have come out in any narration. S. Mukherjee told the writers, 'I have seen this picture three times to try to see why it's successful, but I can tell you that if you had come to me with this script, I would not have taken it.'

After two of Salim–Javed's films got a lukewarm reception from critics, *Trishul* got some great reviews, and was praised for the direction, acting and the overall finesse of production. *Screen* called the film a 'High voltage emotional drama' and praised it without reservation. The *Sunday Statesman* compared the film to Harold Robbins' bestselling novel from the previous decade and said *Trishul* is 'Bombay's answer to *The Carpet Baggers* . . . made with the same style and opulence. A powerful plot, tautly woven and executed by Salim–Javed. It is indeed one of the assets of the film that transferred to the world of Indian high finance; it still seems credible and convincing.'

Trishul—while a brilliant film—tends to be overshadowed by the intensity of *Deewaar* on one side and by the entertainment of *Don* on the other. Nevertheless, the impact of the film has carried far beyond, as was seen in Anurag Kashyap's *Gangs of Wasseypur*, where Nawazuddin Siddiqui's character was shown modelling himself on Amitabh Bachchan's role in *Trishul*.

In fact, *Deewaar* and *Trishul* have a lot in common, as pointed out by film writer Jai Arjun Singh. He writes, 'In a commercial movie culture founded on the star system, actors can sometimes be the real *auteurs*—their personalities shaping not just a film but in some cases an entire filmic movement. A classic example is Amitabh Bachchan as Vijay, the outsider-vigilante of the 1970s. In *Deewaar* and *Trishul*, Bachchan played a Vijay constantly haunted by an injustice-ridden past. Both narratives are built on the theme of a son trying to erase his mother's sufferings by rising in the world, even literally (to the extent that he can sign deed papers for new skyscrapers, the sort of constructions she might have once worked on as a labourer). Both were directed by Yash Chopra, but few people I know would think of Chopra as their chief creative force. Their mood—which also became the dominant mood of mainstream Hindi cinema in that decade—was created by the writing of Salim Khan and Javed Akhtar in conjunction with the many tangible and intangible aspects of Bachchan's personality; the two things came together in a way that became a fine expression for the societal and political frustrations of the time, proving cathartic for lakhs of viewers.'

The iconic role of the film was, of course, played by Amitabh Bachchan. This was a solid platform from which to showcase his performance with his trademark smouldering intensity. And perform he did. In 1978, he was at the peak of his stardom and had starred in the three top grossers of the year. Each of the films won him a Filmfare Award nomination for best actor. *Trishul* was probably his best performance, where he gave credibility to a character with such strong negative vibes. His role in *Muqaddar Ka Sikandar* was loaded with emotion and the film was the most popular of the year. But Amitabh Bachchan won the award for best actor for the third film, where he played two contrasting roles—an international crime boss and a village bumpkin—with equal ease. Also written by Salim–Javed, that film was *Don*.

Don

'*Don* has become a cult figure, a franchise. Today, Shah Rukh is playing him. Tomorrow, somebody else will take over'—Chandra Barot, director of *Don*

On 6 December 1974, the day *Majboor* released in Bombay, a full-page ad appeared in *Screen*. Issued by the producer of a forthcoming film, it announced: 'Box-office Conquerors Salim–Javed now present Nariman Films' DON'. The ad did name the three leading stars (Amitabh Bachchan, Zeenat Aman and Pran) and the main crew, but the names of Salim–Javed were bigger than all of them, and appeared above the title of the film.

In 1974, Bachchan was still not the star he eventually became but with *Zanjeer* under his belt, he was no pushover. Everyone else—Zeenat, Pran, Kalyanji–Anandji—was already a big star. And yet, *Don* was Salim–Javed's film right from the word go. Actually, even before the word go.

The story of *Don* began with Manoj Kumar's crew, particularly with his assistant director Chandra Barot and his cinematographer Nariman Irani. And like most stories in 1970s Bollywood, there was also Amitabh Bachchan.

In 1968, when Manoj Kumar's *Upkar* won two prizes at the National Awards, his assistant director Chandra Barot (and singer Mahendra Kapoor) went to Delhi to collect the prizes. Teji Bachchan—one of the jury members—told Barot about her son who was going to join films. The son duly visited the assistant director in Filmistan Studio and was introduced to Manoj Kumar who decided to cast him in *Roti Kapada Aur Makaan*.

While working in the film, Amitabh Bachchan became friendly with both Barot (who was the chief assistant director on the film) and Nariman Irani, the director of photography. At the time of filming *Roti Kapada Aur Makaan*, Nariman Irani—affectionately called Bawa by all—was under severe stress because his recent production, *Zindagi Zindagi* starring Sunil Dutt, had flopped and he was heavily in debt. The Hindi film industry usually solves these problems with good-natured enthusiasm. Two stars of the film—Amitabh Bachchan and Zeenat Aman—offered to act in Irani's next film, the potential success of which would help pay off his debts. Pran, who knew Irani well, and Chandra Barot, a Manoj Kumar regular, also agreed to be a part of the film.

Simple, yes. But there was a minor glitch. They did not have a script.

While *Roti Kapada Aur Makaan* was still being shot (in 1974), they wanted to approach Salim–Javed for a script because they were fast becoming the hottest writers in the industry and that would make it easier to finance the film. (Upfront cash to pay off old debts, remember?) Nariman Irani's wife, Salma, was Waheeda Rehman's hairdresser and through her, they got the actress to put in a word for them to her neighbour—one Salim Khan.

Irani and Barot went to meet Salim–Javed at Salim's Bandra residence. The writers did have a script, but they warned the team of newcomers that it had been rejected by pretty much the entire industry, including stars like Dev Anand and Jeetendra. Salim Khan asked them honestly, 'We have a script that has been rejected by everybody in the industry . . . *Chalega?*' And the team—Irani and Barot—said, '*Chalega.*'

Salim then looked at Javed and said, 'So let's give the *Don* script to them . . .'

The *Godfather* had released some time back and the word 'don' stuck in Irani's mind. He went ahead and registered the title as *Don.*

Don (Amitabh Bachchan) is an international crime boss, wanted in eleven countries. He kills one of his associates and the man's sister, Roma (Zeenat Aman), joins his gang to avenge her brother's death. Indian DSP D'Silva (Iftekhar) is on Don's trail and finally manages to kill him in a chase. But he doesn't make the news public. Instead, he gets hold of a roadside singer Vijay (also Amitabh Bachchan), who looks exactly like Don, to impersonate him and infiltrate the crime syndicate.

Vijay agrees to do this because he needs money to take care of two children he took in off the streets. The children's father Jasjit (Pran) was arrested by DSP D'Silva for a crime and had sworn revenge.

Vijay and Roma orchestrate a raid on the gang, in which DSP D'Silva is killed. Without him, Vijay can't convince the police that he's not the real Don, and meanwhile, the gang realizes he is an impostor. To save himself from both, he escapes from police custody. He then runs into Jasjit and they join hands to destroy the crime syndicate and its moles in the police force.

In hindsight, it is easy to see why so many heroes refused to play Don. Here was an international criminal who takes sadistic pleasure in killing police informers, is brutal with gang members who don't do his bidding and uses women for casual sex while being absolutely blasé about it. In the image-conscious industry of the 1970s, these were huge negatives for a hero to take on.

However, the villainous Don is on screen for less than a third of the film before the do-gooder Vijay takes over. After Don's chilling menace, it is the street singer's rustic charm which dominates most of the film. This—and the powerhouse possibilities of a dual role—should have been enough reason for any hero to sign on. In addition, the film had breathtaking pace, superb dialogues and a very modern feel to it. Unfortunately, none of that probably came through in the narration done to convince a star.

Don's biggest strength was the 'coolness' about the film. Amitabh Bachchan as Don exuded the suave charm that Ajit had made famous (in films like *Zanjeer* and *Yaadon Ki Baaraat*), but also made it smarter. Don's lingo had a smattering of English and he spoke with a drawl that sounded very convincing on a gangster wanted across the globe. Amitabh Bachchan clearly relished this role of a megalomaniac villain and delivered the lines with aplomb.

In fact, Don was somewhat like James Bond in his delivery of pithy one-liners. When a business associate tries to steal his gold, Don says: '*Yeh dus lakh ka sona toh main bhul jaoonga, Raj Singh. Magar tumhe yaad rakhunga.*'[xxix] He kills off a police informer and reveals his identity with a cryptic line: '*Mujhe iske joote achhe nahin lage.*'[xxx] When he is in bed with a woman, he drawls over a post-coital drink: '*Mujhe do tarah ki ladkiyan pasand nahin aati. Ek woh jo mere paas aane mein bahut der lagaye aur ek woh jo bahut jaldi aa jaye.*'[xxxi] He welcomed beautiful women to his gang by comparing them to wild cats: '*aur mujhe junglee billiyaan pasand hain*'.

And there is the killer line he quips when he is informed that the police has him surrounded: '*Don ka intezar toh gyarah mulkon ki police kar rahi hai, lekin Sonia . . . ek baat samajh lo: Don ko pakadna mushkil hi nahin, namumkin hai.'*[xxxii]

With simple tricks like showing his associates to be mortally scared of him even when he isn't around and by getting everyone to say Don's name with a sense of announcement, Salim–Javed created a massive mystique around the character.

As far as the screenplay was concerned, a few changes were made from the first draft. In the original screenplay, Jasjit was a perfectly fit person. But Pran, who played the role, had been in an accident, which required him to use a walking stick for quite some time. This necessitated changes in the plot to give Jasjit a defective leg so that Pran could shoot with his handicap.

Before the shooting of the song 'Main hoon Don', Zeenat Aman had to leave for a shooting schedule in Shimla for the Dev Anand-starrer *Kalabaaz*, which she could not postpone. When Salim–Javed were told about this, they smoothly inserted a dialogue in the conversation between the DSP and Vijay/Don just before the song. The DSP instructs that Roma be kept away from the villains' den when he conducts the raid.

These two and some other minor changes—necessitated by logistics—were accommodated ungrudgingly by Salim–Javed. But they drew the line when it came to changes based on whims and fancies, however big the stars in question were.

When Chandra Barot showed the rushes of the film to his mentor, Manoj Kumar, his initial impression was that the second half was extremely tight—not even giving time for the audience to take a loo break. He recommended the inclusion of two songs in the second half to give some relief to the series of thrills. Salim–Javed were not very happy but they did see the merit of the suggestion and wrote in one song situation. (It was agreed that two songs would be too much for the thriller to retain its pull.) This song was 'Khaike paan Banaraswala'[19] and though it was shot and inserted after the main filming was complete, the finesse with which the situation was presented gives no indication of that.

One change was requested by Amitabh Bachchan himself. Since Don was on the run from the police and the smugglers, the entire second half had him wearing the same clothes. As a star, he felt he needed to show off some other threads and suggested that a scene be written in which he requests Zeenat to get him a change of clothes. Salim–Javed put their feet down and insisted that such an 'unnecessary' scene would spoil the mood of the film. The urgency and terror Vijay experiences while being chased would be seriously compromised with a costume change, the writers felt, and held their ground.

The duo's willingness to accept several changes while refusing to make one that would compromise the script is a great indicator of their commitment to the film-making process.

Don was announced in late 1974 (immediately after *Roti Kapada Aur Makaan* was released) and it was three years and six months in the making. Producer Nariman Irani—already handicapped with his earlier debacle—was not flush with funds and that shows in some of the scenes. This financial crunch was further compounded when Irani was killed in a freak accident on a studio set in December 1977, a few months before *Don* was scheduled for release, but the film was wrapped up somehow.

The crisis of the producer's death was again handled pragmatically, with the writers taking the lead. In a meeting

---

[19] 'Khaike paan Banaraswala' was actually composed by Kalyanji–Anandji for the Dev Anand-starrer *Banarasi Babu*. When the producers did not use the song in that film, it was used in *Don*.

convened at Salim's residence, a clutch of people interested in helping out Nariman Irani's family came together. The most momentous decision taken at this meeting was to hike the price of distribution rights from Rs 12 lakh per territory to Rs 21 lakh, and pass on the incremental amount to the Irani family. Salim–Javed's own box-office clout (along with Amitabh Bachchan's) was the reason why they could renegotiate with the distributors, who had already agreed to the lower price.

Don released exactly a week after *Trishul*. Coming from one of India's top producers, *Trishul*'s advertising campaigns had run for nearly two months before its release while *Don*'s campaign—due to the producer's sudden demise and a shoestring budget—was low-key and started just a couple of weeks before the film opened.

Released along with major big-budget films, *Don* was written off within a week and there was hardly any money to promote it. Luckily, the song 'Khaike paan Banaraswala' took off like a rocket and that word-of-mouth started bringing in audiences. Collections began improving from the second week onwards and *Don* went on to become the third-highest-grossing film of the year. It was a phenomenal achievement, even for Amitabh Bachchan because *Don* was his only solo-hero hit that year. (*Trishul* and *Muqaddar Ka Sikandar* were multi-starrers.) The icing on the cake was the Filmfare Award Amitabh won for *Don*, becoming the best actor of 1978.

What was interesting in the sparse promotion of *Don* was Salim–Javed's position. Given that the director was a debutant, they, understandably, overtook even him in the publicity material. A double-spread ad in *Screen* on the day of the release had 'Written by Salim–Javed' in bold font just below the film's title. All the other stars' photographs appeared down the left side while Amitabh Bachchan's figure occupied the right. *Don*'s

Delhi release ad followed the same pattern with Salim–Javed's name right on top, even before the director's.

Farhan Akhtar's announcement in 2006 about producing a remake of the 1978 original guaranteed *Don*'s cult status in Hindi cinema history. Akhtar said, 'I think *Don* is the one film from that time that in my mind lends itself to being remade today. For me, it is a film that, back then, was a little ahead of its time. The way the story was told, the language the characters spoke, the writing style there was, it was very modern even for its time. So today, when you adapt it, it fits very easily into a contemporary space . . . and I think it fits into the modern sensibility of movie viewing quite well.' By saying this, he doffed a hat to the writers and gave them almost the entire credit for conceptualizing *Don*. Javed Akhtar, on his part, said that the original *Don* suffered a little from budget constraints and a lavish remake could make the film look really good.

Farhan Akhtar added a very cool sheen to the story by shooting the film overseas, giving *Don* (2006) a distinctive and contemporary look and packing the film with gadgets and gizmos. He also tried to avoid comparison with the original by changing the ending but that didn't work beyond a point. Fans of the original jumped up to defend their favourite film and flayed Farhan's film, somewhat unfairly.

The remake and the associated buzz elevated the original *Don* to an even higher level than where it initially was. From being merely one of Salim–Javed's many successes, *Don* suddenly became their most modern—and, dare I say, coolest—script.[20]

---

[20] The remake rights of *Don* were purchased from Nariman Films and permissions were taken from Salim–Javed by Farhan Akhtar's Excel Entertainment. However, when *Don 2* was made, Nariman Films filed a suit for copyright infringement citing that they had only given the right to remake the movie and not the rights to make a sequel.

The last word on *Don*'s enduring impact comes through an anecdote recounted by the director, Chandra Barot. After the remake was released in 2006, Barot met Shah Rukh Khan and Priyanka Chopra at Dilip Kumar's birthday party and complimented SRK on the film's success. SRK replied, '*Sir, original toh original hai.*'

From the fantasy world of international crime, Salim–Javed turned to the gritty and dirty reality of contemporary India in their next film. When Don kills his enemies, the writers made it look like a sport, but when dark coal mines close around hapless miners, Salim–Javed's script was like a helpless cry for survival. That script was *Kaala Patthar*.

Kaala Patthar

On 27 December 1975, hundreds of miners were working at Indian Iron and Steel Company's (IISCO) Chasnala colliery when an explosion shook the large mine, causing millions of gallons of water from a nearby reservoir to flood the mine. The ensuing destruction left no survivors; only a few of the dead bodies could be recovered. The company claimed an official figure of 372 dead while the workers' union claimed that 700 miners had perished in the accident. The record of the number of mine workers was kept so poorly that neither claim could be verified. While the exact cause of the explosion remains a mystery, four officials of IISCO were charged with negligence based on the findings of the probe done by a former Patna chief justice. The verdict was finally delivered in March 2012, thirty-seven years after the tragedy. Two of the accused had died during the course of the trial.

The Chasnala disaster and its even more tragic aftermath received a Salim–Javed makeover that was by and large reflective of the real conditions of miners, with some filmi concessions. While *Kaala Patthar* was found to be quite realistic, Javed feels that wasn't completely the case. 'I learned from *Kaala Patthar* that instead of sitting in a hotel room writing about a coal mine, if we had treated the script a little more realistically, it would have worked better. Either you don't use a realistic plot or have a realistic locale in the first place, or if you do, you have to be very convincing.'

Inputs about the coal-mining fraternity came from an unusual source. When Amitabh Bachchan was working in Calcutta before joining films, he had worked in the Coal Department of Bird & Company, a leading managing agency of the 1960s. Soon after joining the firm, he was sent to the mining areas (in present-day Jharkhand) to familiarize himself with the processes. He was in the mines observing the installation of a new machine when a portion of the mine collapsed and two miners got trapped underneath. Relief came quite quickly and Amitabh Bachchan lent a hand to the efforts. He was about to start pulling out one of the miners when the man said it was pointless because he was mortally wounded and asked him to help the other miner instead. The actor remembered this incident more than a decade later and recounted it to Salim–Javed when they were working on *Kaala Patthar*. After hearing about his experience, they took several inputs from Amitabh while writing the script.

This story of camaraderie and support among miners in the face of cavalier treatment by the mine owners is somewhat representative of *Kaala Patthar*'s plot.

The movie opens on a brooding miner Vijay (Amitabh Bachchan), who risks his life to save people at every possible opportunity, winning the admiration of his fellow workers. His daredevil acts are actually attempts to redeem himself for his past, when he abandoned his post as captain of a ship and put his own safety above everyone else's in a crisis. Soon, an idealistic engineer Ravi (Shashi Kapoor) joins the mining company and becomes a hero to the miners because he takes up their cause of fair pay and better working conditions. The mining town goes through more than its fair share of misfortune due to poor safety measures, bad equipment and complete apathy on the part of the owner, Dhanraj Puri (Prem Chopra), who unsuccessfully tries to pit Vijay and Ravi against each other in an effort to weaken the miners' unity. Meanwhile, a flamboyant fugitive Mangal (Shatrughan Sinha) escapes from prison and becomes a miner in the same town, and a dramatic rivalry begins between him and Vijay. One of Dhanraj Puri's big projects involves extracting the maximum amount of coal from a mine next to a massive water body. When his unscrupulous practices result in the flooding of the mines, Vijay, Ravi and Mangal enter the mine to save the workers and, after a heroic effort, even manage to rescue a sizeable number.

Amitabh Bachchan's backstory in *Kaala Patthar* was very similar to Joseph Conrad's *Lord Jim,* where a naval officer is disgraced for abandoning his ship, and then redeems himself with acts of bravery. The climax was somewhat similar in structure to Hollywood disaster movies (the *Towering Inferno,* for example) where a group of bravehearts unite to save the victims of a terrible tragedy through reckless heroism.[21]

These two elements were brought together in the familiar landscape of an Indian industrial backwater. This transportation and linkage to a recognizable tragedy was the Salim–Javed touch in a well-known story.

The writers' strong messages of socialism and comments on the role of the state—either positive or negative—seen in all their films, came to the fore in *Kaala Patthar,* where two of the heroes

---

[21] The climax of the film, where water floods the mines, was shot with the help of foreign technicians who created Hollywood-style special effects. The 'mine' sets were created by Sudhendu Roy in Film City. In fact, *Kaala Patthar* was the first-ever film to be shot there, even before the studio had been inaugurated.

are champions of socialism, fighting vehemently to secure the rights of the downtrodden. Even Rakhee's character—Dr Sudha Sen—is shown to be an idealistic doctor who gave up a lucrative practice in the city to help miners in a far-off town.

Parveen Babi as Anita, Ravi's love interest, is a journalist reporting on the plight of the miners. Eventually, she writes a story that makes a case for Dhanraj Mines to be nationalized, since public sector mines have much better working conditions.

All of this is done through some outstanding lines, which dramatically expound the poor working conditions of the miners. And, as was their style, much of it was couched in everyday conversations. For example, Dhanraj Puri's opening scene has him talk dismissively about the colony in which his miners live (*'Iss area se guzarne se dam ghut-ta hai. Bada ganda atmosphere hai.'*[xxxiii]) and sets the tone for his future apathy that is bordering on cruelty. This exaggerated villainy was written to drive home the point.

The ideal foil for this character was Vijay, the hero, fighting what he was convinced was a losing battle. Several of his almost wistful comments about the miners' hapless conditions were in the context of bangle-seller Channo's (Neetu Singh) sales pitches spoken within his earshot. To explain the futility of dressing up in such depressing conditions, he says, *'In koyle ke khaano mein aaye din marne waalon ki auratein chudiyaan pehanne ke liye nahin, todne ke liye kharidti hain.'*[xxxiv] With this one line, Salim–Javed summarized the cycle of desperate life and easy death in the mining community. And towards the end, Vijay describes the mine as a python which sucks away the life blood of the miners in a chilling scene: *'Yeh koyle ke khaan ek ajgar hai, Seth Sahib, jo roz anginat mazdooron ko nigalta hai aur unhe chabaake peeske kuchalke, unke jism se zindagi ka ek ek katra chooskar ek laash ki soorat mein wapas ugal deta hai.'*[xxxv]

Kaala Patthar was also a study in the utilization of the strengths of stars in a multi-starrer—the case in point being Amitabh Bachchan and Shatrughan Sinha's casting at a time when their professional rivalry was at its peak.

The two stars had started off as very good friends when they acted in *Bombay to Goa,* because Shatrughan knew Jaya Bhaduri very well from his Film and Television Institute of India (FTII) days. Both actors had become top heroes by the end of 1970s and their rivalry had intensified by the time they locked horns in *Kaala Patthar*. According to Shatrughan himself, 'All the spontaneity was gone. We were concerned about how many punches each one of us had to throw.' He went on to say, 'I think *Kaala Patthar* was the last nail in the coffin of our friendship. He was very against my doing the film. I was in it much against his wishes.' Now imagine this context for the writers. Amitabh Bachchan was clearly their 'protégé' and there would have been unofficial pressure to give him the stronger role since he was also the bigger star. However, the roles they wrote for Amitabh and Shatrughan were perfectly suited to the two actors. Both played to their strengths and became the two opposing sides of an explosive conflict.

Yash Chopra's long-standing assistant, Ramesh Talwar says, 'Salim–Javed had conceived the differing styles of the three leading men and discussed the same with Yashji, so that the three actors would be available and agreeable to do the film. Once an initial agreement was reached, they started writing the detailed script. All the stars were given the script narration separately. Amitji was part of the first sitting itself while Shatrughan Sinha and Shashi Kapoor heard the script later. All of them were told of their "scoring points" and each of them liked their individual roles. All these narrations were done by Salim–Javed together, along with Yash Chopra.'

Amitabh's diction and voice modulation were used in the many monologues he delivered while Shatrughan's flamboyance made way for the perfect one-liners. On one hand, there is Vijay's fatalistic streak ('Pain is my destiny and I can't avoid it') and on the other, there is Mangal's cocky confidence ('*Duniya mein aisi koi jagah nahin bani jahan se Mangal na nikal sake*'[xxxvi]). Vijay's best moment is a near-silent one where he wrenches a knife from a goon with his bare hands while Mangal's audience-pleasing scene is a teen-patti session where he loses the hand but wins with his chutzpah ('*Mere taash ke tirpanwe patte, teesre badshah hum hain*'[xxxvii]).

These two contrasting characters—as Hindi film scripts ordain—were destined to clash, and clash they did. The battle between Vijay and Mangal (that takes place just before the stroke of the interval) is probably the best-executed on-screen rivalry in Hindi cinema. Over a screen time of nearly thirty minutes, the two adversaries circle each other like prizefighters and clash in a fight sequence so explosive that only the third hero can separate them. The whole execution of the fight was the scriptwriters' triumph as they got two of the industry's biggest stars to play to their strengths, create a reservoir of tension and then dissipate it with breathtaking action.

Writer–director Sriram Raghavan feels that this contrast in the characters may have been one of the problems of *Kaala Patthar*. 'One of the reasons *Kaala Patthar* didn't work that well is probably because Amitabh's is very subdued character. The audience expected him and Shatrughan to trade punches and dialogues, which did not happen. This was right for the movie but the friction between two actors is somewhat expected by audience.'

Nevertheless, *Kaala Patthar* finds resonance in varied places and connects with diverse milieus. Post Punk Cinema Club, a popular blog about movies from across the world, writes, 'What's so enjoyable about *Kaala Patthar*, and what makes it resemble M*A*S*H,[22] is the wide variety of well-developed characters who mingle around in this precarious and dangerous environment. The interactions between these characters are believable and, with the exception of the Big Bad Boss, everyone has more than a touch of humanity.'

By the time *Kaala Patthar* was released, Salim–Javed's stardom was almost equal to that of the top stars in the industry. In trade circles, their names drew as much commercial confidence as Amitabh Bachchan's. *Kaala Patthar*'s pre- and post-release ads had their names right on top, just after the director's, which had become the norm by then.

Kaala Patthar was—given the weight of expectations from it—a moderate success. It was the seventh-highest grosser of the year. Despite a strong script and taut direction, it did not do too well; Amitabh's *Suhaag* and *Mr Natwarlal* turned out to be bigger crowd-pullers. This also became the last time Yash Chopra worked with Salim–Javed as a team.

The subdued success of *Kaala Patthar* was in no way a dampener on Salim–Javed's box-office clout. They were massive stars in their own right. Since their fees for *Kaala Patthar* had been negotiated earlier, it is estimated that they received around Rs 7.5 lakh—an astronomical sum in the late 1970s—for the script, but by this time, their asking price for other films had shot up to Rs 21 lakh. In fact, they pegged their fees with Amitabh Bachchan's (who was charging around Rs 25 lakh per film at the time) and always asked for a comparable amount.

---

[22] *M*A*S*H* was an extremely popular American TV series (that ran from 1972–83) about a group of army doctors, nurses and soldiers stuck in the middle of the Korean war, who created morbid dark humour to escape the tragedy of their daily lives.

While this confidence great, it also heralded the beginning of the end. Firstly, the two started growing apart as now each had his own coterie, which told him that he was the real reason for the duo's success. Secondly, their price and their scale led to greater scrutiny on how their films were mounted and who they starred instead of focusing on telling the best possible story.

Salim–Javed would remain together for a few more years, during which they would write big successes. But in comparison to their initial assembly line of hits, these were mostly disappointments. The lavish sets, the massive congregation of stars, the booming music and breathless anticipation took audience frenzy to such a height that the films' actual performances at the box office never quite matched the monumental expectations from them.

They had reached the zenith of their stardom. And it could only go downhill from here. However, with Salim–Javed, you could be certain of one thing: even their ordinary scripts had more twists and more audience-pleasing moments than any other.

Nothing showed this better than their next release, which came a year later: *Dostana*.

Dostana

While Salim–Javed were at the height of their powers by 1980, the quality of their scripts had begun to deteriorate. Javed dates the start of this decline even earlier and says, 'After 1975–76, our scripts lost that intensity. I don't think our work was good after the mid-1970s. I could see it. The fire wasn't raging any more . . . you become complacent . . . and that spirit of adventure, that daring quality, that devil-may-care attitude disappears.'

Given the long gestation period of Hindi films at the time, this is entirely possible since scripts written in 1977–78 were actually releasing in 1980—which was when the decline became apparent. Also, it could be a sense of discomfort only a craftsman feels about his craft.

Their first release in 1980, *Dostana*, was also Yash Johar's first film as producer, though the mounting of the film was so lavish that a debutant producer's fears and insecurities were not visible at all. Yash Johar's career as a production controller on large-scale films like *Guide*, *Jewel Thief* and *Prem Pujari* proved to be a good training ground for him as *Dostana* had two major actors, a top-notch music composer and some breathtaking action sequences filmed outside India. It helped that Johar was great friends with Amitabh and Jaya and Javed Akhtar and Honey Irani, often partying with them through the night. It was, therefore, easy for him to bring them on board.

Dostana—written at the peak of Salim–Javed's stardom—was a very important milestone. The fact that they had agreed to write the script for the first-time producer's film was supposed to be a big draw for the distributors. Salim–Javed told Yash Johar that they should be paid more than the lead star—Amitabh Bachchan. They had earned more than Amitabh in some of their earlier films as well but *Dostana* was being discussed at a time when the actor too was reaching the peak of his stardom. Negotiations ensued and Salim–Javed were signed for a princely sum of Rs 12.5 lakh, marginally more than the Rs 12 lakh Amitabh was getting. With the success of this negotiation Salim fulfilled a long-standing promise he had made to himself. He remembered the conversation he had had with Abrar Alvi nearly two decades ago, and called the senior writer to ask if he recalled Salim's prediction—that writers would one day be paid more than the top stars of the time. When Abrar Alvi said that he did indeed remember, Salim Khan told him, '*Abrar sahib, aaj humne woh kaam kar liya hai* . . .' The genial Abrar Alvi was extremely happy to hear the news and blessed Salim for the achievement.

Dostana was directed by Raj Khosla, known for huge successes like *CID*, *Woh Kaun Thi*, *Do Raaste* and *Mera Gaon Mera Desh*. Khosla was very impressed with Salim–Javed right from the time when they handed over the script to him. The veteran director had said, 'I have been in the industry for so many years but this is the first time I have seen a script which has "The End" written on it.'

Salim–Javed's promise to deliver a complete script was something that did not change even at the height of their fame. They had probably started taking fewer risks with the plot but did not compromise on what they set out to do.

Police officer Vijay (Amitabh Bachchan) and criminal lawyer Ravi (Shatrughan Sinha) are childhood buddies who don't let their professional differences affect their friendship. Though Ravi uses his legalese to free his clients, most of who are smugglers whom Vijay has arrested, they do not let their professional differences affect their friendship. However, their bond is tested when both men fall in love with the same girl, Sheetal (Zeenat Aman). A notorious smuggler Daaga (Prem Chopra) uses this to create a misunderstanding between the two, which causes them to break off their friendship. When the villains manage to frame Vijay for murder, Sheetal approaches Ravi for help. Ravi agrees but only on the condition that Sheetal will sleep with him after he gets Vijay acquitted. However, before Sheetal is compelled to fulfil her promise, Ravi becomes aware of the causes of misunderstanding between the two and tries to reach out to Vijay. But Daaga and his gang kidnap him and Sheetal, whom Vijay rescues in the climax.

This was the writers' second film with Amitabh Bachchan and Shatrughan Sinha as joint leads, but unlike *Kaala Patthar*—where both the actors' strengths were utilized very well—*Dostana* was largely an Amitabh Bachchan film. He had the better lines, got to sing the songs, offered to sacrifice his love for friendship and even got to hang from a helicopter in the climax. In fact, it is a wonder that Shatrughan Sinha at all agreed to do a film in which he was clearly playing second fiddle.

Shatrughan Sinha claims that Amitabh did not want to work with him at the time because he was getting overshadowed and used the excuse of Shatrughan's tardiness on sets to refuse future films with him. This is not discernible in the script of *Dostana*, though the tension between the two leading men was palpable throughout the shoot.

Dostana—despite having two action heroes—was the first time several romantic scenes were written and brought in focus.

Even when Salim–Javed wrote for a romantic hero like Rajesh Khanna, their scenes had an undercurrent of humour and were never mushy.

In *Dostana*, they created two types of lovers. Ravi is the more sentimental one, who gets tongue-tied in the presence of women (despite being an articulate lawyer by profession). Vijay is the more suave one, with the gift of the gab and a way with women. He even offers to speak to the object of Ravi's affection on his behalf. This is often a very common basis for a bond between friends in real life too, where the more eloquent one helps out his bashful friend(s) with girls.

Salim–Javed wrote a few extended romantic scenes where Vijay woos Sheetal in Amitabh's fabled baritone. The scenes were a deft mix of casual conversation, bragging ('*Mere chehre mein ajeeb si kashish hai, khaas taur se meri aankhen.*'[xxxviii]) and humour—while apologizing to Sheetal with red roses, Vijay writes in the accompanying note, '*Yun toh yeh phool hain halke gulabi rang ke, lekin is waqt woh gusse mein hain. Isi liye laal dikhai de rahe hain.*'[xxxix] The romantic scenes were important because they established the strength of Vijay's relationship with Sheetal and the importance of his sacrifice.

Salim–Javed effectively brought about the action revolution in Hindi cinema that signified a generational shift from the prevalent romantic themes. Quite surprisingly, *Dostana* revealed their 'romantic' side and is an interesting example of their versatility. Thus far, they had kept the love talk to a bare minimum in their films, even those with romantic themes or subplots—*Seeta Aur Geeta*, *Andaz*, *Yaadon Ki Baaraat*—but with this film they managed to show a new facet of their writing quite late in their career.

Despite not meeting expectations, *Dostana* was a major commercial success in 1980, being the fourth-highest grosser of the year, and becoming a major triumph for the debutant producer. Salim–Javed's reputation remained untarnished, though the strain of criticism and—more importantly—their inflating egos had started to show. That, coupled with the tension of their personal lives at that point in time, would have affected their output.

Despite the tensions of *Dostana*, Amitabh Bachchan and Shatrughan Sinha came together in their final Salim–Javed script two months later. The film was arguably the most-awaited film in five years and easily the biggest canvas Salim–Javed worked on in their high-profile career. The film was *Shaan*.

Shaan

'The films which conform a 100 per cent to what the audiences are supposed to want, more often than not, fail'—Javed Akhtar

In December 1980, Bombay's Minerva cinema did a strange thing. They were showing a film where two young wastrels come to the rescue of an older idealistic man tormented by a villainous megalomaniac. They replaced that film with another where two young wastrels come to the rescue of an older idealistic man tormented by a villainous megalomaniac. Both films had a talkative heroine, a strong supporting cast, a young man who is brutally killed, the two heroes singing a song on a two-wheeler and the villain doing his version of a Russian roulette to punish traitors.

In many ways, *Sholay* and *Shaan* were essentially the same movie.

Both were huge multi-starrers with special effects and breathtaking production design that single-handedly set new industry standards. The producers bet the shirts on their backs to make both movies. And consequently, each came with the burden of being the most-awaited film ever. Not to mention the most expensive.

Sholay's success had affected everyone associated with it. Distributors, exhibitors and black marketeers had secured the futures of several generations on the strength of the film's earnings. Ramesh Sippy was no longer the upstart son of a rich producer; he was a box-office god expected to work magic. Amitabh Bachchan—who had been a promising newcomer in *Sholay*—also became, well, a box-office god. And Salim–Javed were no longer a pair of young writers hankering for fame. *Sholay* had changed all their lives. And *Shaan* was meant to be nothing but a vehicle to trump *Sholay*. Everything related to the film was high octane and everybody knew it.

The brief to the writers was to recreate action inspired by James Bond movies, complete with newfangled gadgetry and slick styling. International talent was used a lot more than in *Sholay*, with foreign action directors, special-effects directors, camera operators and sound designers brought in. They stuck to this brief quite well and even managed to pay tribute with a Bond-style opening scene.

Initially, Dharmendra and Amitabh Bachchan were considered for the two leads, with Dharmendra slated to play the character Amitabh Bachchan portrayed. However—with Amitabh becoming the bigger star—it would have been very difficult to balance the two roles. So Shashi Kapoor—no pushover himself in stardom stakes—was brought in. Shatrughan Sinha appeared in a guest role (which was pretty meaty in the end).

Although Ramesh Sippy packed the main cast with stars, he repeated the trick of having a rank newcomer—Kulbhushan Kharbanda—in the role of the villain. He managed to get the same level of audience surprise that he had got by having Amjad Khan play Gabbar. Well, almost the same level.

Salim–Javed, for their part, named the villain Shaakaal (from *Yaadon Ki Baaraat*) and gave him reasonably good lines, including one that was picked up verbatim from the earlier film—'*Shaakaal ke haath mein jitney patte hote hain, utne hi patte uski aasteen mein hote hain.*'[xl] There was massive curiosity around the new actor and several newspapers ran profiles of Kulbhushan Kharbanda before the release (something quite unheard of in those days, when people were less smitten by Bollywood than they are now).

Upright and honest cop, DSP Shiv Kumar (Sunil Dutt) has two brothers—Vijay (Amitabh Bachchan) and Ravi (Shashi Kapoor)—who are conmen. They go around duping people till Shiv Kumar comes to their city and arrests them. They promise to reform their ways. Soon after, mega-villain Shaakaal (Kulbhushan Kharbanda), whose illegal businesses were being shut down by the police officer, has Shiv Kumar killed. Vijay and Ravi swear revenge and are joined by Rakesh (Shatrughan Sinha), a sharpshooter who was doing Shaakaal's bidding because the villain was holding his wife hostage. They storm Shaakaal's island den in disguise and destroy it completely.

Salim–Javed took this simple (simplistic?) plot and created a massive film with several side stories, supporting characters, interesting situations and clever gimmicks.

Shaan has some of the cleverest lines Salim–Javed have written. When heroine Renu (Bindiya Goswami) pulls up in a white convertible, Ravi is smitten by her and Vijay by her car. Smoothly and seamlessly, they carry on a long conversation wherein each describes their respective object of desire—the girl and the car—without realizing that they are talking about different things altogether. Even a seemingly insignificant role like Johnny Walker's (who plays Renu's conman uncle) had really witty lines. But after the flood of memorable lines in *Sholay*, *Shaan*'s script did not seem to crackle enough.

The biggest weakness of the script was probably the need to show off 'cool stuff', with very little attention paid to the story and characters.

For example, DSP Shiv Kumar is killed off by Shaakaal but not before he jumps off an island skyscraper after being kidnapped by four trucks, and is chased by a pack of wild dogs (much of this was shot in the UK). The inherent tragedy of the honest police officer's death somehow gets lost in the whirlwind action.

In terms of character development, this is the most inconsistent of the writers' films. *Kaala Patthar*—for example— had characters which stayed consistent throughout the film. Amitabh Bachchan was a depressed introvert while Shatrughan was the garrulous aggressor and they remained true to their characters till the end. Amitabh did not sing any songs in *Kaala Patthar*, *Deewaar* and *Zanjeer*. Though he did sing a song in *Trishul*, it was an anti-romantic number that actually shows his indifference towards love.

When asked about his strength, Salim Khan says, 'Our forte was characterization, which was a weakness of Hindi films. A guy who loses his father in one scene is seen dancing in the next . . .' Coming from someone so conscious of maintaining character graphs, *Shaan* was a big aberration. In the film, Vijay flirts with unknown women and he and Ravi sing a song with their girlfriends, within a few scenes of their brother's death (which they have sworn to avenge). Vijay's anger seems to switch off whenever the situation demands it. All this contributed to *Shaan* becoming a mish-mash of amazing technical finesse and a very loose script.

Writer–director Sriram Raghavan sums up the typical audience reaction when he says, 'I enjoyed *Shaan* for several great sequences, set pieces and all that but by the time they had the climax at the island, it was no longer real—even emotionally. There were logical flaws even in *Sholay* but you didn't notice them. The loopholes of *Shaan* got noticed because the emotional impact was low.'

Sholay was 'The Greatest Story Ever Told' while the posters of *Shaan* called it 'The Greatest Show on Earth'. In a way, this difference—between a great story and a great spectacle—was what separated *Shaan* from *Sholay*.

And this was caught out by the reviewers, who were quite brutal.

Screen said, 'For the majority of filmgoers, Shaan will offer audio-visual experience that will be quite extraordinary and, indeed, exciting enough to lure them back to the cinema for a repeat viewing.' However, it also said the 'camera wizardry hitherto unequalled in the Hindi screen' and 'lavish settings, plus with dazzling contraptions [sic]' were 'used very imaginatively and deftly to wrap up a pedestrian, oft-repeated narrative of vendetta . . . which is taking too much advantage of the characteristic docility of the Indian audience.' It specifically mentioned the writing by complaining about 'a lack of originality in the conception of the theme' and 'a total absence of vitality which shows up painfully in the dialogue'. It went on to compare the film with *Sholay* ('the director's triumph, which literally bristled with vigorous and sparkling dialogue').

The other major trade magazine, *Trade Guide,* also echoed this. 'Compared to Sholay, this film is far superior in technical values. In this aspect, Shaan is 200% of Sholay. Runwise, it may run 30% of Sholay. At the box-office, it may do 40% of Sholay. In repeat audience consideration, it is 20% of Sholay.'

Shaan is often referred to as a 'flop'. It wasn't that by any stretch of the imagination but nevertheless, it was a colossal disappointment. Ramesh Sippy sees it as falling short of expectations. He says, 'At a cost of Rs 6 crore, *Shaan* doing business worth Rs 12 crore is nothing when *Sholay*, a film costing Rs 3 crore, does something like Rs 25 crore in its first run.'

Amitabh Bachchan sees it differently. He says, '*Shaan* was an elegantly presented caper movie. At that time, the James Bond movies were doing exceedingly well the world over. Ramesh Sippy wanted to do something in the same genre. When it was released, it did seem to lack soul as it was replete with gizmos. It didn't work but today it is widely circulated on video and DVD and often shown on the television and cable channels.'

Every time Salim–Javed came under pressure, they always bounced back. While *Shaan* was a major disappointment, their next release—fourteen months later—went on to become the biggest hit of 1982. That film was also fraught with accusations of a shoddy script but it managed to bring about newness by virtue of being set in a different point in history, when it was time for a revolution. The film was *Kranti*.

Kranti

In 1949, a little boy called Harekrishna Goswami saw Dilip Kumar in the film *Shabnam*. He was already very fond of the star and after that film, he became such a big fan that he began calling himself Manoj—the name of Dilip Kumar's character in *Shabnam*—and eventually joined films as Manoj Kumar. For him, the opportunity to direct Dilip Kumar in *Kranti* in the early 1980s was a dream come true. This was the period when the veteran actor was transitioning from leading roles to very strong character roles. *Kranti* marked the beginning of his second innings.

Like Nasir Husain in *Yaadon Ki Baaraat*, this was the first time Manoj Kumar sought the help of other writers for his own film. Prior to this, all his directorial ventures—*Upkar, Purab Aur Pachhim, Shor* and *Roti Kapada Aur Makaan*—had been entirely written by him. Even *Kranti*'s dialogues are officially credited to him. Like all their screenplays, Salim–Javed did write the basic dialogues, which were then worked upon by Manoj Kumar. Javed said, '*Kranti* was completely Manoj Kumar's baby . . . We wrote the story and screenplay, but according to what he wanted . . . Incidentally, Manoj Kumar himself wrote the dialogues of the film, and whatever changes were made were improvised by him.'

Unlike Salim–Javed's usual insistence on not changing anything in their scripts, they were uncharacteristically pliable with this film—probably in deference to Manoj Kumar's stature.

The theme of patriotism that Manoj Kumar was associated with got a masala makeover in *Kranti*. From the quiet idealism of *Upkar*, he had upped the decibel (and glamour) somewhat in *Roti Kapada Aur Makaan*. With *Kranti*, he pulled out all stops, using extravagant sets, elaborate action and a packed multi-star cast. Even by the high standards of 1970s multi-starrers, *Kranti* was a biggie. And in order to pack all those stars in, the story was quite complicated.

Set in the princely state of Ramgarh in the nineteenth century, the film begins with a coup engineered by Shambhu Singh (Prem Chopra) to install Shamsher Singh (Pradeep Kumar) as the king. The British also support this move because they gain control of the port. Sanga (Dilip Kumar), a citizen of Ramgarh, discovers that the British are using the port to smuggle arms into and artefacts out of the state but before he can do anything, he is framed for the murder of the dethroned king. Sanga escapes from prison, but is separated from his wife (Nirupa Roy), his older son and newborn baby boy, who is taken to the palace by the deceased king's sister and raised as her own.

Sanga becomes a pirate and a rebel against the British rule, going by the name Kranti. His older son Bharat (Manoj Kumar) also becomes a freedom fighter, and saves another rebel Karim Khan (Shatrughan Sinha) from execution. Sanga's younger son Shakti (Shashi Kapoor) is now the general of the Ramgarh army and is ordered to capture Kranti. The female leads are Surili (Parveen Babi), who is part of Bharat's team, and Rajkumari Meenakshi (Hema Malini), who starts off as an Anglophile princess but joins the 'kranti' and falls in love with Bharat.

Father and sons clash as the British discredit the freedom fighters. Both Bharat and Sanga believe that the other is sabotaging the freedom movement, while Shakti tries to capture them. After many skirmishes, the freedom fighters finally meet the British and Ramgarh forces in a pitched battle on the ramparts of the fort. Bharat is killed during the battle, while Meenakshi gives birth to Bharat's son. The film ends with Sanga passing on the flame of Kranti to Bharat's son.

It is to Salim–Javed's credit that what sounds almost incomprehensible in description works better on screen. With easy-to-recognize set pieces, familiar situations and memorable dialogues, the writers tried their best to make it palatable to the typical Hindi film audience. One of *Kranti*'s weaknesses was a dragging climax with all the stars doing much more than they should have.

Incidentally, *Kranti*'s final story was completely different from when it began. 'It will be about seventy years in the life of a village, the change that has at last come. The change for the better in which the farmer can breathe fresh air, away from the clutches of the moneylender and the zamindar, tentacles holding him as bonded labour,' Manoj Kumar had said in a 1977 interview about his then-current production *Naya Bharat* which had the same star cast. Clearly his original vision went through a significant change once writing commenced.

An element of *Kranti* that was quite incongruous for a Salim–Javed film was the primitive treatment of women. While it was common for women to have marginal roles in multi-starrers, *Kranti* had a fair bit of gratuitous skin show, which was new for a film written by the duo. And in an inexplicable bit of misogyny in the garb of patriotism, Bharat points to the foreigners' disregard for Indian traditions by speaking ill of the British for saving a woman from a sati pyre. While the demonification of the British was done because they rape the woman they save, Bharat ends up defending sati by calling it '*apne parivar ki parampara*' [xli].

Interestingly, Kranti is presented as a concept or character, which is passed from one generation to the next—much like Phantom from the eponymous comic series—to carry on the struggle for freedom.

The template for *Kranti* was used in *Mard* a few years later—with several similarities between the two films. Both films have obnoxious Britishers perpetrating unspeakable atrocities on hapless Indians till two generations of freedom fighters take them on. Add to that the age-old favourite lost-and-found saga and subplots of expatriation of priceless artefacts and shrewish Anglophile women tamed by patriots, and you pretty much have identical films. Incidentally, *Mard* was also among the top-grossing films of 1985.

While *Kranti* was a huge commercial success, it got a poor critical reception. The reviews—while praising some aspects of the film—were almost unanimous in criticising the screenplay. *Screen* said, 'If, in spite of its grand sweep and technical brilliance, Kranti has failed to impress, it is largely because it has for its foundation a weakly and amateurishly written screenplay. A film of Kranti's dimension and sweep should have had a well-knit screenplay with powerful characterisations and situations. The grandeur of the settings, the technical brilliance and Manoj's sensitive direction are all at a disadvantage in telling a predictable story set against the backdrop of the freedom struggle in the middle of the nineteenth century.'

K.M. Amladi, writing in the *Hindustan Times*, felt, 'For all the time, money and talents that have gone into the making of it, Kranti is in a word magnificently shallow . . . The film's weakest point is its script for which Salim–Javed and Manoj must share the blame. It is riddled with that depressingly predictable missing-brothers syndrome—another down-the-line product from the Salim–Javed script conveyor belt. What it lacks is any spark or any cutting edge.'

Manoj Kumar's own acting and his heavy-handed direction have ensured that *Kranti*'s appeal does not endure. In fact, it is probably the most dated of Salim–Javed's films, which is strange because the period setting should have made the movie timeless. But the overdone emotions, theatrical acting and the bombastic dialogues—hallmarks of the worst of 1970s Hindi cinema—can be found throughout the film.

What is undeniable is the laboured feel of the script— possibly a factor of Salim–Javed's strained relationship and the pressure on them to write big films. Risk-taking was something they had completely eschewed and once-novel ideas had become predictable now as Amladi's review in the *Hindustan Times* pointed out.

However, the poor reviews don't take away the box-office impact of the film—it was the top grosser of 1981, bigger even than some of Amitabh Bachchan's greatest hits at a time when the actor was at the peak of his popularity. *Kranti*'s collections surpassed those of Manmohan Desai's *Naseeb*, Prakash Mehra's *Lawaaris* and Tinnu Anand's *Kaalia*—three of Amitabh's biggest successes. It also beat two debutants' films—Kumar Gaurav's *Love Story* and Sanjay Dutt's *Rocky*—not to mention south Indian star Kamal Haasan's first Hindi film *Ek Duuje Ke Liye*.

One of the positive things that critics had to say about *Kranti* was in praise of Dilip Kumar's performance, complimenting him for 'bringing a measure of plausibility to [the] role . . . having lost none of his old charm or his screen presence'. Salim and Javed were huge fans of the veteran actor but several previous attempts to work with the thespian hadn't borne fruit. *Kranti* came towards the fag end of their partnership, but this role was nothing compared to what the writer duo would write for him next. Considered one of the classics of Hindi cinema and probably the greatest casting coup of the 1980s, this film was *Shakti*.

Shakti

If there is an actor Salim–Javed admire more than Amitabh Bachchan, it is Dilip Kumar. And he is the same actor who pretty much inspired Amitabh Bachchan to join films. In many ways, then, *Shakti* was a dream come true for both the writers and the younger star. In fact, Salim–Javed had tried to get Dilip Kumar to do *Zanjeer*, but it wasn't until much later that they finally managed to get the actor in films of theirs— coincidentally, one of them for the role of a police officer.

Salim–Javed, being the cocky upstarts that they were, had said in a 1974 interview, 'Dilip saab is a very involved person when he is doing a film. The trouble is he thinks only in terms of his scenes and not the complete film. Nobody has so far had the courage to tell him so. Everyone says "wah wah" and he naturally likes it. Maybe we will succeed in convincing him about our point of view.'

With *Shakti*, they actually delivered on what they had claimed, successfully balancing their hero worship with a role that fit the story completely.

After the disappointment of *Shaan*, Ramesh Sippy mounted the biggest casting coup in the industry by pitting Hindi cinema's two biggest actors against each other; the standard publicity line 'Clash of the Titans'—for once—seemed like an understatement.

Amitabh Bachchan says, 'It was a dream come true to be teamed with Dilip Kumar whom I'd admired from my childhood. I'd often bunked college to see *Ganga Jumna*, I've seen it twenty-five times at least. To find him in the same film, the same frame, was unbelievable. The mahurat was done dramatically on Juhu beach outside Holiday Inn. Dilip Kumar drove up in a jeep, I flew in on a helicopter. We said our lines of dialogue to each other. The mahurat became the talk of the town.'

The starting point of *Shakti* was a Tamil film starring Sivaji Ganesan—*Thanga Pathakkam* (Gold Medal), which was a huge hit in 1974. The title referred to the gold medal a dutiful police officer receives for shooting down his errant son in the line of duty. When Salim–Javed were asked to render this basic plot in Hindi, they ended up changing it significantly. The result was a completely new story; the only similarity being that both films end with the father shooting the son.

The Tamil film was essentially a vehicle for Sivaji Ganesan. Similarly, the original plan for *Shakti* was for Dilip Kumar to shine opposite a less prominent actor—Raj Babbar—in the son's role. In fact, Javed Akhtar had said, 'When we were writing *Shakti*, we didn't know that Amitabh Bachchan would be in the film—we had no idea . . . *Shakti* was basically a vehicle for Dilip Kumar; it was planned for him, not for Amitabh.'

This imbalance in the roles of the father and son led to a fair bit of soul-searching for the writers, as they believed it was poor casting. Their commitment to the script was so strong that they considered having the industry's biggest star in the lead role of this film a mistake.

When asked if casting had spoiled any of their films, Javed Akhtar brought up *Shakti* and said, 'I really wonder what

Shakti's fate would have been if the son's role had been played by some other actor who didn't have Amitabh Bachchan's status. Perhaps that would have been better because the role was not big enough for Amitabh. I believe that *Shakti* was one of his good performances but it's sad that many people didn't appreciate his work in the film . . . In spite of being a mega-star, he did not let his stardom come in the way of playing the role of the son. And he played the son and looked submissive, or passive, or frightened or intimidated—as a son should look in front of a powerful father. Some people confused this with some kind of weakness. He showed he's an actor first, then a star. But the fact remains that he was a superstar, and people expected more from him than the script or the role offered. But I wonder if an actor of lesser stature had played that role, perhaps *Shakti* could have been a more satisfying film.'

The writers told both actors exactly how the script was supposed to unfold. Amitabh Bachchan recalls, 'When you're working with Dilip Kumar, you can't expect an equal role. In fact, Salim–Javed had told me that there would be an *unnees-bees ka farq* between the roles of the father and son . . . and that my role would be *unnees*.'

Of course, with Amitabh Bachchan in the lead, *Shakti* became a huge commercial venture and that led to certain other compromises, like having songs in the film. Javed Akhtar says that he tried to (unsuccessfully) persuade Ramesh Sippy to cut out the songs. He felt that the film would run better without them. Although commercial considerations dictated otherwise, Javed maintains, 'I don't think *Shakti*'s songs drew the audience to the theatre for a single show.'

Like *Deewaar*, *Shakti* was conceived as a songless film to give it a stark, brooding touch. Film critic Sukanya Verma writes, 'At a time when most Big B's introduction scenes involved applause-designed daredevilry or punch lines, his subdued entry in Shakti reveals the screenplay's intention to keep it dark, hard-lined.'

But when *Shakti* was released, Amitabh was a massive star, doing everything—comedy, tragedy, action, romance—in the other films that were hitting theatres around the same time. It was imperative for the success of a film that he be given a wide range of crowd-pleasing things to do on-screen that utilized his full potential. This obviously did not happen with *Shakti* and the audience felt short-changed.

Writer–director Sriram Raghavan says, '*Shakti* released a few months after *Namak Halaal*, where Amitabh was doing so many things—action, dance, comedy—and masses would have compared the two.'

Police officer Ashwini Kumar (Dilip Kumar) is very fond of his wife Sheetal (Rakhee) and son Vijay but also completely bound to his duty. When a gang of smugglers led by J.K. (Amrish Puri) kidnaps Vijay to get Ashwini to do their bidding, he refuses and says he would rather lose his son than compromise on his ideals. The young Vijay overhears this and develops a deep-seated resentment towards his father. Vijay manages to escape with the help of one of the kidnappers, Narang (Kulbhushan Kharbanda). But by the time he becomes an adult, Vijay's (Amitabh Bachchan) bitterness towards his father has grown, in part due to Ashwini's dedication to his duty and in part because of his own preconceived notions. When Vijay gets a job in Narang's hotel, Ashwini asks him not to accept it since Narang is a known smuggler. Vijay refuses and walks out of the house. In a bid to take revenge against J.K. and defy his father, Vijay too becomes a smuggler. Ashwini eventually catches up with him and arrests him. While Vijay is in jail, J.K. kills Sheetal. On hearing this, Vijay escapes to avenge her death. In a climax at the airport, Vijay kills J.K. and Ashwini shoots Vijay, finally managing to articulate his fatherly love when it is too late.

Shakti's critical acclaim was unanimous. *Screen* called it 'an outstanding cinematic event' and said that 'Both actors use their voices to supreme effect and inject varying depths of meaning to the lines Salim–Javed have written for them, making it hard to decide who does better, each equally adept at scene-stealing from the other.'

K.M. Amladi wrote in the *Hindustan Times*, 'the real strength of Shakti comes not from the overall magnificence of the production values . . . but from Salim–Javed's delving into psychological insights without losing the popular dramatic structure of their tale . . . Salim–Javed . . . deserve credit for weaving a not too implausible narrative with some psychological weight.'

Javed Akhtar had once said, 'In different corners of the world I have met people who believed that *Shakti* was the best film written by our team.'

The film also won the Filmfare Award for best screenplay—a prize which had eluded them since *Deewaar*—and Dilip Kumar won the award for best actor, beating his co-star to it.

Javed Akhtar says about the performances, 'In acting you don't work against your co-actor but work with him. And their coordination was superb.' Each one of their confrontations was wonderfully written and perfectly fit in with the narrative. Both actors showed a remarkable grasp over their craft by delving much deeper into their characters and rising even above the great screenplay. In fact, nothing explains this fact better than the performance they delivered in the scene where Sheetal lies dead in their home. Without speaking a word, the two actors just looked at each other and wept. Their tears, their body language and their timing were so good that they conveyed their

grief perfectly without the support of well-written lines. This
was a suggestion from Amitabh Bachchan himself. He says, 'On
Rakhee's death, I had to deliver a four-page dialogue. I suggested
that the scene be done in pin-drop silence instead. Rameshji and
Salim–Javed agreed to that right away. The scene came across as
poignant and unique.'

The three characters—Ashwini, Vijay and Sheetal—had
their own quirks and dynamics, which never wavered through
the film. For example, Ashwini is shown to be slightly immature
and socially inept in his personal life right from the first scene
when he reaches the hospital where Vijay is born. That he is
incapable of expressing himself is established very well, and is
critical in his relationship with Vijay. It is the writers' master
stroke that Ashwini's love for Vijay is apparent only when Vijay
is absent. Right from the time when Vijay is a schoolboy till he
grows up, that awkwardness remains uniform and well etched.
When Roma (Smita Patil) comes to meet Vijay's parents at
their home, Ashwini is brusque initially. But the moment he
finds out she is Vijay's wife, he is immediately affectionate and
welcoming.

Vijay's resentment, which is shown to stem from his
perception of his father's indifference towards him, starts
simmering from his childhood, reaching a crescendo when he
delivers a drunken monologue—'*Mere baap ne do shaadiyan
ki . . . Apni maa ka beta main hoon. Meri sauteli maa yani mere
baap ki doosri biwi ka beta hai, kanoon.*'[xlii] —that perfectly sums
up his feelings.

Rakhee did an excellent role as the mother torn between her
husband and son. This role would have been a tricky decision
for her since she was acting as Amitabh's heroines in a couple
of films (*Barsaat Ki Ek Raat* and *Bemisaal*) in the same year.
But her chemistry with Vijay in the film was pitch-perfect. In

a seemingly insignificant but extremely well-written scene, she goes to meet Vijay who is staying at a lady friend's house. The lines convey exactly what a mother would say to a mildly truant son, as well as the son's embarrassment at having to explain living with a woman.

Shakti is a brilliant film, an iconic one in fact. It falls short only when you compare it with the other film it pays subconscious tribute to—*Deewaar*. After two brothers on either side of the law, we now had a father and son locked in a tragic battle. Several scenes and dialogues are extremely close to each other, making it impossible for audiences to not recall the earlier classic.

The character of the mother is similar, weighing in on the side of righteousness. While Nirupa Roy refuses to be a 'thief's mother' and walks out with her honest son, Rakhee does the same by delivering a brilliant line: '*Main abhi itni kamzor nahi hoon ke apne pati ke imaandari ka bojh na utha sakoon.*'[xliii]

So were the characters of the girlfriends. Both Parveen Babi in *Deewaar* and Smita Patil in *Shakti* were modern, working women, subtly acting as the voice of conscience. Sunita inspires Vijay to return to a respectable life in *Deewaar*. And while Roma doesn't directly do that in *Shakti,* she is clearly a stabilizing influence on him.

In fact, the scene in *Shakti* where Ashwini meets Vijay to inform him of Sheetal's illness is an almost exact replica of the bridge scene from *Deewaar*—though, needless to say, the *Deewaar* scene was much better. Film critic Sukanya Verma says, 'The Salim–Javed script resonates better with Yash Chopra's *Deewaar* about the discord between two brothers on different sides of the law. A couple of dialogues—"*Jao pehle unse kaho sabse pehle mere khilaaf saboot laayein, gawah dhoondein,*"[xliv] or "*In usool adarshon ka bojh uthane ka shauq jisse hai usse uthane do*"[xlv]—pay subconscious tribute to the 1975 classic.'

These similarities only serve to draw attention to the fair bit of tiredness that had crept into Salim–Javed's writing by now—especially in scenes audiences were already familiar with. Smugglers landing at the same location as they did eight years earlier, heists that did not have the earlier ingenuity and most importantly, the anger that now had a touch of arrogance. Both the writers and their most famous protégé were struggling within the very successful mould they had created.

For all practical purposes, *Shakti* was the last film Salim–Javed wrote as a team. By the time the film was released, they had been officially split for more than a year and Javed's solo credits had started appearing in trade magazines.

It is an apt tribute to their talent and understanding that the final film they wrote was such a nuanced yet dramatic script. When they first entered the film industry, they had to fight to put their names on posters and when they exited, their names appeared right after the director's. More than their critical and commercial successes, this tectonic shift in the industry's attitude towards writers is what they can be credited with.

But they weren't done yet.

Part III:

SPLIT WIDE OPEN

Personal Lives

When Javed was working on *Seeta Aur Geeta*, he jokingly recommended Honey Irani to the makers, saying that she was just the girl required to play the role of (Seeta's bratty of cousin). They got to know each other better on the sets of the film, liked each other's sense of humour and soon fell in love.

Javed proposed to her during a game of cards they were playing on the sets. He was losing, and when she offered to pull a card for him, he said, 'If it's a good one, I'll marry you.' The card was good and he proposed, 'Chalo, chalo let's get married.' The shooting for *Seeta Aur Geeta* began in October 1971 and the two got married on 21 March 1972.

There is also the famous story about Javed requesting Salim to take his proposal to Honey's mother, Perin Irani. Since Javed did not have a cordial relationship with his own father, Salim was the 'elder' in his family. Salim's conversation with Perin Irani was not unlike the immortal scene the duo would later write for *Sholay*:

– '*Ladka kaisa hai?*'
– '*We are partners and I wouldn't work with anyone unless I approve of him. Lekin daaru bahut peeta hai.*'

  – *'Kya? Daaru bahut peeta hai!'*
  – *'Aaj kal bahut nahi peeta, bas ek do peg. Aur is mein aisi koi*
    kharabi nahin hai. Lekin daaru peene ke baad red light area
    bhi jaata hai.'

Honey was only seventeen then and her mother was not very happy about her marriage to a struggling writer. In fact, Perin Irani is believed to have said, 'Let her get married, she'll learn a lesson and come back.' The first few months of married life were terrible as they had to stay with Honey's elder sister Maneka, who was married to film-maker Kamran Khan (Farah and Sajid Khan's father). They stayed in a room meant for film props for a year till *Zanjeer* was released and subsequent successes allowed them to move into a place of their own. Honey remembers, 'Javed made me promise I wouldn't accompany him to parties, apply make-up or hire a maid. So I'd get up at 4 a.m. to fill water. Of course, when I got pregnant, we had a maid.'

After Javed's success, they bought a flat in Bandra Bandstand and never looked back. They became a popular filmi couple, partying every night till the wee hours of the morning. Amitabh and Jaya Bachchan, Yash and Pamela Chopra, and Yash and Hiroo Johar were part of their group.

Zoya and Farhan were born soon after (in October 1972 and January 1974, respectively) and the family was complete. They became friends with other star children—Shweta and Abhishek Bachchan, Hrithik Roshan, Aditya and Uday Chopra—all of whom are pretty close even today.

As Salim–Javed became more and more successful, Javed and Honey's marriage hit a rough patch. Honey Irani said in an interview, 'The initial years were wonderful. I don't really blame Javed for what happened later. He was young when he got such huge success. It's not easy to handle that. He used to drink a lot too. That was one of the major problems.' And Javed agrees, 'I always used to drink but began drinking more. This is one phase of my life I am ashamed of and if people tolerated me during this time it was their benevolence.' (He eventually gave up alcohol completely and remains a teetotaller to this day.)

They separated in 1978, which was then rumoured to be due to Javed's relationship with Shabana Azmi. Though Javed knew Kaifi and Shaukat Azmi, and often went to their home, since Shabana was very busy with her work the two never really connected for the longest time. According to Shabana, they only got close after 1980, when her film *Sparsh* was released. Javed really liked it, and talked to her about it at length at a party. Since he was still officially married, she did not want to pursue a relationship and contemplated taking a step back—especially as his children were very young then. However, that didn't happen and they married in December 1984, around the time his divorce formally came through.

Javed's father Jan Nisar Akhtar died in August 1976. Just before his demise, he had given Javed a copy of his last book with the inscription: 'You will remember me when I am gone'. These words indeed stayed with his son and Javed wrote his first poem in 1979 to 'make peace with both my father and my inheritance'. His desire to write poetry would eventually become an important turning point in Salim–Javed's partnership.

Salim's life also saw a fair bit of turmoil after several years of a stable family life. After his marriage to Salma in 1964, their three sons were born by 1970. They also had a daughter, Alvira, later. This was a difficult period for the couple as Salim's earnings from films weren't very substantial. On top of that, there was a lot of tension in the family because Salma's father had cut off all communications with her for marrying outside her religion.

Success brought stability and the family moved into their flat in the now-iconic Galaxy Apartments in 1973 on Dussehra, shortly after the release of *Zanjeer*.

Sholay took Salim–Javed to new heights and it also brought Salim back in touch with Helen, who had just come out of a long relationship with director P.N. Arora (which she broke off in 1973). Helen's career had stalled at this point and Salim recommended her to several directors, including Ramesh Sippy. The song 'Mehbooba mehbooba' resurrected her career and she was in demand once again, for the next five or six years, doing 'item numbers' as well as short acting roles. *Sholay* was the first Salim–Javed film Helen worked in,[23] following it up with several others, including *Immaan Dharam* (in an important role opposite Amitabh Bachchan), *Don* (in a pivotal role as Kamini who is killed while trying to catch Don) and *Dostana* (as Prem Chopra's moll, a role that wasn't in the usual mould).

During this period, Helen was like a family friend—often visiting Salim's home and interacting with them. While Salim and Helen had known each other from the time they were both strugglers in the early 1960s, it was only now that they fell in love; Salim calls it an 'emotional accident'. He honestly explained the situation to his children and married Helen in 1981. In a later interview, Helen said, 'I got married to a beautiful human being by the name of Salim Khan, who is one of the best writers . . . He has given me all the confidence and contentment in life and the best role is what I am playing right now.' While it all worked out amicably later on, the first few years of Salim's relationship with Helen—both courtship and marriage—were quite stressful.

Salim and Javed have always accepted that the intensity of their scripts decreased towards the later part of their careers

---

[23] Interestingly, Helen had worked in both *Adhikar* and *Yakeen*, films written by Salim and Javed respectively, before they teamed up.

for which they cited several reasons, such as complacency and the inability to experiment. However, they were experiencing turmoil in their personal lives in the late 1970s—that period of separation (for Javed) and a second marriage (for Salim) would have been mentally draining for both of them—and it is conceivable that those issues affected their professional output, at least on a subconscious level. Success brought with it a lot of prestigious projects, but they came with the attendant problems of high expectations and pressure which would have further strained their working relationship. While their respective personal relationships overcame the strain and even flourished in later years, their professional relationship didn't survive.

The Split

'I suppose when people can no longer communicate with one another, they part. Be it Nehru and Jinnah or Salim and Javed'—Gulzar

One superstar—Rajesh Khanna—asked Salim Khan and Javed Akhtar for a script that brought them together as Salim–Javed. A script that Salim–Javed wrote for another superstar—Amitabh Bachchan—separated them into Salim Khan and Javed Akhtar once again.

The seeds of a rift were probably sown over a longish period of time as both writers became major stars in their own right and found their own circles of friends. The age difference between the two (Salim was ten years older than Javed), was also partly responsible for this split, for they had completely different family cycles (Salim's eldest child was eight years old when Javed got married) and wholly different sets of friends. While they worked together and spent long hours ideating and writing, and in business meetings, their personal lives did not coincide. Their different lives also brought hangers-on who individually convinced each that his talent was the driving force in the partnership, while the other one was just along for the ride. This was the likely psychological background to a series of events that acted as the final trigger for their separation.

In her Marathi book *Yahi Rang, Yahi Roop* journalist Anita Padhye, who did a long interview with Salim, describes the sequence of events from his point of view.

Salim–Javed approached Amitabh Bachchan with the script of a film that would eventually become *Mr India*. Bachchan declined, citing the invisible-man concept as a deterrent since— he believed—the audience came to *see* him in a film and not merely to hear him. Salim–Javed's conviction that Amitabh's voice would bring a lot of value to the role was not something the superstar shared. According to the book, Javed felt that the duo shouldn't work with Amitabh any more after this 'insult', but Salim was not in complete agreement with this suggestion. A few days after this, Javed was at Amitabh's Holi party and told the star that Salim wasn't keen on working with Amitabh any longer. This misunderstanding caused a considerable strain in the duo's working relationship.

Meanwhile, Javed had also started penning lyrics for films (Yash Chopra's *Silsila* being his first) and he proposed to Salim that they write lyrics under their joint name as well. His plan was to offer a complete script and the song lyrics as a package from Salim–Javed but Salim refused. Salim says, 'I don't consider it right to take credit for something I didn't do. Javed would write lyrics, have meetings with music directors and I would sit there contributing nothing. This was not acceptable to me.' Besides, he explained further, if there was one aspect of their job to which he made no contribution, outsiders might assume that was the case with the other aspect as well.

According to him, it was Javed who proposed that they split. Salim remembers that day vividly. They were at Javed's residence, discussing and brainstorming on projects. After a full day's work, when it was time for Salim to leave, Javed said, 'I was thinking that maybe we should work separately.' Salim took a few moments to digest this and replied, 'I am sure you have said this after considerable thought and nothing I say will change your mind,' and began walking towards his car. When Javed, as was his habit, joined him, Salim turned to him and said, 'I am old enough to take care of myself,' and sent him back.

That was the exact point in time when the split happened.

Over the next few weeks, gossip columns speculated about the reasons and trade magazines 'announced' solo projects, but the moment they shook hands in front of Javed's Juhu home on the evening of 21 June 1981, Salim–Javed once again became Salim Khan and Javed Akhtar.

The date is so easily identifiable because it was the same day that Salim Khan got news that Helen's mother was seriously unwell and had to leave Bombay. She passed away later that evening and he became busy with her funeral, remaining away from Bombay and unreachable for a few days. When he returned, he started getting calls enquiring about the split, as Javed had already talked about it to some people in the industry.

Javed seemed to manage the post-split period much better as several directors announced prestigious projects with him immediately afterwards. This was possibly because he was already actively soliciting work as a lyricist and was in talks with directors. In the two years after the split, he had writing projects with Ramesh Sippy, Rahul Rawail, Yash Chopra and Subhash Ghai. Most of these films also had lyrics by him, thus making him the single-point writer he had proposed Salim–Javed become. In a November 1981 interview, Javed said, 'I really don't know how I will fare on my own. I have signed four films which, considering my past record, is a lot for me!'

Salim, on the other hand, was less prepared for the split and did not go around asking for work. In fact, he was quite frustrated with the entire episode and took a long sabbatical in London. He felt at peace in his new surroundings till someone referred to him as 'Helen's husband'. That was when he decided to return to Bombay and seek work. He expected his past reputation would precede him and imagined producers would be lining up like before to work with him. However, the industry where heroes changed every Friday had moved on. As many past stars have found out—to their dismay—the industry can be extremely generous to those in favour and just as ruthless to those out of circulation.

Salim speaks very bitterly about this phase. 'When I returned, it was the telephone that reminded me how easily people forget. There was a time when I'd make my drink, and then keep the phone off the hook. And here I was, checking the phone every now and then to see if it was working.'

After *Shakti*—where he had shared credit with Javed—Salim's next release came nearly four years later. *Naam* turned out to be Salim's super comeback, putting him firmly back on the radar of all major producers. He established a successful working relationship with Mahesh Bhatt and soon enough, all the well-known directors of the time—Ramesh Sippy, Rahul Rawail, Manmohan Desai—were working with him as well.

Post-split, Salim and Javed's relationship went from bitter to neutral to cordial. In October 1981, Salim said in an interview, 'If we have split today, it is only because we, without the interference of a third party, have decided to call it a day. I too don't know the real reason for this break-up. One day, Javed came to me and told me he wanted to operate separately. Since I respect his decisions, I did not even ask him why he wanted us to split! It's sad we had to break up our team, but I'm very happy that we are still friends!' A few months later (in February 1982), he was more abrasive—'I don't ever want to make up with Javed even if Javed were to apologise or suggest a patch-up.'

This continued through the 1980s. A gossip column in *Hindustan Times* (in 1987, after the release of *Naam*) reported, 'Salim exudes a new confidence now. Till the release of *Naam*, the uncertainty would show on his face, though he says it did not affect him at all. The man does not mince words, especially when it comes to his feelings about Javed. When asked what he thinks of Javed, he said bluntly: "I dislike him. I won't say I hate him, because it is not good to hate anybody." He not only dislikes Javed but everything that has anything to do with him. He thinks all Javed's films—*Saagar*, *Arjun*, etc., were bogus, with the exception of *Betaab*.'

Both their individual careers saw a fair degree of success in the 1980s, which is considered to be the most derivative of all the decades of Hindi cinema. This led to considerable speculation about an alternate time in which Salim–Javed did not split. One of the proponents of this line of speculation has been Amitabh Bachchan, who has been known to wonder if his career would have seen a different trajectory had the split not happened. Bachchan openly admitted the vacuum in his career due to the split: 'It's a shame that they parted ways, they were truly unbeatable. Quite often, the media would conjecture—what will happen to Amitabh Bachchan without Salim–Javed? Really, once they separated I couldn't ever get that kind of intensity again, that power was missing.' Javed Akhtar had once half-jokingly said that Amitabh Bachchan should have found other good writers since they had failed.

Film critic and director Khalid Mohammad says, 'If Salim–Javed had continued as a team, perhaps they would have become jaded. Yet, it can't be denied that their parting was premature. At least half a dozen films could have emerged from them as a team.' There are still others who believe the poor quality of writing in the 1980s could have been improved if only Salim–Javed hadn't split. This is interesting because the writers' last few scripts had clearly not been among their best. Yet, many people believe that the output of an entire industry over a decade would have been better if two—just *two*—people had continued to work together.

There is obviously a fair amount of nostalgic romanticism attached to this train of thought but that was exactly what Salim–Javed brought to the profession of writing, which continued to build their mystique well after their joint careers ended.

They featured regularly in gossip columns till the late 1980s, whenever Salim's rise coincided with a downturn in Javed's career or vice versa. Many such items even 'blamed' the women in their lives—Shabana Azmi and Helen—for the split, but both men steadfastly denied any such insinuations.

Script writers being written about in gossip columns, that too years after they had split—such was the power of Salim–Javed.

Interim Films:
Zamana and *Mr India*

Post their split, two films—*Zamana* and *Mr India*—were released (in 1985 and 1987 respectively) that were credited to Salim–Javed. These were conceptualized and partially written when they were still a team.

Zamana went through a lot of interruptions; its development began long ago, at a time when Salim–Javed were among the top movers and shakers in the industry. A friend of Salim Khan's, who had business interests in steel and hospitality and wanted to invest his money in films, came to him seeking advice about an entry into the industry. The duo offered him a script—a complete screenplay that had scope for two male leads, one older and one younger.

The story was about two brothers who get separated in childhood after their father is killed by the villains. The brothers grow up to be a police officer and a gangster. Soon enough, the gangster is given a contract to kill the police officer by the same criminal responsible for their father's death. All the while, everybody—including the two protagonists—is unaware of the two brothers' identities.

Salim put the financier in touch with the producer (Jagdish Sharma) and they chose Rajesh Khanna and Rishi Kapoor for the two leading roles, which was something of a casting coup. At this point, Ramesh Talwar—Yash Chopra's long-time chief assistant director—was brought in. He had worked with Rajesh Khanna while assisting Yash Chopra on *Daag* and with Rishi Kapoor on his directorial debut *Doosara Aadmi*. Talwar was good friends with both stars and seemed a good candidate to handle them.

The director took on the script with some trepidation since he felt the lost-and-found formula was more up Manmohan Desai's alley; his own preference was towards offbeat love stories. But the film's cast (two of the industry's biggest stars) and the writers made it look like a sure-shot commercial success and he took it up. This is an interesting case where the project originated from the scriptwriters and went on to find a producer, director and actors.

The shooting started and twelve reels—about three-fourths of the film—were canned in the first schedule itself. But after that, the financier's other businesses ran into rough weather and he couldn't fund the rest of the shoot. By the time he managed to arrange funds, the actors were busy with other projects and the film was massively delayed. Shooting was resumed more than three years later, during which time Salim–Javed had separated, Ramesh Talwar had made two more films (including one written by only Javed Akhtar) and the box-office draw of the stars had diminished. Even fashion trends had changed so much that the film looked horribly dated.

Salim and Javed worked on two different segments when *Zamana* was being shot. The screenplay was given right at the beginning but the dialogues, written as the shoot progressed, were penned by Javed. Salim assisted the director during the editing to suggest minor changes in the plot to help stitch the sequences together. This was critical since many of them were shot quite far apart. Salim's involvement in the editing—partially due to his relationship with the financier—was again very unusual for a writer in the industry.

Zamana—as is evident—suffered from several drawbacks that resulted in a dismal performance at the box office and poor recall. Along with *Aakhri Daao*, it is one of Salim–Javed's least-known scripts. Their separation cannot possibly be cited as a reason for this since they were still partners when they wrote it. However, *Zamana* suffered from the same problems that some of their later scripts had, where they had lost their appetite for risk and were using old formulae without any innovation to essentially create star vehicles.

*

Mr India—with the basic idea of the 'invisible man'—was jointly conceived by Salim–Javed and eventually picked up by Boney Kapoor and Shekhar Kapur for the former's home production.

After two low-budget successes (one of which was *Woh 7 Din*, starring brother Anil Kapoor), Boney Kapoor was ready to play for higher stakes. He bet on the sci-fi plot with lots of special effects, lavish sets and costumes—all towards making what is known in the industry as a 'badi film'. The director chosen for this venture was Shekhar Kapur, who had started off as an actor but had just delivered a massive critical and commercial success in *Masoom*.[24]

---

[24] Javed was approached for writing the dialogues of *Masoom* but he turned them down because his price did not fit into the film's small budget.

The story was simple enough. An impoverished violin teacher Arun Verma (Anil Kapoor) stays in a rundown seaside house with several orphan kids he has picked up off the streets. While resisting villain Mogambo's (Amrish Puri) attempts to gain control of the house and convert it into a smuggling base, the young man stumbles upon his father's discovery—a bracelet that turns people invisible. With the help of this bracelet, he becomes Mr India—the invisible man who takes up arms against smugglers, black marketeers, gambling den owners and their supreme boss Mogambo.[25]

While the concept had been written jointly, the script was detailed out single-handedly by Javed. Shekhar Kapur says of him, 'I know very few scriptwriters who have an understanding of how to create mythology through dialogue. It's no coincidence that both Gabbar Singh (with his then co-writer Salim Khan) and Mogambo were his creations . . . What's even more startling is the fact that when you look carefully, Mogambo actually does not do much. He talks, he threatens, he clicks his fingers on a globe on his throne, he strides, he builds missiles and threatens to blow up India. He threatens and he threatens and threatens. But actually does nothing . . . At least Gabbar Singh cut off Sanjeev Kumar's arms, ruthlessly killed his own men, killed a son and sent the body back to the blind father . . . But poor Mogambo? Nothing but empty threats, other than where he causes a few beautiful-looking and well-fed kids to go hungry. How on earth then did Mogambo become one of the greatest villains of Hindi commercial cinema?'

The mythic quality of Mogambo's villainy can be summed up in three words. When Shekhar Kapur asked Javed Akhtar

---

[25] The name Mogambo was also the villain's name in a film called *Maha Badmaash* (1977), where a mysterious criminal kingpin remained hidden in the shadows and instructed his minions in a booming voice.

to explain the character of Mogambo to him, Akhtar replied with '*Mogambo khush hua*' [xlvi]. The explanation being that it was the signature line of a megalomaniac who used verbal approval to reward his gang. To convince a very incredulous Shekhar, Javed Akhtar told him, 'Shekhar sahib, when Kapil Dev hits a sixer over the ground, people will shout "*Mogambo khush hua*". When people play teen patti and they get three aces, they will say "*Mogambo khush hua*". Trust me on that.' Shekhar Kapur was initially convinced but at the time of editing, he felt the line was being repeated too many times in the film and wanted to cut it out from a few scenes. Javed convinced him not to. 'This is going to become a kind of buzz line,' he predicted.

These words have the same swagger that Salim–Javed displayed during their heyday, while narrating their big films. They had started off with Gabbar, Teja and Shaakaal, creating some of Hindi cinema's biggest, baddest villains (though the mega-villain had become something like a caricature by the time they wrote yet another Shaakaal in *Shaan*). But for *Mr India*, Shekhar Kapur says, 'Javed sahab completely understood the "comic-book" pitch of the film, knowing that in this tongue-in-cheek film, the villain can be bloodthirsty only in intention, but never in action.'

Of course, Amrish Puri brought a new dimension to those three words by speaking them with great relish. When Puri asked Shekhar Kapur how he was supposed to interpret the part, the director said, 'Imagine you are playing Shakespeare to nine-year-old kids and they have no idea who he was. Imagine you have to make it feel mythic and entertaining.' With this brief, Amrish Puri completely 'got' the part and managed to make the three words sound new every single time he uttered them. This whole 'comic-book' treatment was also given to the other characters, the most memorable among them being Miss Hawa

Salim-Javed in their early days, looking lean and hungry for more.

At the premiere of *Deewaar*, the star writers and the star actor with director Yash Chopra (extreme left) and producer Gulshan Rai (extreme right).

Don was announced in 1974 (before *Deewaar* or *Sholay*) and Salim–Javed were the biggest draw of the film, ahead of Amitabh Bachchan, Zeenat Aman and Pran.

786

THIS IS A PREDICTION

BY

SALIM-JAVED

THEIR PERFECT DREAM

SHOLAY

EXACTLY AND BEAUTIFULLY CONVEYED TO THE
SCREEN BY THESE GREAT FILM MAKERS

Mr. G. P. SIPPY
Mr. RAMESH SIPPY

AND

THE UNIT

WILL BE A GROSSER OF
RUPEES **ONE CRORE**
IN EACH MAJOR TERRITORY OF INDIA

Two writers taking ownership of their film's business. A never-before,
never–after ad for *Sholay* that left the industry spellbound.

Aakhri Daao had a pretty strong star cast but the makers chose to pitch it as a 'smash hit from Salim Javed'.

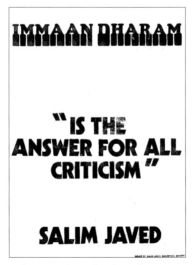

Ad taken out by Salim-Javed on the day of *Immaan Dharam*'s release, which showed the opposition they faced in the industry and the attitude with which they took it.

Amitabh Bachchan shares a joke with his favourite writers at the premiere of *Sholay*.

Salim-Javed popping champagne at one of the many success parties they attended.

Today, the only time the industry remembers Salim Khan is when his better/worse ex-half, Javed Akhtar, bags a prestigeous assignment. Reading announcements of the latter's films, hearing his lyrics set to music, watching him going all out to attract attention at the mahurats of Dharmendra's 'Betaab' and Ramesh Talwar's 'Duniya', the first question on every filmwalla's lips is—'Where is Salim these days? Does he have any films on hand? Is his career finished?'

The questions are justified in the wake of the controversies surrounding the Salim-Javed break-up. While Salim has stuck to his side of the bargain and remained evasive and non-committal on the subject, it's doubtful if Javed has done the same. For it can't be merely a coincidence that whatever stories have arisen after the split, have all been pro-Javed and anti-Salim....

.... Javed was the real writer of the duo; Javed was the poet with the literary background; Javed was the lyricist—poor Salim was dismissed off as "creatively impotent"!

Previously, the industrywallas had greatly admired Salim's shrewd business acumen and smooth p.r. relations. Some had even declared that they'd put up with the nasty-tongued Javed only because of Salim's charming efforts to make amends. People really believed that without Salim, Javed would be nowhere in the industry.

Yet, the situation seems to be the opposite today. Salim has yet to sign a single film on his own merit. His overtures to old colleagues have been ignored, pleas to new producers turned down. When six months of work-soliciting paid no dividends, a thoroughly disheartened Salim went into hiding—in shame and frustration. Industrywallas insisted that in sheer desperation, he'd even gone to Javed's house, begging for a patch-up....

That was when Salim broke his silence and retaliated in his defense.

SALIM: THE BITTER HALF CONFESSES –

"Our Split Was Not Mutual......"

Post the split, Salim Khan expressed his bitterness in a few interviews while Javed Akhtar never spoke about it. [Interview source: *Stardust*, February 1982]

The story of *Sauda* was credited to Salim–Javed but the duo refused to acknowledge it as their film because the makers had changed the script.

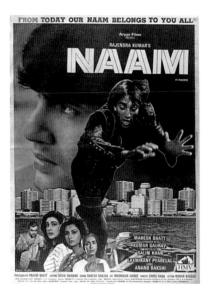

Naam–Salim Khan's first solo project–put
his name back on top of the heap.

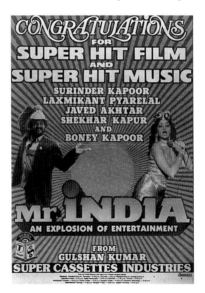

Mr India was the last film to be jointly credited to Salim-Javed though
the final touches to the script and dialogues were given by Javed.
And yes, he got their usual top billing.

Hawaii—a short segment in which Sridevi enters the villains' den as a dancer. Javed explains the origins, 'In Urdu, we have an expression—"*Bhai, kahan hawa hawaii ghoom rahe ho?*"[xlvii] It's a UP expression. The sound of Hawa Hawaii was rather interesting. So Sridevi became "Miss Hawa Hawaii from Havana".' Whether as Hawa Hawaii, or the batty child-hating reporter, or the sensuous girlfriend, or the whip-wielding dominatrix—the actress was an absolute scream, pulling out all the rabbits from her bag of performances.

The cast of children—many of whom grew up to become stars themselves—had wonderful roles, with each of them performing differently instead of the cutesy cookie-cutter style in which Hindi films portray child actors. The editor of Sridevi's newspaper (Annu Kapoor), the minor villains Daga, Teja, Walcott (Sharat Saxena, Ajit Vachani, Bob Cristo) and even the house butler Calendar (Satish Kaushik) had well-etched roles, quirks, dialogue tics and all the things that were the hallmark of Salim–Javed films.

Mr India opened with massive buzz and a lot of interest. The uninformed masses were curious to see if the film was around bodybuilding while the industry marvelled at its lavish scale. The gossip column of *Hindustan Times* reported, 'The talk of the town in Bombay is Boney Kapoor's Mr India. The man to make it a hot topic is none other than Amitabh Bachchan, because when Amitabh talks about a film, everyone does so, too. Amitabh saw the film last week, and after trial surprised the unit members present, when, as is usual with him, instead of leaving the venue immediately, he stayed on for half an hour, discussing the film in detail and outlining its merits.'

Mr India was a huge hit, Anil Kapoor's biggest till then and along with subsequent hits like *Tezaab* (1988) and *Ram Lakhan* (1989), it set him up for stardom. It is important to say 'set him up for stardom' because in this film, he was completely overshadowed by Sridevi and Amrish Puri in roles that have become part of Bollywood history. In a way, Amitabh Bachchan was right: the hero was indeed invisible.

We can only wonder what changes might have been made to the script to accommodate Amitabh Bachchan. Given that the charm of the film lay in the fact that the hero was a commoner, one can't help but wonder if the superstar would have played the common man the way Anil Kapoor did. Fortunately, Salim–Javed always put the script before the star. And *Mr India*—released five years after their split—carried on this legacy.

Salim Khan:
After the Split

As mentioned earlier, when Salim Khan returned to Bombay after his long sabbatical in London, things were bleak for him.

Many of his past directors were already working with Javed Akhtar and Salim was left out in the cold for a long time. He did work on *Zamana*, assisting Ramesh Talwar in completing the long-delayed film, but that was more out of obligation for having initiated the film for a friend and it was not a new project. After that, he worked—unofficially—on a couple of films being directed by friends where he gave suggestions to improve scripts. Raj Khosla's *Maati Maange Khoon* and Yash Chopra's *Vijay* were two such films. His true 'break' came at last when he partnered with a maverick young director.

Mahesh Bhatt had been around for a considerable period of time, having directed six films in the 1970s. None of them had made a major impact at the box office, though at least one of them (*Manzilein Aur Bhi Hain*) had raised eyebrows— and conservative society's hackles—with its bold themes of prostitution and promiscuity. He hit the big time with a succession of three films, each based on a different aspect of his controversial life—*Arth*, *Saaransh* and *Janam* (the last one was made for TV). All three films received critical acclaim, and the first two were among the top grossers of 1982 and 1984 respectively. With his less-than-pristine reputation, Mahesh Bhatt partnered with Salim Khan to make *Naam*, which was—in a way—a morality tale about a new-age Angry Young Man.

Salim Khan's innate confidence comes across when he explains why he chose *Naam* to be his 'return film'. 'I was not working for quite some time and decided to wait for the perfect vehicle I would return with. I wanted my return to be with a strong film whose success could be solely ascribed to me. *Naam* was Mahesh Bhatt's first commercial venture and he was yet to prove himself at the box office. Sanjay Dutt had just returned from drug rehab and faith in him wasn't very high. Kumar Gaurav and the film's producer Rajendra Kumar were no longer top stars either. I realized that if *Naam* did well, I would get most of the credit.'

While *Naam* was produced by Kumar Gaurav to relaunch himself as a hero, it was Sanjay Dutt, his brother in the film (and his brother-in-law in real life), who walked away with all the accolades for his edgy performance as a lovable goon forever on the brink of falling apart. *Naam* did not have any majorly memorable dialogues but it brought out the angst and frustration of the time's rudderless youth exceptionally well. Sanjay Dutt's journey from a roadside ruffian to a false job in Dubai to a criminal's henchman to redemption was both frustrating and gritty, drawing the audience into this compelling story. The standard themes of brothers with contrasting characters and the fallible hero were given a fresh lease of life in the film, and became wildly popular once again.

Naam was another triumph—becoming the third-highest grosser of the year—beating massive star vehicles and turning Sanjay Dutt into a superstar. Apart from that, what *Naam* also did was put Salim Khan's name right after the director's once again. He had achieved exactly what he wanted—the gossip columns were talking about the rivalry between Salim–Javed once again.

Hindustan Times' gossip column reported (in May 1987), 'Salim is on a signing spree . . . He and Mahesh Bhatt seem to operate as a team, signing films in a package deal. There are not many good writers in the industry and if Salim has signed a dozen films, it is because producers infer that if Javed has failed, Salim must succeed.'[26]

After *Naam*, Salim worked with Mahesh Bhatt on two more films—*Kabzaa* and *Jurm*. Neither was as successful as their first venture together but they were reasonably interesting.

Kabzaa was adapted from *On the Waterfront*, starring Sanjay Dutt as the hero, played by Marlon Brand in the Hollywood version, who takes on Paresh Rawal and his cohorts after an initial period of indecision and petty crime. It was again a congregation of familiar characters—the two brothers, an apparently benevolent crime boss, the do-gooder—appearing in a tale of evil forces trying to evict the poor and righteous from their homes. Many of the devices were familiar from earlier Salim–Javed films, right down to the hero's name—Sanjay Dutt's name was Ravi Verma in the film. *Kabzaa* suffered from an indifferent performance by Sanjay who, after a stint of stardom, could not recreate his earlier intensity, causing at least some of the scenes to lose their punch. Overall, *Kabzaa* was not a major success.

---

[26] The reference was to Rahul Rawail's *Dacait*, written by Javed, which had released around that time and had not done well.

Jurm was more of a Hollywood thriller, both in treatment and plot. A police officer (Vinod Khanna), deputed to protect a murder witness (Sangeeta Bijlani) gets into an adulterous liaison with her while murderous villains keep trying to eliminate her. Loosely based on the 1987 Hollywood thriller *Someone to Watch Over Me*, *Jurm* was a tightly scripted, fast-paced thriller that held interest by smartly mixing a love triangle with a murder mystery. It was conceived as a quickie at a time when Mahesh Bhatt was directing some three or four movies simultaneously. Shot on a small budget, it made decent money on the investment but wasn't a particularly memorable film. (*Jurm*'s biggest claim to fame is the song *Jab koi baat bigad jaaye* lifted from the hit single, '500 miles').

Having secured a foothold in the industry once again, Salim Khan wrote two films for Amitabh Bachchan—reuniting with the star after several years for two very absorbing films. Unfortunately, neither of the films did too well commercially but they are both important milestones in the evolution of Amitabh Bachchan as a Hindi film hero.

The first film was *Toofan*. It was the typical Manmohan Desai formula but with several interesting twists—including the device that was the eponymous hero's superpower. Whenever the caped superhero attacked the villains, a massive storm was always at hand to disorient them. In the standard-issue story of two brothers separated at birth taking up arms against dacoits, Salim Khan managed to rummage through his bag of tricks and come up with several cool gimmicks. A villain with a wooden hand, a bumbling magician as hero, a superhero with a storm at his beck and call and a high-tech bow and arrow, and several complicated subplots made *Toofan* somewhat distinctive among similar films of the time.

The other Amitabh film he wrote soon afterwards was *Akayla*, a project by yet another old-time favourite, Ramesh

Sippy, where the hero had evolved from being an angry young man to an angry middle-aged one. Amitabh was Vijay yet again but this time, he was an alcoholic cop—somewhat inspired by *Dirty Harry*—of indeterminate age. A backstory traced back to his college days meant he was not really middle-aged but his brooding demeanour made it seem so. Along with *Agneepath* (written by Santosh Saroj and Kader Khan) and *Main Azaad Hoon* (written by Javed Akhtar), *Akayla* was the actor's exploration into slightly older roles and flawed characters. Unfortunately, none of these films did very well at the box office—even though the actor's performances were hugely appreciated—and Amitabh's transition to these kinds of roles had to wait for nearly a decade.

In a way, Javed and Salim writing *Main Azaad Hoon* (1989) and *Akayla* (1991) respectively in quick succession resulted in two different interpretations of the Angry Young Man coming to the fore. In the former, the hero was non-violent, almost like a satyagrahi, while in the latter, he was battle-scarred, cynical and brutal. The anger poured out in very different ways and they could be seen as Salim and Javed's individual interpretations of the iconic character.

Salim's other scripts were not at all commensurate with his reputation and the fatigue (or perhaps it was his disinterest) showed.

While he was not involved in launching Salman Khan into films in any way, Salim wrote the script for one of the actor's earlier films, *Patthar Ke Phool*, which was also the much-anticipated debut of Raveena Tandon. The teenage love story graduated to being a police story–cum–revenge drama, with several subplots churned in. With teenage heart-throbs Salman and Raveena in the lead, this movie was supposed to be a huge box-office success but it didn't do too well. The plot had been in circulation for nearly three decades by then, and the expectation of cool gimmicks and dialogues was not met by the fairly predictable script. (Salim also named Vinod Khanna's character—Salman's father in the film—Vijay Verma.)

The four films Salim wrote in the first half of the 1990s—*Mast Kalandar*, *Aa Gale Lag Jaa*, *Majhdhaar* and *Dil Tera Diwana*—did not do well at all, though they are unique because some of them were out-and-out love stories, something Salim–Javed as a team and Salim Khan as an individual hadn't tried at all.

Majhdhaar was a love triangle while *Dil Tera Diwana* was a love story in the face of a family feud. *Aa Gale Lag Jaa*[27] was the only one with a twist as it was advertised as 'a love story with 9 songs and 11 murders'. However, none of the films made much of an impact.

After the mid-1990s, Salim Khan went into retirement—content to watch his eldest son achieve superstardom and younger sons dabble in acting and production.

Over the last two decades, he has been a vocal proponent of quality in screenwriting. He has been unfailingly generous whenever he has come across a good script. In the recent past, he complimented Shoojit Sircar and Juhi Chaturvedi—director and screenwriter of *Vicky Donor*—called them home and presented the duo with one of his own Filmfare trophies. In a statement, he very humbly stated that he himself wouldn't have been able to handle such a topic and was amazed at the sensitivity and humour with which *Vicky Donor* was written.

However, this wasn't the first award Salim Khan was bestowing on new writers. Prior to *Vicky Donor*, he had met with the team of *A Wednesday* and given them a trophy (the one which he received for the screenplay of *Zanjeer*)

---

[27] *Aa Gale Lag Jaa* is remembered for being the adult debut vehicle of *Masoom*'s child stars, Jugal Hansraj and Urmila Matondkar.

for making 'a very special film'. For *Chillar Party*, a film produced by Salman Khan, he again had some words of praise and a trophy for the director duo, Vikas Bahl and Nitesh Tiwari. The first time he gave away one of his trophies was after seeing Farhan Akhtar's performance in *Rock On*. Some of his home productions—most notably the *Dabangg* series—have his inputs in the script though he has graciously refused to take any credit for them. Speaking about Abhinav Kashyap's script for *Dabangg*, he said, 'It is his script. When you produce a film, you give inputs to the writer and sometimes he accepts them. So did Abhinav but that doesn't take away from the fact that *Dabangg* script was his and the film was his.'

Javed Akhtar:
Going Solo

After the split, Javed Akhtar hit the ground running. Already in talks with film-makers for writing lyrics, he bagged several massive projects with big banners almost immediately.

He had already started writing lyrics while they were still a team, and his first release was *Silsila* (1981). '*Dekha ek khwab toh yeh silsile hue*' to the tune composed by Shiv–Hari[28] became the first song he ever wrote. In fact, he had written this song purely on the insistence of Yash Chopra who had heard the poems Javed had penned and recited at private gatherings. After Chopra's repeated entreaties, Javed ended up spending a day with the composers and came up with the words that became a huge hit.

That Javed was able to compose to the tune given to him was not surprising since he came from a family of poets and had the talent, further honed in the company of legendary poets and song writers like Kaifi Azmi and Sahir Ludhianvi. Writing lyrics for Hindi film songs requires creativity in highly constrained

---

[28] Shiv-Hari were two reputed classical musicians—santoor player Shiv Kumar Sharma and flautist Hariprasad Chaurasia—who composed music for Hindi films (almost exclusively for Yash Chopra) as a team.

circumstances—the tune to which the lyrics must be matched and the speed with which the words have to be turned in being just two such constraints. It is not unusual for many accomplished poets to throw up their hands and quit writing songs. Javed was apprehensive of this and therefore, reluctant to start. However, his father's death in 1976 and Sahir's death in 1980 were events that made him acutely aware of the creative legacy he was part of and became a catalyst in his taking up lyric writing in a bigger way.

Post the split, Javed's first film was a romantic launch vehicle for an actor who would become one of Hindi cinema's top stars in the coming decade. Produced by Dharmendra and directed by Rahul Rawail, *Betaab* was the perfect debut in which Sunny Deol romanced, sang, danced (a bit), rode, fought and generally saved the day. Javed wrote the film (though not the lyrics, which were by Anand Bakshi) and continued the same bound-script tradition by providing an end-to-end script. *Betaab* turned out to be a dream debut for Sunny Deol and became one of the top grossers of 1983, sealing Javed's reputation as a solo writer in the bargain.

While *Betaab* had some great action scenes, it was essentially a romantic film—the standard Hindi film formula of love in the face of parental opposition. What Javed wrote after this were essentially reinterpretations of the Angry Young Man theme. The situations changed as did the motivations of the characters. The actors varied in age significantly, going from absolute newcomers to living legends. What was common between these characters and the heroes of *Zanjeer* and *Deewaar*, though, was the unfair treatment meted out to them by their adversaries, their society, their country.

One of the earlier films in his solo writing career was *Duniya*, where the man was angry but not really young—Dilip Kumar.

Javed Akhtar teamed up with Ramesh Talwar, who had become a close friend (the writer and the director had worked together on several Yash Chopra films), and with whom Javed's wife Honey Irani worked as an assistant director. *Duniya* was the standard revenge plot typical to Hindi cinema, written with a lot of intelligence and sophistication. Dilip Kumar returns from prison as an old man to take revenge against the people who ruined his business and destroyed his family. While the plot was old, what was new was the cleverness with which the acts of revenge were planned. Dilip Kumar got a great platform to display his histrionics, the villains got their just desserts and Javed had come up with yet another memorable script for the thespian after *Shakti*.

After *Duniya*, Javed wrote mainly for Sunny Deol and Anil Kapoor—both of whom attained stardom on the strengths of the iconic roles he scripted for them. His contribution in turning them into top movie stars is immense.

Javed Akhtar reunited with Yash Chopra in *Mashaal*, which was an intelligent take on the death of innocence and how cynicism was digging deeper roots. Dilip Kumar is the idealistic newspaper editor, who is 'angry' to start with; his run-ins with the crime-infested system cause further frustration and lead him to cross over to the dark side. His protégé—Anil Kapoor as a reformed petty criminal—takes over the crusader's mantle and becomes his mentor's nemesis. One of Anil Kapoor's earliest successes, the film saw the actor going from a typical tapori (a character he has become associated with) to a responsible journalist.

In *Meri Jung*, Anil Kapoor played a criminal lawyer—a role originally written for Amitabh Bachchan. This angry young man goes to court—an unexplored territory in Salim–Javed's films—to squeeze justice out of a heartless legal system. The familiar story of revenge acquired a new dimension as the tussles were played out in words instead of fists and in courtrooms instead of dockyards. A trial is the perfect situation for great dialogues and the writer did not disappoint. *Meri Jung* turned out to be a massive success for Anil Kapoor, Subhash Ghai and Javed Akhtar.

Almost simultaneously, Javed wrote two brilliant scripts for Sunny Deol, giving the young star a character progression from an orphan in love (*Betaab*) to an urban vigilante (*Arjun*) to a full-blown dacoit (*Dacait*). All these films were directed by Rahul Rawail, with whom Javed Akhtar and Sunny Deol formed quite the team.

In *Arjun*, Sunny Deol's character is an amalgamation of the two brothers from *Deewaar*. He is educated and trying unsuccessfully to find a job but there is also a volatile anger in him, waiting to explode. The modern urban landscape remains the same, though, unlike Vijay Verma, who was an immigrant, Arjun Malvankar is a Marathi manoos, probably disenchanted with the encroachment of 'outsiders' in his city. The rampant crime and corruption turns him into a vigilante, who eventually becomes a political henchman. For the first time in Hindi cinema, the Ugly Politician was the main villain and his backroom wheeling and dealing was what the new angry young man was fighting. In fact, Arjun becomes a politician's right-hand man to change the system but soon realizes the dirt may be too pervasive, even for him. Film critic Sukanya Verma says, 'Seeking justice single-handedly isn't new but what sets *Arjun* apart is how shrewdly writer Javed Akhtar constructs a specific milieu, its growing unrest and plays on the politics of it.'

The anger found immediate resonance among the youth and *Arjun* was among the top grossers of the year.[29] This rage was not only communicated through the lines they spoke but

---

[29] Javed Akhtar had three major hits in 1985—*Saagar*, *Meri Jung* and *Arjun*, in that order.

the ones they sang as well. Writing the lyrics along with the screenplay, Javed Akhtar came up with '*Mammaya kero kero kero mamma*',[30] which became hugely popular as a youth anthem, not only because of the catchy tune but the devil-may-care attitude it portrayed—'*Duniya bura maane toh goli maaro/Dushman ko yeh bata do dushmani hai kya.*'

In *Dacait*, Sunny Deol is the idealistic, peace-loving, city-educated villager who is wronged so brutally by society and the justice system that he has no recourse other than becoming an outlaw. The violence in the film was quite unnerving and the innocent youngster's descent into a murderous bandit was portrayed with amazing finesse. In fact, *Dacait* was the first film to show the 'modern'/'real' dacoit, who was a far cry from the moustachioed, dhoti-wearing, Kali-worshipping caricatures usually seen in Hindi cinema. *Dacait* was an extremely well-written and well-directed film, which—surprisingly—did not do too well at the box office. But it was the first film that showed frustration and anger turning a law-abiding citizen into a gun-toting outlaw with a death wish, before *Paan Singh Tomar* nearly thirty years later.

After writing individual hits for Sunny Deol and Anil Kapoor, Javed Akhtar wrote *Joshilaay,* which brought the two together. The film was a revenge drama that became quite extraordinary when transported to the rugged terrains of Ladakh. In Jogi Thakur (played by Rajesh Vivek), Javed created one more of his fearsome villains, and the two heroes chasing him were somewhat reminiscent of the duo from *Sholay*. Anil Kapoor was the brooding, laconic one while Sunny Deol was the garrulous bundle of energy. They both made a cool pair pitted against a formidable villain in hitherto unseen locales. The film suffered

---

[30] This is actually a Portuguese phrase (*Mama yo quiero quiero quiero mama*) which means 'I want my mother'—taken from a popular song.

a major reshuffle as Shekhar Kapur—the original director—left the film midway due to creative differences and producer Sibte Hassan Rizvi took over direction as well.

Towards the end of the 1980s, Javed Akhtar reunited with his original favourite—Amitabh Bachchan—for *Main Azaad Hoon*, a massive departure from the action-romance-melodrama masala the star was doing at this time. Loosely based on Frank Capra's *Meet John Doe*, it was the story of an impostor thrust in the role of the titular Azaad, a crusader who takes it upon himself to correct the ills of a town. Amitabh Bachchan switched off the star and gave a fabulous performance based on a great script. Rousing lines and a fast-paced plot powered the story through but the art-house treatment and the sad ending did not generate much of a positive response at the box office. But Javed successfully manage to reprise his and Salim's original creation into a new, relevant avatar, nearly twenty years after it was created.

The only romantic film Javed wrote in this period was *Saagar*, a love triangle set in Goa. Ramesh Sippy directed Rishi Kapoor and Dimple Kapadia in the lead roles, along with Kamal Haasan, who overshadowed both the stars with his performance in an author-backed role. Javed created a nice backdrop for the film—by managing a perfect balance of escapist fare in a real setting, and also wrote the lyrics for R.D. Burman's brilliant score. A great script backed by remarkable acting and chartbusting music ensured that *Saagar* became one of the biggest hits of 1985.

After a fairly successful run in the 1980s, Javed Akhtar was credited with *Jeevan Ek Sanghursh* and *Jhoothi Shaan* in the early 1990s. It is difficult to understand how Rahul Rawail and Javed Akhtar could come up with *Jeevan Ek Sanghursh* after the superb *Dacait*. One possible explanation is that when the latter's unusual treatment did not do well at the box office, they just put pretty much everything from the Bollywood formula cupboard into this film to make it work and ended up making a big, fat star vehicle.

Jhoothi Shaan is said to be 'Written by' Javed Akhtar though he himself says he had no contribution in the film except for the lyrics of a song. His name was probably included to improve the saleability of the film.

In 1992, Javed Akhtar wrote *Khel* for Rakesh Roshan, starring the reigning box-office pair of Anil Kapoor and Madhuri Dixit. While it came on the heels of a few underperformers, Javed's equity as a writer was still solid and he continued to attract top producers and stars. *Khel* was a sophisticated film about three scamsters trying to cheat an ageing dowager out of her fortune. The film was full of clever lines, smooth cons and an energetic cast. While it did not perform too well commercially, it was liked for its 'coolness' and still enjoys a bit of cult following.

Sometimes, the decline comes like an abyss, unexpectedly, and immediately, after an intoxicating high. Failure is a rude awakening, often causing people associated with it to re-evaluate priorities and change course altogether. This is exactly what happened with Javed Akhtar after two of his biggest films in the mid-1990s did very badly. After the super success of *Mr India*, Javed Akhtar signed up with Boney Kapoor to write Anil Kapoor's magnum opus, *Roop Ki Rani Choron Ka Raja* (*RKRCKR*), along with Sanjay Kapoor's debut film, *Prem*. And unfortunately for all concerned, both the films crashed and burned.

In many ways, *RKRCKR* was *Shaan* redux. All the pieces were the same: the same writer reuniting with the same director–producer, the same cast in a bigger, more expensive production after a massive hit. *RKRCKR* was cleverer and had more 'events' in the story but—in hindsight—that's what made it bloated. It sorely lacked the lightness of touch that *Mr India* had. The need to have too many costumes, sets, stunts and stars led to a heavy production—both for the viewer and the producer. The most expensive Hindi film when it released, *RKRCKR* had a disastrous run at the box office, setting everyone associated with the film back by a lot.

Producer Boney Kapoor's bad luck continued with *Prem*, his youngest brother Sanjay's debut vehicle (that was also supposed to launch Tabu but whose other films released much earlier due to the delays with filming *Prem*). The film went back to the reincarnation plot, which has been an extremely popular theme in Hindi cinema but had no new twists to make it attractive to the new audiences. In fact, another reincarnation drama—*Karan Arjun*, released in the same year—buoyed by the presence of two major stars (one of whom was Salim Khan's superstar son Salman) did phenomenally well, adding to *Prem*'s woes. A not-so-charismatic hero and the attendant issues of a much-delayed production made matters worse.

In the wake of these two disasters, Javed Akhtar stopped writing scripts for the most part. In 1998 he was credited with Priyadarshan's *Kabhi Na Kabhi*, which had none of the felicity and finesse Salim–Javed collectively—and even Javed Akhtar singly—were famous for. It was a tired, hackneyed revenge drama that sank without a trace.

After that, Javed slowly cut back on his scriptwriting assignments and concentrated on lyrics instead. He says, 'I can't tell you the exact moment or the date or the day [that I stopped writing screenplays] but I was becoming mechanical. Producers were paying me so I had to write. There was no sense of achievement or discovery. So I thought I'd give myself a break.'

In the decade of the 2000s, Javed Akhtar has hardly written scripts—making exceptions only for family members. His first outing after this long hiatus was for Honey Irani's directorial debut, *Armaan* (2003). Based on a story by Honey herself, he essentially wrote the dialogues for the film, though Honey Irani said, 'He even helped me with the screenplay. Javed was a great help primarily because he is a writer and could see more nuances in the script than I could. His contribution has really been valuable.' He is also credited as a co-writer of the screenplay. The film—a relationship drama—did not do too well and Honey Irani takes a large part of the blame herself: 'The first half was boring. There was not one but three, four operations. The performances were fabulous but I blundered in the screenplay.' While the star cast was impeccable—Amitabh Bachchan, Anil Kapoor, Preity Zinta and Gracey Singh—none of them seemed to be playing to their strengths and there weren't any memorable 'highs'.

His next writing assignment was for son Farhan Akhtar's second directorial venture—*Lakshya* (2004). He wrote the entire film (including the lyrics), taking an aimless young man to his final redemption in the battlefields of Kargil. There was extensive research about the war, the arms and ammunition and setting that went into the script. While the first half of the script was breezy with Javed Akhtar evoking a youngster's lack of ambition with sensitivity and humour, the second half lost steam with a couple of songs, messages of patriotism and pacifism—all interrupting some much-needed battle action. And like always, he did give his inputs while finalizing the cast; Farhan Akhtar says the decision to cast Hrithik Roshan in the film was based on Javed's idea of the physicality of the role. While the film did not do too well commercially, the reviews were by and large positive. Mayank Shekhar accurately said the 'screenplay achieves a war-movie without ever degenerating into blind glorification of battle-gore or chest-thumping jingoism.'

Javed Akhtar's most recent writing assignment was for daughter Zoya's directorial debut—*Luck by Chance* (2009). He wrote the dialogues for the film, a beautiful gem which could only have been made by someone who has always been on the periphery of the industry and is in love with it. Among all the lines Javed wrote for the film, there was one which harked back to a previous film. In a scene portraying the graduation ceremony of an acting school, character actor Macmohan comes to give away the certificates and takes pleasure in repeating his most famous line to the budding actors: '*Pooray pachaas hazaar*'[xlviii], which incidentally, was written by the same dialogue writer. A line that—like many others—has passed into Hindi cinema legend.

Part IV:

THEMES AND MESSAGES

The Angry Young Man

'Any kind of image attributed to an actor, like the Angry Young Man, concerns not only that actor, but also the environment that prevails in that period of history in which the people are functioning. If there is a certain anger in the minds of the people, against certain kinds of system or against some kind of governmental policies or social norms, or taboos, and if somebody expresses it . . . if the actor is able to convey the anger effectively, then he's actually expressing the anger of the pent-up emotions of his own generation'—Govind Nihalani

Possibly Salim–Javed's most significant cinematic contribution, the Angry Young Man redefined Hindi cinema of the 1970s and was a phenomenon unlike any other. It was in *Zanjeer* that this phenomenon first came to the fore, but its origins can be traced to a few decades earlier.

In 1956, British playwright John Osborne wrote a play, *Look Back in Anger,* to express what it felt like to live in England during the 1950s. The messages of the highly successful play were 'impatience with the status quo, refusal to be co-opted by a bankrupt society, an instinctive solidarity with the lower classes'. The protagonist of the play was an embodiment of the rebellious, post-war generation. He was called the Angry Young Man.

When *Zanjeer* was released nearly two decades later, the situation in which the protagonist operated and the reactions he had towards the ills of society were similar to the original theme, and Amitabh Bachchan became the face, the embodiment of the Angry Young Man.

In the twenty-five years or so that had passed since Independence, the idealism of the freedom struggle had been eroded and the promise of a socialist utopia had become completely out of sync with reality.

In the immediate aftermath of Independence, Hindi cinema was greatly concerned with society and the changes it could foster. The onus of building a nation and inspiring citizens was taken up by the optimistic film-makers of the time, who were great believers in the power of cinema. It had the benefit of being a medium of entertainment, and thus was the perfect platform to convey important social messages in interesting formats. Hence, film-makers like Bimal Roy and V. Shantaram took up themes like criminal reform and industrial progress at the cost of agriculture in some of the defining films of the times—*Do Ankhen Barah Haath* and *Do Bigha Zamin* respectively. There were many other notables in this genre—*Boot Polish*, *Mother India*, *Naya Daur*, *Jagte Raho*; every major director made films with messages.

After the social themes of the 1950s, Hindi cinema entered a phase of high-octane entertainment using romance, melodrama, comedy, action (to a relatively lesser degree) and, of course, music. The social and historical stories that were a legacy of the freedom struggle gradually faded away. The biggest stars of the decade—Shammi Kapoor, Dev Anand and Rajesh Khanna—all projected a picture of unreal romantic love that was more escapism than anything else.

Historian Ramachandra Guha writes, 'The late 1960s are reminiscent of the late 1940s, likewise a time of crisis and conflict, of resentment along lines of class, religion, ethnicity and region, of a centre that barely seemed to hold.' Elaborating on these tensions, Javed Akhtar says, 'For the first time, since the high of Independence, people started feeling that law and order were breaking down and extra-Constitutional powers were taking over. Is it a coincidence that the vigilante hero became popular when people felt there was no justice and one had to take law in one's own hands?'

In this depressing political situation, the anger against the hopeless system was channelized from within by certain leaders and they—sometimes—did take the law in their own hands.

In Bihar, freedom fighter Jayprakash (JP) Narayan returned to active politics in the late 1960s and his call for revolution found many takers. The momentum reached its peak in 1974 when inflation, unemployment and black-marketeering were rampant. In a massive rally in Patna, JP called for 'total revolution' and initiated a struggle to have the Vidhan Sabha dissolved. Students were the most active participants of this movement and the youth of the entire country saw a hero in the angry septuagenarian JP.

Far away in Maharashtra, discontent of a different kind was being fermented by a new organization called the Shiv Sena, founded by former *Free Press Journal* cartoonist, Bal Keshav Thackeray. Thackeray's stated aim was to ensure job security for Maharashtrians, and he managed to wrest control of Bombay's trade unions from the communists by actively—and often violently—campaigning against 'immigrant' Gujaratis and south Indians. It was a sign of the times that a cosmopolitan city like Bombay got mobilized behind such blatant regionalism and rallied behind Thackeray, who was in his early forties and projected himself as the 'angry, irreverent and defiant voice of the people'.

In another part of the country—Bengal, most prominently—a radical brand of leftist ideology was inspiring young people to take up arms and attack the system. Naxalism found—and still finds—acceptance among those completely deprived of the benefits of governance.

There were different kinds of anger in different parts of India but the country's dominant popular culture—Hindi cinema—was depicting none of that. It was into this atmosphere that Salim–Javed's films arrived.

The writers have repeatedly said that they had no intention of passing on a message through their films. They were merely looking to present an interesting character in an interesting setting. The volatile situation in India during the early 1970s was like a simmering cauldron in which they brewed their potion of discontent. What needs to be noted is that their backgrounds, their eye for detail, their rebellious temperaments and—not least—their youth (Javed was about twenty-five and Salim about thirty-five when they wrote the character) made them better suited than anybody else to create an iconic figure like the Angry Young Man. Salim Khan, growing up in the care of his police officer father had heard many stories of ill treatment of honest officers and the rage building within the system, which was being hijacked by corrupt ministers and bureaucrats.

Javed Akhtar says, 'It was neither a conscious decision, nor a coincidence. People have written theses on these films and their socio-political relevance, but we were blissfully unaware. I am happy that we had no idea, because if we had, it would have meant that we were looking at society from outside. We were a part of it, breathing the same air, living the same life.'

However, like many of their creations, Salim–Javed were not the first to develop the idea of the Angry Young Man. There were precedents that the writers were aware of and from which they took bits and pieces to give shape to the iconic figure which reigned for more than a decade and spawned many imitations. Javed Akhtar has himself said that *Mother India*'s Birju (Sunil Dutt) was a character he loved because of his rebellious streak and that he had made a deep impression on him. He has even wondered if Balraj Sahni's character in *Do Bigha Zamin*—another favourite of his—should have revolted against the system instead of being a mute victim.

In Hollywood of the 1950s, James Dean had a very brief but influential career playing angst-ridden youngsters (most notably in *Rebel Without a Cause*). He was often called a replica of Marlon Brando, who again portrayed characters violently angry with the system (in films like *The Wild One* and *On the Waterfront*).

Back home, Gulzar's *Mere Apne* (1971) was one such film in which the plight and the misguided energy of the unemployed youth were portrayed quite brilliantly. Vinod Khanna and Shatrughan Sinha—still known for their negative roles—made two awesome anti-heroes, Shyam and Chheno. The supporting cast of youngsters (Paintal, Danny et al) was disillusioned bunch of people though their anger was channelled through sarcasm ('*Haal chaal theek thaak hai . . .*') and they were not violent (or at least not demonstrably so) towards the system.

Mere Apne was a remake of the Bengali film *Apanjan* (1968). The Bengali film industry had smelled the anger a little earlier. Satyajit Ray's acclaimed *Pratidwandi* (1970) was another superb depiction of the Angry Young Man, albeit in a more realistic way. A scene from *Pratidwandi* shows the protagonist Siddhartha (Dhritiman Chatterjee) facing an interview panel where he does quite well till he cites the 'war in Vietnam' as the significant event of the past decade. The panel construes his eloquent answer to be a sign of communism and potential activism.

This scene finds resonance in the scene in *Deewaar* where Ravi (Shashi Kapoor) does very well in an interview till nepotism rears it ugly head and a candidate with connections in the company beats him to the job.

All these characters were cut from the same cloth—recent graduates in search of employment; intelligent, sensitive and yet ignored in the rat race because the establishment wants people who will toe the line, who won't think independently or challenge the status quo.

The success and appeal of Salim–Javed's films and the recognition they received as creators of the character are due to their near-perfect blend of realism and escapism.

Their Angry Young Men were born in very real circumstances—the honest police officer fighting the unresponsive system; the dockyard coolie being extorted; the bastard son growing up to be vengeful because his father abandoned his mother; the disgraced naval captain seeking redemption.

And they took the system on mostly successfully. Theirs was not the 'anger of the taut bow' (as Satyajit Ray once described his wronged character in *Sadgati*) but the anger of an exploding bomb. Their characters did not tremble in impotent rage. They picked up a gun and mowed down the villains. Their smouldering eyes were backed by hard fists.

Salim–Javed's Angry Young Man was inconceivable for the Hindi cinema audience of the time and yet when he appeared, it seemed they had been waiting for him.

Angry Young Man Redux

'So many other actors have tried to ape Amitabh, but they've failed. Because they didn't have the sophistication and the tehzeeb that Amitabh grew up with. As an actor, Amitabh's anger was never ugly. Other actors mix anger with arrogance. But Amitabh's anger was mixed with hurt and tears'—Javed Akhtar

In *Arjun* (1985), there is an almost exact replica of the 'job interview' scene that Shashi Kapoor was seen in in *Deewaar* (1975). But while in the earlier film, the interviewer was somewhat embarrassed about taking the job away from the deserving candidate, the interviewer in *Arjun* is absolutely blasé and throws back the file containing the certificates without even opening it. '*Naukri kisi aur ko de di gayi*'[xlix] is the common response in both places, but the intervening decade had institutionalized the unfairness.

When Salim and Javed started writing independently, Indian society and politics had changed a lot from their initial days as a team. In the early 1970s, there were still some vestiges of idealism left that made people feel extremely frustrated and angry at the sight of corruption and crime. Thus, for the average Indian a man taking the law into his hands or taking on the establishment became a hero—almost a messiah. It was this feeling of awe that was behind the mass appeal of diverse characters like Jayprakash Narayan, Bal Thackeray and Amitabh Bachchan's Angry Young Man.

By the mid-1980s, the decline in public morality had become much worse. Corruption in politics had become so widespread that anger had given way to cynicism. The lumpen elements of society had started to receive political patronage and the nexus between crime and politics had becoming very strong.[31] Politics in India had never been free of unsavoury characters but the criminal links had become more overt now.

In fact, the smugglers and criminals who made their ill-gotten fortunes in the 1970s were now seeking legitimacy through elections. The best example of this is one Haji Mastan Mirza, who started off as a smuggler but 'reformed' after a period of incarceration and ventured into politics by forming a party and forging alliances with existing leaders. In more ways than one, the smuggler of *Deewaar* had been replaced by a more powerful character who was no longer the anti-hero but a full-blown villain—the 'dirty politician'.

Salim and Javed read this mood perfectly—nearly as well as they understood the mood in 1970s. The people's idealism had given way to hardened cynicism, the employment situation had become grimmer and the subversion of justice had become easy to the point of being laughable. And, in their best traditions, they built these elements into scripts that brought realism without sacrificing entertainment or pace. For example, the Middle East

---

[31] The 1970s decade had three extremely hard-fought elections (1971, 1977 and 1980), which saw major upheavals in political fortunes. With higher stakes and the need to turn tables on bitter rivals, politicians started using criminals for more and more 'ground work'.

job scam (where youngsters were sent to Dubai with promises of jobs that didn't exist) formed the backdrop for *Naam*, while the dying small-scale industries of Bombay were a key element in *Arjun*. The results were some very interesting characters that utilized the actors' talents very well. The Angry Young Man was still a wronged individual out to seek revenge or redemption, but now he was appearing in different avatars.

Anil Kapoor played characters that were aggressive and intelligent. In *Mashaal*, he was the tapori who was inspired by an idealistic newspaper editor to become a journalist, whereas in *Meri Jung*, he was the hotshot lawyer taking on impossible cases to ensure truth triumphed over manipulated evidence. And in *Joshilaay*, he was the strong, silent type, going after a bandit to avenge his parents' death.

Sunny Deol was the gullible idealist who turns vigilante after run-ins with corrupt politicians (*Arjun*) or village despots (*Dacait*).

Sanjay Dutt was the forever-in-trouble youngster teetering on the wrong side of the law, before deciding to reform. Sometimes he got hired by international crime bosses (*Naam*) and sometimes by local dadas (*Kabzaa*).

Most often, the common factor—like earlier—that served as a catalyst for the underdog to take on the system was a tragic death. Just as the death of a fellow coolie at the hands of the dockyard goons shakes *Deewaar*'s Vijay, similarly, Arjun is traumatized when his friend is killed by a politician's henchmen.[32] Be it Alok Nath's death in *Kabzaa* or the father's unjustified hanging in *Meri Jung*, it was death that brought out the fighter in the young man.

---

[32] In a superbly choreographed scene in the rains, the friend Mohan (played by Satyajeet) is chased and killed by the goons in a maze of black umbrellas.

The mother figure—a central character in Angry Young Man films like *Deewaar* and *Trishul*—was no longer the inspiration, at least not overtly. For example, in *Dacait*, the mother (Rakhee) loses her senses in the attack that destroys her family. She is a victim of atrocities along with the rest of her family but she doesn't inspire her son to take up arms.

Even in *Meri Jung*, the mother (Nutan) loses her memory and is missing from her children's lives for a major part of the film. While the injustice against his father and mother propels the hero (Anil Kapoor) to become a legal crusader, she is not the prime mover, as Waheeda Rehman's character was in *Trishul*.

And while the mother figure does make an appearance in *Mashaal*, she (Waheeda Rehman) has a benign impact on Anil Kapoor, who is more inspired by Dilip Kumar. Her death triggers a different kind of reaction in her husband, as his disillusionment with the system is complete and he turns into a criminal. The wife here is not only *not* the beacon of morality she was in Salim–Javed's films, but in fact she propels the hero in the wrong direction.

In *Naam*, the mother figure is present but is neither as crucial to the plot nor as critical about her son's wayward behaviour as we saw in her earlier avatars.

And, finally, in *Arjun*, the mother figure is actually a stepmother (Shashikala)—a harsh and irritating background presence in the hero's life. She has no interest in him or in his career choices as long as he brings in a salary. She has no message, let alone a positive one, for her stepson and is reduced to just a grating noise in his life.

Sunny Deol, Anil Kapoor and Sanjay Dutt turned out to be the new avatars of the Angry Young Man in most of their earlier films. Sunny Deol's performances in *Arjun* and *Dacait* laid the foundation for *Ghayal*, his career-defining film. Similarly, Anil

Kapoor was brilliant as a tapori in *Mashaal* and his exceptional dialogue delivery in *Meri Jung* set him up for *Tezaab*, the film that made him a superstar. Even Sanjay Dutt, whose subsequent career was riddled with interruptions, got a great launching pad in *Naam* that signalled his return to Bollywood after his dream debut (*Rocky*) went sour due to his drug problem.

And it was not only the youngsters whose careers got a boost with Salim Khan and Javed Akhtar.

Dilip Kumar established himself as an exceedingly strong character actor in the 1980s with his roles in *Mashaal* and *Duniya*. In both cases, he was the centre of attention (despite the presence of a younger hero) and brilliantly played the Angry Old Man out for revenge.

Amitabh Bachchan, grappling with poor health and a disastrous stint in politics, did films with both writers that gave his anger as well as his youth a new twist. In *Main Azaad Hoon*, he was a bystander who became the face of a revolution against corrupt politics. He went from being an ordinary man with no point of view to a vocal critic of the establishment, but his anger was not about fists and guns any more. Here, the Angry Young Man got a Gandhian twist as it was more about inspiring people with words. In *Akayla*, the anger and bullets remained but the character was a jaded police inspector. Repeated run-ins with powerful criminals and a failed romance had turned him into a hardened man with a drinking problem. The man was angry, still going after criminals, but was not so young after all; it was an intelligent way to project the ageing Bachchan.

The Angry Young Man returned in the 1980s with a bang, and made careers once again. Unfortunately, the popularity of the character led to its becoming commonplace, for film after film flogged it to death. Conceived by master writers like Salim–Javed and brought alive on screen by a talented director like Yash

Chopra, the character became a caricature as the anger ceased to be impactful and the violence was no longer worth even the fake blood it spilt. This cycle of violence in Hindi cinema continued for most of the 1990s, ending only when three men—each about five years apart—brought in a fresh burst of stylish romance that not only revived Hindi cinema but also made it cool in the years that followed. These three men were Salman Khan (*Maine Pyar Kiya*, 1989), Aditya Chopra (*Dilwale Dulhania Le Jayenge*, 1995) and Farhan Akhtar (*Dil Chahta Hai*, 2001).

Villains

An honest police officer is wrongly incarcerated due to the
machinations of a crime boss. When the seething officer
is released from jail, the first thing he does is walk into a
restaurant where the villain, protected by his bodyguards,
is having dinner with his moll. He sits down at the villain's
table, and announces, '*Teja, main aa gaya hoon.*'[1]

The villain looks up from his soup. 'Hello,' he
replies coolly.

—from *Zanjeer*

When Salim–Javed started writing, Ajit was one of
the top 'villains', playing smuggling kingpins and
unscrupulous industrialists in his trademark cool-cat style.
Two out of his three best-known roles were written by Salim–
Javed. *Yaadon Ki Baaraat*'s Shaakaal (he of different-sized
shoes) and *Zanjeer*'s Teja (he of molls called Mona) formed the
crux of his characterization which would eventually become
the subject of 'Ajit jokes'.[33]

---

[33] His most quoted line and the best-known character were both from
Kaalicharan where he drawled, '*Saara sheher mujhe Loin ke naam se jaanta hai.*' [li]

For the first time, villains were intelligently devious. They had interesting tics and their speaking styles were eminently imitable. They even had backstories to explain their villainy. *Zanjeer*'s Teja, for example, rises from being a faceless mercenary in a spurious medicine racket before he kills his own boss (played by Sapru) and usurps the throne.

In creating the character of the Angry Young Man, Salim–Javed built an entire mythology around him, making him a superhero hitherto unseen in Hindi cinema. A core part of creating this mythology was to invest the hero with a worthy adversary.

Film historian Kaushik Bhaumik says, 'Salim–Javed had a very strong understanding of the extremely popular nautanki culture where Raavan is as much part of the attraction of Ramleela as Ram is. In fact, Raavan has to be the spectacular pivot around which the Ramleela revolves.' He further elucidates that the myth-making with which the Angry Young Man flourished needed everything to be hyperbolic and exaggerated.

The duo realized that for the heroes to be big, the villains had to be as big—if not bigger. If the hero was to be someone audiences would not forget in a hurry, the villain he vanquished had to be memorable. This process of building the villain as painstakingly and meticulously as creating the hero is something that is taken from the mythology of our country.

To take forward Bhaumik's Ramayana analogy, in the epic, Raavan is presented as a great king and a formidable foe, an opponent worthy of Vishnu's incarnation. His son Meghnad and brother Kumbhakarna have their own strengths and get their own build-ups. This myth-making has been perpetuated— and to a large extent, exaggerated—by the annual Ramleela festival across the country. The visual spectacle of Raavan and his cohorts being constructed over an extended period of time is something we have become used to, right from our childhood.

And eventually, on Dussehra the huge figure of Raavan looms over all of us as the symbol of evil. The heroes—Ram and Laxman—have only cameos in the programme as they arrive right at the end to finish off the villains in a grand spectacle of colours and fireworks.

In a way, in several of their films, Salim–Javed mimicked this slow construction of the Raavanesque figure and his larger-than-life presence. In *Sholay*, we are treated to an edgy mix of ominous music, a very unusual voice, a pair of boots and a scraping belt for an extended period of time before Gabbar Singh erupts on to the screen with an explosive '*Sooar ke bachche!*'[lii] The fact that Thakur Baldeo Singh hires the two heroes to catch him alive makes the 'mashhoor daku' a *presence* in the film even before his first appearance. There are hints of an old enmity and there is a king's ransom—'*pooray pachaas hazaar*'—as bounty on the villain. By the time Kaalia openly threatens the villagers with Gabbar's wrath, the audience is dying of curiosity to see him. More than an hour into the film, we are at last 'treated' to Gabbar Singh in a six-minute long introduction sequence, that certainly blows away more than a few minds.

Five years after *Sholay*, we have Shaakaal in *Shaan*.

The entry of Shaakaal is even grander as we follow his lieutenants—formidable villains themselves—on a long journey to the mega-villain's lair that looks like it is straight out of a James Bond film. Again, the villain, the fearsome 'Shaakaal saab'—played by then-unknown theatre actor Kulbhushan Kharbanda—builds on his mystique for quite some time before he swivels into view with a huge control panel in front of him and sharks swimming in the ocean behind him. Shaakaal's version of Russian Roulette was even more elaborate than what we had seen in *Sholay*, as were his army, his network of informers, his array of gadgets, his physical presence and—eventually—his end.

This creation of an iconic villain was taken up a notch with Mogambo in *Mr India*. The super villain wanted to rule India by spreading murder and mayhem, even destroying the country with his nuclear missiles if the need arose. Even before we see the hero (or rather, the common man who eventually becomes the hero), we see Mogambo's den, his army, his Führer-like command over loyal subjects and hear the three words that will transcend time—'*Mogambo khush hua*.' Mogambo's entry is framed—rather, choreographed—through long shots as we are given vague hints about the villain till he leans into the screen with this trademark line.

It was not only the build-up that Salim–Javed gave the mega villains, but the general strain of intelligence that ran through almost all their villainous characters that made the difference. The Hindi film villain has always been a snarling buffoon who brings misfortune through brute force before being beaten into submission.

Not in Salim–Javed's films.

Yaadon Ki Baaraat's Shaakaal is perceptive enough to recognize the faint sound of a passing train during a phone call from an adversary, and dispatch his henchmen to kill the man when he appears to make the next phone call.

Chacha Bhatija's Jeevan is the proverbial 'asteen ka saanp' who weaves an elaborate web of deceit to control his brother-in-law's property. While this act is not new to Hindi cinema, the initial scenes have him fooling most of the audience as well.

Don's Amitabh Bachchan is a master of escapes, hoodwinking the police in style and identifying traitors in his own gang with ease—sharp, ruthless and a million times more glamorous than the hero. The other villain—kingpin Vardhan, impersonating an Interpol officer—is again a very cool customer who does not get flustered by the fact that

Vijay knows his real identity. He plays a cat-and-mouse game with him, leading both the gangsters and the police down the garden path without compromising his cover.

While it takes most of the other characters a lot of time to figure out that Mr India is visible in red light, Mogambo gets it in a flash. He sees Mr India at the edge of his steaming red cauldron of acid and immediately switches on all the red lights in his hideout.

Even a minor character like Madho Singh (Shetty) in *Trishul* seems formidable because he isn't merely a neighbourhood tough but someone who has managed to keep an industrialist like R.K. Gupta (Sanjeev Kumar) at bay for a very long time.

Be it their less famous but very impactful villains or biggies like Gabbar Singh and Mogambo, Salim–Javed invested their baddies with a level of charisma and intelligence that was usually the exclusive preserve of heroes.

The entire process of creating the villain—from finding a name like Gabbar (which was a real bandit's name), to giving him a new vocabulary while writing the dialogues, to recommending a completely new actor to play the very unconventional part—was anchored by Salim–Javed. The result was such a magnetically evil character that Gabbar Singh (the character and not Amjad Khan the actor) became the face of Britannia Glucose D biscuits, a brand that was a favourite among children and families.

This journey of creating a charismatic villain was a definite first in the history of Hindi cinema, and also the very first time audiences started rooting for the villain. This was something that took a while for people to get. Naseeruddin Shah—not a fan of *Sholay* at all—explains this wonderfully in his memoir when he talks about watching *Sholay* in its second week (in a half-empty theatre): 'I saw with my own eyes the rejection by an audience of an effective actor in a movie because he was upstaging the ones they identified with. His later applause-inducing non sequiturs were that day being greeted with stony silence or hostile rejection by the majority of the Dharmendra/Bachchan fan club present. It took a week or two for the audiences to cotton on to the fact that, hey, they had been rooting for the wrong guys all along. Gabbar was their man.'

In fact, this inability of audiences to process a larger-than-life villain had been a problem for the makers as well, because the Sippys had seriously considered dropping Amjad Khan halfway through the shooting. From being a towering figure in the script to the difficulties in filming to the initially muted audience reactions to becoming an icon, the reactions to Gabbar Singh were as complex as the character itself.

Here was a role which all three male leads—Dharmendra, Sanjeev Kumar and Amitabh Bachchan—coveted when they first heard the script. Here was a character that took the longest to cast. Here was a newcomer who was almost dropped due to his inability to project menace in the initial days of shooting. Here was a character who was called 'a short fat lout, is a far cry from the much-feared dacoit. The man cannot even run or fight and only keeps ordering or grimacing', in one of the early reviews (in *Star and Style* magazine). And here was an icon who became so popular with kids and adults alike that advertising agencies made ads around him. And continue to do so.

The process of creating Mogambo was as interesting.

While the character was jointly conceived by Salim–Javed, they had split long before the film went into final stages of script development and Javed Akhtar wrote the final draft. The villain became a legendary character not through his actions but through words, just three of them—'*Mogambo khush hua*'. Be it the power of the words or the charm of that gargantuan character, Amrish Puri just sank his teeth into the role. Shekhar

Kapur says, 'Each time he brought a new flavour, a new emotion, a different resonance in his voice. He became threatening and lovable at the same time. Each time bringing something out of the ordinary for those lines that have now gone down in history.'

Javed Akhtar was right about Mogambo's impact. Shekhar Kapur recalls watching a cricket match in Sharjah several years later when a six was hit and a huge banner proclaimed, 'Mogambo khusha hua!'

Gabbar Singh:
A Villain, They Wrote

'Gabbar Singh yeh keh kar gaya, jo dar gaya woh mar gaya . . .'

Line from a song in the film *100 Days* (1991)

During a Twitter Q&A, film director Anurag Kashyap was asked who his favourite movie villain was, and he replied, 'Gabbar Singh.' When asked why, he said, 'Because when I saw him the first time, I was only six years old.' For him and many people who started watching movies in the 1970s, Gabbar Singh is their first abiding movie memory. He was indeed the scary figure who was invoked to get children to sleep.

But is Gabbar Singh the most memorable character of Hindi cinema?

Well, he is certainly the only villain—if not the only character—whose lines are repeated in daily conversations as well as popular culture even forty years after the film's release. A survey done by the *Economic Times* in 2005 (just after the film's thirtieth anniversary) suggested that there were fifty ads in circulation that were inspired by *Sholay* for top brands like Maggi, Britannia,

Clinic Plus, Alpenliebe and Tetley. A large number of these ads depended on Gabbar Singh and his iconic '*Kitnay aadmi thay?*'[liii]

Javed Akhtar says he and Salim were influenced, to a large extent, by Sergio Leone and his brand of Western movies. 'There is some Mexican blood in Gabbar. He's a bandit, not a daku (dacoit),' he says. They gave a lot of thought to Gabbar's persona.

Because Amjad Khan was an absolute newcomer in films when he played Gabbar, he spent a lot of time on the sets observing the other actors, helping out as an assistant and talking to the writers about the script. Since Amjad was Salim–Javed's recommendation, both parties felt a certain sense of responsibility towards each other and that led to more thought around the character and better preparation. The blackened teeth, unwashed look, stooping gait and even the unusual language formed a character that was quite unlike any Hindi film audiences had ever seen. No longer did the daku wear a turban and tilak, and pray to Maa Kali before embarking on his adventures. The honour code of the dacoits was thrown out of the window as well; Gabbar was completely okay with attacking his enemies' families. In fact, that seemed like his strategy. He almost relished killing a small child, something that was out of bounds for even the most hard-core villains till then.

This incarnation of evil was written as the antithesis of the moral Thakur—the two characters who formed the axis of the film.

The character of Gabbar was conceived as inherently unpredictable. Just before shooting Kaalia, he feigns concern: '*Ab tera kya hoga, Kaalia?*'[liv] Immediately after the three dacoits think they have escaped death in his version of Russian Roulette, he explodes into a manic burst of laughter and then shoots them. He doesn't merely tell us the bounty on his head but arrogantly asks a minion to do so.

Even his language—his vocabulary—wasn't regular Hindi. Javed Akhtar says, 'He became alive . . . There are so many words in Gabbar's vocabulary that I wasn't even conscious of. I didn't even know for sure if I could use those words . . . Gabbar had his own language.'

For example, Gabbar—when describing his arrest—says, '*Aur kacheri mein aisa taap mujhko, aisa taap mujhko.*'[lv] Literally, 'taap' means fever and the way it is said, it is not even a properly formed sentence but it communicated Gabbar's unconventional anger remarkably well. Gabbar threatens to skin Basanti alive—'*khurach khurach ke*'—a word that perfectly brings out Gabbar's sadism.[34]

The language gave an additional dimension to the scary, evil characterization of Gabbar. And if his lingo was unpredictable, his actions were even more so. Right from the manic laughter in his first scene (nearly a third of the way into the film) to his brutal murder of innocents, Gabbar is that rare villain who repulses you with his cruelty and yet holds your attention with his magnetism.

Apart from the language, Gabbar's backstory—never mentioned in the film—found some interesting expressions.

To coincide with the release of *Sholay* in 3D (in January 2014), a graphic novel called *Sholay: Gabbar* was published, which traces the origins of Gabbar Singh. Author Saurav Mohapatra says, 'Gabbar is a groundbreaking character in Hindi movies as he was the first "no explanations given, he's just evil" character in our movies. When I was asked to write about his origin, it was tricky. I decided to stack the narrative evenly so that the reader has to make a choice towards whether

---

[34] Javed Akhtar is referring to the line where Gabbar tells Basanti, '*Dekho chhamiya, zyada nakhra mat karo humse nahin toh yeh gori chamdi hai na— saare badan se khurach khurach ke utaar doonga.*' [lvi]

or not to believe in the truth of his story. Everyone is a hero in their own eyes and why should Gabbar be different, I thought. I treated him similar to the Joker in the *Dark Knight*.' Mohapatra's story has a young Gabbar becoming bitter after his father dies from police atrocities and joining the army, which he deserts to become a dacoit. His gang of friends—Sambha et al—come together during childhood and they stick through many upheavals though there is no doubt about who the leader of the gang is.

Director Soumik Sen independently wrote another origin story for Gabbar where the dacoit is born Gulab Singh and has frequent run-ins with the oppressive Thakur families before being disowned by his father and joining the Indian army.

It is interesting that with the sketchy details provided in the film (e.g. Gabbar's father's name, the army fatigues he wore, the anger he has against the Thakurs), two independent writers came up with stories that were similar in many respects. The multiple viewings of *Sholay* ensured that these details were absorbed and their presence pointed towards a character that was bigger than the sum of its parts.

The impact Gabbar Singh has had is immense and his charisma has not petered out over time. Much has been spoken about the famous Britannia Glucose D biscuit ad[35] endorsed by Gabbar Singh (and not Amjad Khan) that came immediately after the film was released and continued to run for nearly a decade after.

Early in 2015, Akshay Kumar starred in Sanjay Leela Bhansali's production of a Hindi remake of a Tamil film. The film is about a vigilante forming an anti-corruption force to

---

[35] Incidentally, the Glucose D campaign was executed by Britannia's then group product manager, Sunil Alagh, who went on to become the biscuit company's managing director.

weed out dishonesty in society. While the original was called *Ramanna*, Bhansali chose to name the Hindi film *Gabbar* in—increasing the curiosity value.

Beyond the Hindi-speaking belt, Gabbar Singh has fans even in south India. Telugu superstar Pawan Kalyan acted in a remake of *Dabangg*, where he played the Robin Hood cop's role who went by the name Gabbar Singh. The reason for the name was that the film's hero—as a child—was impressed by the *Sholay* character. If you know the plot of *Dabangg*, you'll realize there is no reason to take up this name except to pay homage.

Gabbar Singh's character was charismatic enough that a talented performer like Amjad Khan became one of the country's top villains after just that one role and was hailed as an excellent actor. There are two strange epilogues to the Gabbar casting story.

Satyajit Ray—a fan of *Sholay*—liked Amjad Khan so much that he offered him the role of Nawab Wajid Ali Shah in his first Hindi film, *Shatranj Ke Khiladi*. The film-maker said, 'I took Amjad on the strength of his performance in *Sholay*. I hope you know that his characterization of Gabbar Singh did not go down well with the public for the first few weeks. It caught on later. But I thought if an actor could be so good and so rangy, why not cast him against the grain and see how it works.' Gabbar went from playing a macho villain to an effeminate king who sang and danced. The role did not go down well with the cow-belt audience and there were reports of people storming out or ransacking theatres because their 'Gabbar Singh' was playing something so radically different. The critical acclaim the film received did not translate into commercial acceptance.

Denied the opportunity of being Gabbar in *Sholay*, Amitabh Bachchan finally fulfilled his dream of playing the iconic villain later in his career when he was able to break free from the shackles of his heroic image. He brought a different kind of menace to Babban, who ran an underworld empire in 2000s Mumbai, but the film—*Ram Gopal Verma Ki Aag*—turned out to be one of the biggest disasters of Indian cinema, faring terribly with both critics and audiences.

Like the film he appeared in, there is only one Gabbar Singh. Intimidating and inimitable.

Violence of the Mind

'The leading exponents of the current screen cult of bloody reprisals are scriptwriters Salim and Javed, whose none-too-original scenarios only succeed in stating the obvious: that the defence against violence must always be more violence . . . Sholay manages to raise screen violence to almost unimaginable heights'—From K.M. Amladi's review of *Sholay* in *Hindustan Times*, titled 'Uncensored Violence'

'The film could have gone easy on the depiction of the violence. There is a pronounced sadistic touch to the last-reel encounter between Sanjeev Kumar and Amjad Khan's villain, the episode having the sort of violence that borders on the sickening'—From Bikram Singh's review of *Sholay* in *Filmfare*

Sholay had violence well above what the average Hindi cinema audiences were used to in the 1970s. Starting from the train robbery right in the beginning to the gritty shoot-out in the climax, the film is full of violent scenes. But there is hardly any blood. Despite bullets flying thick and fast, bandits and bystanders being cut down every now and then, there is no sign of the diluted version of tomato ketchup that we have now got used to. The first signs of blood are introduced in the very last scenes when Thakur uses his nail-studded shoes to squash Gabbar's hands to a pulp. A major reason for this was to keep the censor board at bay but, as it turned out, the impact was more devastating this way. Because the violence was psychological.

Cutting off a proud man's arms is such a distressing act of violence that one doesn't have to show the severance in all its bloody, gory glory. The horror of a whole family being wiped out is again not linked to the extent of bloodshed. Especially when a child's head is blown off from point-blank range. Even Ahmed's death—a shocking end to a young man with potential—is not shown but symbolized through the killing of an ant.

Each one of these scenes is unimaginably violent without focusing on the actual act of violence.

In many ways, *Sholay* marked the pinnacle of the series of violent films that Salim–Javed were accused of writing. *Sholay*'s violence was a 'choreographed ballet' that was created with the help of mega-budgets and foreign technicians and equipment. However, Salim–Javed's forte was not the elaborately mounted 'fight scene'. In fact, the real speciality of this dynamic duo was conjuring the kind of violence that played on your mind rather than the sort that played out only in front of your eyes.

Salim–Javed focused on creating a context that affected the audience's psyche and made the actual fights seem far more impactful. The physical violence was accentuated by psychological violence, and this was often achieved long before any punches were actually thrown.

Action was no longer a resolution mechanism, a punishment meted out to the villain at the climax. The fight now came right in the initial scenes and was often used to set up the hero's character. And the hero did not fight with his fists alone; he brought his anger and his psychological scars into battle.

In *Deewaar*, when Vijay Verma fights Peter's goons in the famous scene at the dockyard warehouse, we can sense that his manic anger is not just against these goons (with whom he has no history). He is channelling his anger against the father who abandoned him, a society that thought nothing of punishing a little boy for his father's sins, and a system that is failing him and his brother. At the end of it, when his mother asks why he didn't avoid the fight, Vijay's angry retort is exactly what the audience has been thinking all this while. '*Tum chaahti ho main bhi mooh chhupake bhaag jaata*?'[lvii] *Deewaar* had just this one fight scene but the film always comes across as exceedingly violent because in the viewers' minds, Vijay starts getting beaten up the day the disgruntled workers tattoo '*Mera baap chor hai*' on his arm. It is only now that he is able to give it back and begin the process of finding some sort of closure.

This was a common pattern in Salim–Javed's scripts: the action scene would be announced much in advance and the tension kept simmering till it exploded into the actual fight.

In *Zanjeer*, during Inspector Vijay Khanna and Sher Khan's confrontation in the police station, the police officer—in an unprecedented move for a Hindi film hero—kicks the chair the crime boss is about to sit on. Their tussle begins right then with Sher Khan taunting Vijay that it is only because of the safety of the station and the security his uniform affords him that he can dare to do such a thing. Vijay picks up the gauntlet, walks into Sher Khan's 'ilaaka' sans uniform and challenges him to a bout. The high-voltage fight scene actually takes up only a couple of minutes of screen time but it was written as a well-paced, crackling-dialogue-laced event that seems to last longer on-screen and even longer in our memories. It ends with Sher Khan acknowledging the new hero—'*Aaj zindagi mein pehli baar Sher Khan ki sher se takkar hui hai . . .*'—and bringing the episode to a satisfying close.

In *Trishul*, Amitabh Bachchan's devil-may-care character acts in a similar fashion when trying to evict Madho Singh (Shetty) from the land that he has bought. The standard Hindi film action sequence—where the hero beats up and throws out the villain—is preceded by a sequence that builds the tension, with Vijay walking up to Madho Singh and asking him to leave. Then, of course, he returns with an ambulance to pack the beaten villains into. Again, the violence is made memorable by introducing dialogues and other elements that accentuate both the action and the character. In a way, the violence in *Trishul* is set up by the way Vijay is introduced in the first scene where he lights a dynamite fuse with his beedi and calmly walks away from the danger zone. You get an inkling of the impending violence from the manner in which he explains his fearlessness: '*Jisne pachees baras apni maa ko har roz thoda thoda marte dekha ho, use maut se kya dar lagega?*'[lviii]

The most protracted build-up of an action sequence in a Salim–Javed film was in *Kaala Patthar*, where both Vijay (Amitabh Bachchan) and Mangal (Shatrughan Sinha) were presented as diametrical opposites, shown to be getting increasingly angry with each other, and finally pitted against one another in a pitched battle. Incidentally, this fight (which happens just before the interval) is preceded by two near-skirmishes between the two heroes, both triggered by insignificant things like a matchbox and a cup of tea. Both incidents are diffused in the nick of time by Ravi (Shashi Kapoor) but it all adds towards the explosion of the final showdown.

Not all of Salim–Javed's orchestrated fight sequences were serious, though. In *Don*—a film where the mood was more light-hearted—Vijay/Don taunts villain Shaakaal (played by Shetty) repeatedly in a police van. By now the audience knows a fight is coming, which will facilitate the gang's escape and bring about the climax, and it is brought on by a series of wisecracks made about Shetty's supposed cowardice.

In *Deewaar*, *Kaala Patthar* and *Trishul*, as in a few other films, the initial fight is the biggest action sequence of the film; the first two do not even have a 'resolution fight' at the climax, and the one in *Trishul* seems distinctly tamer than the 'ambulance' scenes. As macho heroes became more and more popular in the late 1970s and 1980s, this became a template for action films, where there was always a fight scene to introduce the hero or set him up as one.

Film writer Jai Arjun Singh talks about *Deewaar* but it could well be about some of the other Salim–Javed classics when he says: 'The movie's power draws as much from its silences as from its flaming dialogue, and the writing of Salim–Javed, in conjunction with Bachchan's incomparable performance, take it to heights Indian cinema has rarely touched since. The power of *Deewaar* lies in its ability to make us *feel* the tragedy rather than present it to us all gift-wrapped on a platter.'

Having said this, Salim–Javed did popularize the genre of Hindi film where the 'fight scene' was no longer a pre-climax formality in which the bad guy is given some half-hearted punches as punishment before being taken away by the police. Since most of their scripts were based on the premise of revenge, they brought in the concept of what film historian Kaushik Bhaumik calls 'proportional justice'.

Bhaumik gives the example of *Yaadon Ki Baaraat* where the violent manner in which the villain Shaakaal is killed is similar to the brutal way in which he murdered the heroes' parents. He meets his end near a rail track, a setting reminiscent of the one where the parents are murdered and the three brothers get separated. Even in *Zanjeer*, Vijay's parents are shot dead by Teja on the night of Diwali, the firecrackers drowning out the gunshots. When Vijay arrives at Teja's den to take revenge, it is yet another Diwali night.

In a way, the blood and gore of destroying Gabbar's hands in *Sholay* is also an instance of 'proportional justice'. Gabbar cuts off Thakur's arms, and he in turn, orchestrates the retribution in which Gabbar's hands are rendered useless. The sudden appearance of blood in that scene seemed to underline the completion of this quest for justice.[36]

By and large, the anger of Salim–Javed's heroes was the result of some serious psychological hurt that was as violent on a mental level as their action sequences were on a physical level. Be it the tattoo in *Deewaar* or an 'illegitimate father' in *Trishul* or a distant father in *Shakti*, the resulting psychological violence inflicted on the hero returned to wreak vengeance and this translated into extremely violent action scenes whose impact was far greater than the screen time they occupied.

In many films this impact was further heightened by the intensity that the writers' favourite—Amitabh Bachchan—brought to the fight scenes. Salim Khan says, 'Amitabh Bachchan is physically very weak in real life but he projects aggression amazingly well. When most heroes pick up a gun, they look as if they don't really know how to handle it and the gun may go off

---

[36] Incidentally, the climax of *Sholay* was supposed to have been even more violent, with Gabbar being impaled to death. The Emergency-era censor board refused to allow the depiction of a former police officer taking the law into his own hands. Hence, the death and Thakur's guttural screams were replaced by a tamer version where the police force walked in and arrested Gabbar. The original version is available quite freely on YouTube and is a gut-wrenching watch. Sanjeev Kumar's measured performance throughout the film has a tragic conclusion when he breaks down and cries at his 'victory'.

accidentally. But when Amitabh picks up a gun, it seems that he really means business.'

At a time when the industry had given up on Bachchan, Salim–Javed were the only ones who kept their faith in him. And coincidentally, it was a fight scene in which they noticed the actor for the first time. Bachchan recalls, 'I had a fight scene in *Bombay to Goa* where I fight while I am also chewing a gum. I get punched in the face, roll over and get up, still chewing gum. Salim–Javed had found this scene quite impressive.' A cursory fight scene in a not-so-successful film was what hooked the writers and inspired them to tie their fortunes to that of a struggling actor. And eventually their gamble paid off: the actor became Hindi cinema's first action hero and Salim–Javed were 'credited' for bringing in a wave of action in Hindi films.

As they say, it is all written!

A Political Awakening of Filmi Proportions

'Independent India presented itself as a mixed economy, partaking of both socialism and capitalism. But, argued [economist Jagdish] Bhagwati, it had failed on both counts. It had grown too slowly to qualify as a "capitalist" economy, and by its failure to eradicate illiteracy or reduce inequalities had forfeited any claims of being "socialist"'—Ramachandra Guha in *India After Gandhi*, quoting a work published in 1973

One of the elements of 1970s Hindi cinema was how mainstream films built in political commentary as part of the natural dialogues of characters. For example, even in a comedy like *Khubsoorat* (1980), Rekha's family—who speak only in rhyme for large parts of the movie—refers to Y.B. Chavan's exit from Indira Gandhi's Congress in one of their breakfast-table 'conversations', after reading the newspaper. In *Andaz* (1971), there is mention of a college strike on the matter of 'border disputes with Mysore or Madras'—again issues that were live in the 1960s.

Strictly speaking, none of these political references were linked to the story in any way but they were an interesting way of bringing in some present-day relevance to the goings on in the film. Salim–Javed did not restrict themselves to merely mentioning political events in passing; rather they made strong comments about them, which revealed their consciousness regarding the state of the nation.

In *Haath Ki Safai*, a random passer-by reacts to a petty theft by saying, '*Din dahade chori? Yeh government nahin chal sakti . . .*'[lix] Written in the early 1970s, this was a direct comment on the state of the country and was a throwaway line, with no connection to the plot. Such a political statement is unimaginable today. Even if it gets past the censor board, there is likely to be an avalanche of protests from the parties in power.

The 1970s were a turbulent decade and problems were aplenty. Unemployment had reached record levels and fresh graduates were not finding any work. The public distribution system had collapsed and food availability—especially for the poor—had become a major problem. As a result, there had been sharp increase in crime—most notably, smuggling and black-marketeering. Simultaneously, the Licence Raj and associated protection of interests led to disproportionate assets in the hands of a few, and that increased the gap between the rich and poor significantly.

Salim–Javed touched upon each one of these everyday issues to include a strong message in their films. The situation was normal, the lines were very well constructed, and together this made the overall message memorable. Salim Khan says, 'Vitamin tablets have to be made palatable by a coating of sugar or something similar. Whatever our message was, we put it in a capsule of song, dance, action and entertainment. And this is how cinema has been.'

Unemployment was the issue that most affected Salim–Javed's core constituency—the youth, the demographic with which the Angry Young Man had the maximum resonance. Add to that their personal travails of having to find work and you hit a raw nerve. While the film industry was completely different from the regular corporate sector, Salim and Javed both had to go through endless meetings with producers to find work in their initial days.

One of the common refrains found in their films was acknowledgement of the hard labour—mental and physical—that a job hunt was. In *Trishul*, Vijay asks Geeta what she is doing (after being fired from R.K. Gupta's company) and she replies, '*Jo kuch nahin karte, woh kamaal karte hain . . . aajkal main kamaal kar rahi hoon.*'[lx] In *Chacha Bhatija* too, Sundar says, '*Kaam dhoondhna bhi kaafi mushkil kaam hai*'[lxi]—indicating a high degree of sympathy for the ranks of the educated unemployed.

The other element that the writers touched upon was work experience. Employers wanted experienced candidates but the graduates fresh out of college could not get any till they found a job. In *Shakti*, Vijay goes for a job interview and explains his lack of experience with rather obvious logic, '*Agar insaan ko kaam nahin milega, toh use experience kaise hoga? Yakeen kijiye, main yeh kaam kar sakta hoon.*'[lxii] Even a minor character like Sachin's in *Trishul* echoes the same sentiment during an interview. In both cases, the 'heroic characters' (Kulbhushan Kharbanda and Shashi Kapoor, respectively) take a call to hire them on the basis of their confidence.[37]

---

[37] In *Shakti*, as well as the lesser-known *Aakhri Daao* (starring Jeetendra), the hero displays exemplary confidence during a job interview by replying to the same question—'*Aap iss kaam ko nahin jaante*'—with the same words, '*Aur aap hume nahin jaante!*'[lxiii]

The final—and probably the most frustrating—angle of a job search that they depicted was how the Indian concept of 'sifarish' brought an insidious nepotism into the corporate sector. In *Deewaar*, Ravi is the perfect candidate who seems capable and has all the necessary qualifications, but just as he is about to be given the job, a phone call from 'general manager sahib' tips the scale in favour of an unseen brother-in-law. In a later scene, Ravi decides to apply for a job in the police force but without the 'sifarish' of his future father-in-law who is a senior police officer. In *Trishul*, Sachin also gets a job in his fiancée's family-owned firm without any 'sifarish' and states that quite proudly. This is a reflection of Salim's and Javed's personal beliefs, for neither man 'launched' his children in the film industry, letting them find their own way instead.

Since employment was hard to come by at the time, an alternate career in crime was the natural fallout for many youth. However, Salim–Javed chose to look at both sides of the coin and the circumstances in which a citizen becomes a criminal. Their view was that there were bigger criminals around, operating within the legal framework. *Haath Ki Safai*'s Raju—when being released from prison—gives a short speech about how god-men, businessmen and politicians are all stealing from the people but only the pickpockets get caught.

Thieves in Salim–Javed films were honourable people. '*Choron ke bhi ussool hote hain*' (in *Yaadon Ki Baaraat*) became '*Choron ke hi to ussool hote hain*' (in *Majboor*), hinting that these were good people who had drifted into a life of crime due to extenuating circumstances.

And how extenuating these circumstances could be was explained in *Deewaar* through a long but gripping sequence in which police officer Ravi shoots down a thief only to find that he had stolen a loaf of bread to feed his hungry family. When Ravi goes to meet and apologize to the thief's family, the boy's father (A.K. Hangal) describes in detail their miserable life but also maintains that nothing really justifies crime—'*Hindustan mein hazaron log bhookhe marte hain toh kya sab chor ho jaye?*'[lxiv]—thus summarizing the writers' point of view. Ravi shoots down another criminal in the climax of the same film, who also had justifications for his crime but could not be forgiven either.

In the same scene in *Deewaar*, the thief's mother appears on-screen for one dramatic outburst where she curses the black marketeers who hoard food grains and are driving the prices up artificially. This issue of food distribution, along with the associated problem of adulteration, cropped up many times in Salim–Javed's films. In *Chacha Bhatija*, as frustration mounts in the long line of people at a ration shop, the hero Shankar arrives and berates the owner—'*Tum logon ki tijori mein rakkha hua paisa nahin gina ja sakta, magar garibon ki jism ki pasliyaa zaroor gini ja sakti hai.*'[lxv] (And being the hero that he is, he vows to give up his own black-marketeering racket in movie tickets right then and there.)

This issue of hoarding and adulteration comes up again in *Chacha Bhatija* when Shankar says, '*Dekh raha hoon ki sethon ke dilon mein lalach aur garibon ke chawal mein kankar badhte hi jaa raha hai.*'[lxvi] In fact, '*chawal mein kankar*' is a metaphor that returned again and again in Salim–Javed's films—even after their separation. In *Arjun*, the hero bites into a 'kankar' in his food. And in *Mr India* (where the film's mood was lighter), there is an entire factory of adulteration with different-coloured 'kankars' for different food grains. But it was always a message of hope because in the end the bad guys got their just desserts. As Kabir says at the end of *Immaan Dharam*, '*Aaj ka Hindustan black marketeers, smugglers aur jamaa khoro ko ab ek pal ke liye bhi bardaasht nahin kar sakta.*'[lxvii]

'*Saathiyon, agar is waqt meri awaaz un malikon tak pahuch rahi hai to wo sun le . . . humein yeh shikayat nahin hai ki unke drawing room ke guldaan phoolon se kyon saje hain. Humein yeh shikayat hai ki humare aate ke canastar khaali kyon hain? Humein yeh shikayat nahin ki yeh koyle ki khaaney unke liye sona kyon ugal rahi hain? Humein yeh shikayat hai ki humare hisse mein sirf raakh kyon aati hai?*'[lxviii]

With this speech, given by labour leader Anand Verma (Satyen Kappu) at the beginning of *Deewaar*, Salim–Javed presented the rich–poor divide starkly and created the anger that they would use time and again.

And they depicted it in rousing language. In *Chacha Bhatija*, Shankar resists the attempts of the rich to destroy their slum with the following words: '*Garibon ke jale hue gharon ki raakh ikkathi karne aaye ho, taki apne seth ki chandi ke bartanon ko ghis ke aur chamka sako?*'[lxix]

The resentment among the general public at the yawning gap between the top and bottom strata of 1970s society was repeatedly reflected in many of their scripts, right from *Haathi Mere Saathi* to *Haath Ki Safai* to their more famous films.

This whole nationalist stand comes together exceptionally in *Kaala Patthar*, a film that highlights pretty much every aspect in which India had failed to become a truly socialist or a truly capitalist country.

Dhanraj Puri (Prem Chopra) repeatedly expresses his disgust for the poor and their living conditions (though it is his company's policies that are keeping them in misery). As the rich oppressor, his disregard for the lives of the miners comes across when they discuss incurring a potential loss of Rs 40 lakh if they consider the safety of four hundred miners. Puri tells his accountant, '*Saxena, tumhara hisaab itna kamzor hai mujhe pataa nahin tha.*

Yeh bhi nahin jaante chaalis lakh char sau se bauht zyada hai.[lxx] And follows it up with his description of the 'ideal miner', one who is not brave enough to raise his voice: '*Humare kaam ka wohi mazdoor hai jo maraa maraa jiye aur sar jhukake sab sehta jaaye.*'[lxxi]

On the other hand, we have Vijay who is forever ready to take up the cause of the miners. In one scene, Vijay compares the mines to a giant python that swallows the miners and sucks them dry. Vijay confronts Puri several times in the film but he—as an aftereffect of his earlier experiences—is forever pessimistic about the long-term welfare of the miners.

If Vijay is the face of the angry miner, engineer Ravi is the sympathetic technocrat no less concerned with their fate. In some scenes, his speeches are reminiscent of *Deewaar*'s Anand babu and though he is part of the 'management', he nevertheless intervenes on behalf of the workers and wins them a positive wage settlement.

The third crusader in the film is Anita, a reporter who writes a scathing report about Puri's mines, proposing that they be nationalized. In a conversation, she presents the benefits that miners working in nationalized mines get and through her, the writers make clear their idea for a welfare state.

Kaala Patthar's overall message was a direct consequence of its setting—a coal mine—and the true story on which it was based. Salim–Javed essentially believed in socialist principles and wrote a script that revolved entirely around their belief that industry practices, if monitored and regulated by the government, could ensure a basic lifestyle for all, which, in turn, would have a cascading impact on society, and India would awaken to a better tomorrow.

As *Deewaar*'s Ravi says, '*Subah to uss din hogi jab har kisi ke paas kaam hoga, ghar hoga, koi footpath pe nahin soyega . . .*'[lxxii]

Women of Substance

'Badkismati se mujhe baatein karna bilkul nahin aata'[lxxiii]
—Inspector Vijay Khanna to Mona in *Zanjeer*

With this one line, Amitabh Bachchan killed any hope of romance for his Angry Young Man avatar, heralding an era of violent action as the main draw for Hindi films. Salim–Javed's scripts were the starting point of this period and, indeed, romance was not their main focus. Film historian Kaushik Bhaumik says, 'With their films, women became less important as there were very few women characters. Most of their films have women in peripheral roles. Hindi cinema lost touch with women in the 1970s because it was completely centred around Bachchan and the audiences all turned male.'

Film critic Sukanya Verma counters this by saying, 'Even if not always central to the story, the girls stood out in many of their movies. Look at Hema Malini's feisty acrobat in *Seeta Aur Geeta*, fearless tangewali in *Sholay*, no-nonsense, poised businesswoman in *Trishul* or Zeenat Aman's vendetta-seeking heroine in *Don*, Parveen Babi's independent, unapologetic young woman engaged in a live-in relationship in *Deewaar* or

Waheeda Rehman and Rakhee in *Trishul*, these women are no wallflowers. Strong doesn't always mean vocal.'

Apart from some very memorable women characters, Salim–Javed managed to bring some interesting twists to romance in their scripts. For viewers brought up on saccharine-sweet romances, the writers brought in a very different, almost matter-of-fact sort. For example, Rajesh Khanna was not his usual flamboyantly romantic self in *Haathi Mere Saathi*. There was a distinctly humorous tinge to his courtship. While proposing to Tanuja, he avoids the usual stars-and-moon metaphors of Hindi cinema and makes a joke about it instead.

This was retained even in their later films. In *Dostana*, Zeenat Aman's cloying call to Amitabh Bachchan is met with a cocky arrogance that actually ends with the hero praising his own eyes instead of trying to look for stars in hers. He woos the lady with confidence, invites her on a date where he professes his love, deduces her affection like a police officer and they become a couple!

There are relatively fewer romantic interludes in Salim–Javed films and in most—*Shakti, Zanjeer, Chacha Bhatija, Haath Ki Safai*—romance happens over a series of 'professional meetings'. Be it a serious interaction like *Zanjeer* (where Amitabh Bachchan meets Jaya Bhaduri to take her eyewitness account for a case) or a comic one like *Haath Ki Safai* (where Randhir Kapoor meets Hema Malini to act in a play for her theatre company), romance unfolds 'on the job'.

Speaking for the Angry Young Man, Javed Akhtar explains the character's reticence, 'Vijay's relationship with the Parveen Babi character in *Deewaar*, or his relationship with the Rakhee character in *Trishul*—it is very difficult for him to tell these women that he loves them . . . [It is as if] They [have created] a Deewaar between themselves and their emotions.'

Sometimes, it is easy for the characters to have sex and use physical intimacy as a stepping stone towards love and mental intimacy. And that brings out something quite unique. What Salim–Javed pioneered in their films was the non-judgemental, mature sexual relationship between two consenting adults. Mainstream Hindi cinema was always made for the 'family audience' and sex was always cloaked in (now laughable) symbols, and almost always associated with sin. Therefore, you had shots of flowers touching and songs shot in the rain to denote intimacy. Sex (including rape) was seen as a 'loss of honour' for the woman and usually ended with punishment in the form of widowhood or ostracization.[38]

In *Trishul*, Shanti (Waheeda Rehman) is shown as modern working woman of intelligence and integrity who approaches her relationship with R.K. Gupta (Sanjeev Kumar) without being the coy wallflower audiences were used to seeing in Hindi films. In a (sort of) romantic scene, the conversation between the two is worth paying attention to:

- '*Lo, ab chai piyo.*'
- '*Tum kehti ho to chai pee leta hoon. Lekin chai peene ka baad mujhe bahut bure bure khayal aate hain.*'
- '*Tum ko sivai in baton ke kuch aata hai?*'[lxxiv]

In their usual realistic style of dialogues, the writers conveyed that the couple have been having consensual sex for some time and Shanti is a willing partner. The subsequent scenes also establish the depth of her involvement with R.K. and that it is not merely a physical relationship she is in.

---

[38] Hindi cinema specialized in 'virginal prostitutes' as several mainstream films have depicted sex workers whose primary draw was their music, without even a hint of sex. *Devdas*'s Chandramukhi (Vyjayanthimala), *Pyaasa*'s Gulabo (Waheeda Rehman) and *Amar Prem*'s Pushpa (Sharmila Tagore) are three such iconic characters among many others. This was an accepted template.

Much has been said about Sunita (Parveen Babi) in *Deewaar*—a 'premium escort' who is in the profession without any apparent justification. She has no brother to put through college or a mother suffering from tuberculosis. She seems to be a carefree, modern working woman approaching her job with a high degree of competence. (Her flirtatious conversation with Bachchan in the bar is masterfully written.) One could argue that her characterization glosses over the real horrors of a prostitute's life but that was not the point of the story. Bachchan's Vijay does not move around in circles where he will find a homely, middle-class girl anyway and the writers did not burden Sunita with homely, middle-class attributes. While the characters' physical relationship is much discussed, their deepening bond is also clearly indicated in the lines Salim–Javed wrote. Sunita is the only person Vijay confides in about his terrible childhood and tormented life, which indicates a high level of trust between the two. Javed Akhtar articulates, 'Heroes like Vijay have great respect for women. But they are too shy, too introverted to show their emotions. Or accept their emotions. The only way that people who have been hurt very badly save themselves is by hiding their emotions.'

Incidentally, the writers also broke the standard Hindi film trope of the unwed heroine getting pregnant on the first night she sings a song in the rain with the hero. *Trishul*'s Shanti and *Deewaar*'s Sunita (as well as *Shakti*'s Roma) get pregnant during the course of an extended relationship and that seems absolutely normal.

And talking of normal women, working women were commonplace in Salim–Javed's films. As more and more women started entering the workforce in the 1970s, both middle-of-the-road and art-house films started depicting middle-class working women. Salim–Javed's were among the first mainstream Hindi films to have heroines in a variety of professions. In fact, nearly all their heroines had an occupation and seldom were they merely daughters of rich men. Sometimes, there was a quirky angle to their professions—Basanti the tangewali (*Sholay*) and Seema Sohni the undercover reporter (*Mr India*), for example. These women were usually shown to be good at their jobs and having strong moral values.

The duo's first film—*Andaz*—has an unwed mother going about the business of raising her child without a fuss and becoming a working woman almost immediately after her fiancé's death. Where *Andaz*'s Sheetal (Hema Malini) differs from a more famous unwed mother—Sharmila Tagore of *Aradhana*—is that there is no air of sacrifice. Incidentally, her first appearance in the film is when she arrives as a teacher in Ravi's (Shammi Kapoor) daughter's school. Her own son and, thus, her single-mother status are revealed later, thereby making her a professional and not an object of sympathy or scorn (which are usually the emotions attached to unwed mothers in Hindi films).

Two very strong women characters appear in *Trishul*—Geeta (Rakhee), R.K. Gupta's secretary (who was instrumental in running his empire), and Sheetal Verma (Hema Malini), the general manager of a large corporation. While *Trishul* is the story of Three Faces of Man, both these female characters are excellent foils to the heroes even though they aren't central to the story. There were some very interesting throwaway lines to sketch these two characters. Geeta is also called 'Computer' as she seems to know everything about her boss' empire and is portrayed as an honest, upright professional who does not compromise her ethics even in the face of heavy monetary inducement. Sheetal, on the other hand, is the modern woman who plays tennis and golf to keep fit and is not coy about accepting lunch invitations from flirting rakes.

Hema Malini's most famous working-woman act is obviously as the batty tangewali in *Sholay*, who knows exactly how to earn her daily bread, keep unwanted suitors at bay, and when to get married and retire to a life of comfort. And she has a ready answer to explain her stand on women's equality: '*Dhanno ghodi hoke agar tanga kheench sakti hai toh Basanti ladki hoke tanga kyon nahin chala sakti hai?*'[lxxv]

Kaala Patthar again has two idealistic working women. Dr Sudha Sen (Rakhee) is the lady doctor who gives up a more lucrative city practice in order to work in a clinic meant exclusively for hapless coal miners. Quite tellingly, she takes over charge from a male doctor (Sanjeev Kumar) who is frustrated with the job and leaves after a very short stint. Anita (Parveen Babi) is an investigative journalist who reports on the malpractices by the mine owners and faces the wrath of Dhanraj Puri, whose guest she is. She stands up to him with an indignant righteousness and refuses to toe the official line, thus becoming a worthy partner to Shashi Kapoor's idealistic engineer. Neither character wears their beliefs on their sleeve and is quite happy to go about their business quietly, taking only short breaks for romantic interludes.

Not all women were perfect but they seemed to listen to their conscience better than the men. *Zanjeer*'s Mala (Jaya Bhaduri) is a single working woman who manages to keep the wolves at bay with a mix of aggression and street smarts. When offered a large sum of money for not testifying against a criminal, she initially accepts it but after a while, the murder of innocent children—the crime to which she was an eyewitness—is too much to bear and she returns to testify. Her justification for her unethical wavering as well as her return to honesty are both very normal.

Don's Roma (Zeenat Aman) infiltrates a gang of international criminals to take avenge her brother's murder. In Hindi films, where any women in the villains' dens were restricted to molls, holding a glass of wine or dancing a cabaret, Roma is completely different from that ornamental variety. She becomes a gangster herself. She trains to become a karate expert and is a pro at handling firearms, not to mention that she has the energy of a '*junglee billi*'.

Talking about unusual professions, we must now talk of *Seeta Aur Geeta*—Salim–Javed's only heroine-oriented film and one of the most rollicking performances given by an Indian film actress. Hema Malini owned this film from the get-go, playing a feisty acrobat by day and a docile (quasi-) housewife *also* by day. It forever changed her position in the film industry as in this film she did all the things normally reserved for the hero— comedy, action, romance, dialoguebaazi—along with all the things usually assigned to the heroine.

Bollywood buff Carla Miriam Levy (aka @filmigeek) says, 'I think there is a good feminist reading of the movie, or at least of some of its elements. For example, Sanjeev Kumar's character *thinks* he wants a seedhi-saadhi Hindustani ladki, until he meets and interacts with a real woman who has some real energy, and then his mind is changed about what kind of woman he wants.'

However, Javed Akhtar has an interesting counterpoint to the 'feminist narrative' of the film. He says, 'If I were to write a script today, my women characters would be even more mature, more independent, more liberated because my perspective on the question [women's status in society] has become slightly clearer. When I see *Seeta Aur Geeta*, there's a scene that makes me cringe. Geeta, who's actually Seeta, has started cooking extremely well and sews clothes. So everyone thinks she's become a model girl as a result. Today, I'd write her character very differently. The way I wrote the Seeta character then wasn't intentional, but it came from my understanding at that time.'

This is a remarkable admission by the writer about the regressive undertones in their work. A more overt depiction of regressive values happens in *Chacha Bhatija*, in which the main characters yearn for a male child, wives are docile to the point of being servile and the husband is set on a pedestal and worshipped. In *Dostana*, matters worsen, and the victim of an instance of sexual harassment is blamed. When Sheetal (Zeenat Aman, flaunting her gorgeous figure in a stunning bikini-sarong outfit) is teased by a roadside Romeo, she catches him and brings him to the police station. Police officer Vijay promptly arrests the guy but offers a rather old-fashioned view to a modern woman and criticizes her choice of clothes as too provocative.

- '*Kuch farz ladkiyon ka bhi hai . . . Agar aise kapde pehen kar aap bahar sadak pe niklengi to gundo ki seeti nahin bajegi to kya mandir ki ghanti bajegi?*'
- '*Kya kharabi hai in kapdon mein?*'
- '*Bahut kam hai.*'[lxxvi]

The woman being a doormat and the modern woman shamed for her lifestyle were both common elements of society and Hindi cinema of the 1970s, but one cannot help but feel a tinge of regret that Salim–Javed—otherwise known for remarkable women in their scripts—did not do better.

When asked if Salim–Javed's notions of a strong woman were dated, Carla Miriam Levy says, 'Perhaps they are, but only in the sense that they were written to be relevant in their time, and this time is not that time. I don't think they are any more or less dated than Vijay, the Angry Young Man they created. He had particular relevance and resonance in the time of the Emergency—today's heroes have little of that anger and anti-establishment force to them—and yet he continues to be a moving and engaging character.'

Missing Father, Iconic Mother

'Aur khush kismati se woh meri maa hain' [lxxvii]
—Inspector Ravi Verma in *Deewaar*

Salim Khan lost his mother to tuberculosis when he was nine; Javed Akhtar to an autoimmune disease when he was eight. Due to the nature of their work, both their fathers had been somewhat distant even before their mothers died. As a police officer in a problematic region of Madhya Pradesh (which included dacoit-infested areas), Salim's father had to travel a lot. Javed's father had to remain underground for extended periods of time because of his affiliation with the Communist Party, which had been declared unlawful by the British government.

Both mothers—in the short time they had with their sons—left indelible marks on them. Salim still recalls his mother's strict lessons in honesty on one hand and how, on the other, she was not able to be with her children due to her illness. Salim's father also passed away within a few years of his mother's death, just as he was beginning to forge a relationship with his youngest son. Thereafter, it was Salim's elder brothers (and faithful family retainers) who took care of him till he became an adult.

Javed's mother Safia was a poet and a college teacher, and held very progressive values. After her death he was sent to live with relatives. Javed was upset with his father for being absent during his childhood. The friction between the two increased when he arrived in Bombay after his graduation to stay with his father. Jan Nisar Akhtar had remarried by then and Javed was unable to live with his father and stepmother for more than a week. He explains that his past baggage was also responsible for him exiting the household, 'I was nineteen when I came to Bombay. I couldn't get along with my father. Perhaps because we had lived so much apart and there were so many unresolved misunderstandings and hurts.' Javed stayed on in Bombay, continuing to work for pitifully small amounts but he never let people know he was famous lyricist Jan Nisar Akhtar's son.

Having spent their childhoods without parental guidance and protection, both men came to depend heavily on their circle of friends for physical and mental sustenance, some of them even becoming mentors for brief periods of time. And many of the duo's experiences found their way into their films.

Deewaar opens with the two sons hero-worshipping their idealist father. The turning point of this traditional relationship comes when, unable to bear the burden of his professional ignominy, the father deserts his family. Vijay—having borne the brunt of the wrath intended for the father—turns away from him and becomes silently resentful of his behaviour. This concept of the 'missing father' was not unique to *Deewaar* (though, admittedly, it was portrayed the best in that film).

Each one of Salim–Javed's films—without exception—has a missing father. Some reviewers have interpreted this as a symbol of the state that was increasingly missing in action, leaving hapless citizens to fend for themselves in burgeoning inflation, corruption and criminalization. But a more direct reason could be the two writers' own traumatic childhood experiences. Salim Khan says, 'I did not lack any material comfort when I was growing up but I cannot call my childhood happy because I did not get the love of my parents.' Salim left his inheritance in Indore and came to Bombay facing an uncertain future—much like the young Shankar (Dharmendra) of *Chacha Bhatija*, who leaves his elder brother's house after his beloved bhabhi is evicted.

The lead characters in Salim–Javed's films have fathers who were either killed (*Zanjeer, Yaadon Ki Baaraat, Kranti*) or who died early, leaving the hero to fend for himself (*Haathi Mere Saathi, Seeta Aur Geeta, Haath Ki Safai, Majboor*). However, the most memorable films were the ones in which the father was alive but had an adversarial relationship with the son.

In *Deewaar*, the father (Satyen Kappu) abandons his son. In *Chacha Bhatija* and *Trishul*, he (Rehman and Sanjeev Kumar respectively) deserts the wife, thus depriving the son of his identity. In *Kaala Patthar*, the father (Iftekhar) takes a principled stand and refuses to accept his disgraced son. And, in the most contentious relationship of all, in *Shakti*, the father (Dilip Kumar) puts his duty as a police officer above his son and alienates him for life. Even when his son is an adult, he shows little respect for his abilities, though he loves him. The relationship ends with the policeman father putting duty first once again.

Even in their later films (after separation), the father continued to be a missing character. The two brothers in *Naam* have to fend for themselves and their widowed mother. Though the father is physically present in *Arjun*, he is unable to protect his son against both internal (stepmother) and external attacks (the local dadas). As the hero grows in strength, the father just vanishes from the scene.

The exact antithesis of the father—missing or antagonistic—was the iconic mother, an epitome of virtue and strength.

Whenever the father was missing, the mother also faced great difficulties but she never turned away from her husband. When his co-workers are bullying Anand Verma's sons, they are also taunting his wife Sumitra Devi, but she does not waver from her devotion. When the younger son speaks about his father's cowardice, the mother reacts violently at first and then explains, '*Unhone jo kuch kiya, hamare liye kiya. Taki hum zinda reh sake, jee sake.*'[lxxviii] Obviously, she understands that her husband was under duress and puts him on a pedestal.

It would be interesting to note here how Javed recalls his mother projecting his father to him. 'While my father was alive she never let us feel abandoned by him. She always made us proud of our father who was a great poet, a communist. She explained that he wasn't at home because of this great cause. We used to hero-worship him, but after she died and we started living with our maternal relatives, I did feel let down by him. And that created a kind of resentment in me, an anger and a who-cares attitude.' The feelings Javed had for his father seem to mirror those *Deewaar*'s Vijay has about his father.

The mother in *Shakti* is very similar to the mother in *Deewaar*—in terms of the balance they have between the love for their sons and their moral sense. In addition, she is the bridge between the two men in her life—both of whom open up to her but never to each other. She dutifully represents both sides and loves both of them equally, taking sides only when her son crosses over to the dark side. Film critic Sukanya Verma feels Sheetal (Rakhee) in *Shakti* probably leaned too much towards her husband. 'I wish her commitment to her husband wasn't so unquestioning. She could have bridged the gap of growing resentment and lack of communication between her husband and son long ago and saved their lives from irreversible catastrophe.' The ultimate tragedy of this character is that father and son finally open up while weeping uncontrollably at her funeral, but even that is not enough to form a lasting bridge between the two.

Much has been said about *Trishul*'s Shanti (Waheeda Rehman), whose son rises to destroy his father because he abandoned her. In a departure from convention, Shanti in fact brings up her son to repay her debt ('*Maa teri hoon, mera karz chukana hoga*') and presumably take revenge against R.K. Gupta. But Vijay's lines—after her death—suggest that it was she who had been stopping him from targeting his father and that barrier no longer existed. Nevertheless, Shanti's strengths as a woman and a mother are remarkable.

There is another mother in *Trishul* who usually goes unnoticed. R.K. Gupta's mother (played by Sudha Chopra) is the pragmatic mother, whose fierce ambition pushes her son to abandon his middle-class fiancée and marry a millionaire's daughter instead. She is the one who spots the 'opportunity' for her son, and in a telling piece of dialogue she 'sacrifices' the life of comfort a daughter-in-law like Shanti would have given her. She believes her son's shot at a business empire is worth much more than that and, in a way, precipitates the rest of the film.

Although the fathers were missing in their films, Salim–Javed created some very memorable 'surrogate fathers' for their heroes in their scripts.

When *Deewaar*'s Vijay is polishing shoes on the pavements of Bombay, a man spots his potential and eventually lays the tracks for this '*lambi race ka ghoda*'[lxxix] to run on. Davar sahib (Iftekhar) is the smuggler who is willing to place his bets on a dock worker who is—in a way—hungry to prove himself to figures of authority. And Vijay, in turn, is willing to give his life for this father figure who pulled him out of the gutter. Kulbhushan Kharbanda's character in *Shakti* was written along similar lines. This Vijay considers him to be more important than his own father because this criminal had helped him when his father had refused.

Zanjeer's Sher Khan (Pran) starts off by challenging Vijay to prove his mettle but once he has done so, Sher Khan becomes his greatest friend and guardian, helping him emotionally as well as financially. *Majboor*'s Michael (Pran) too has a similar relationship with the hero, though his role was shorter. Here was a man willing to go to any length to ensure another man was not wrongfully convicted. Sometimes, the 'surrogate father' is the leader of a gang of pickpockets (*Haath Ki Safai*) and our hero, his favourite student, whom he raises with care and affection. And sometimes, he is a respectable science professor (*Mr India*) who has seen the hero's father getting killed and is carrying a secret invention that only he knows of. As the flamboyant hero (Rajesh Khanna) makes an exit in *Andaz*, a more practical one (Shammi Kapoor) enters and establishes himself as the 'father' whom the unwed mother's son can idolize.

When Javed had just come to Bombay and had turned away from his father, Sahir Ludhianvi became a 'father figure' and helped him in many ways. Even Salim was helped by many such 'seniors' when he was fending for himself. As both of them fought for a foothold in a ruthless industry, these people mentored them and helped them off on the path of success. These people returned—or rather, were immortalized—in their scripts as surrogate fathers.

Dialoguebaazi

'"It's very easy to write in difficult language but it's very difficult to write in easy language because you have to have tremendous command over language to put an intricate or complicated idea into simple words." In my own writing, I have tried to develop a diction which is simple so it communicates, it reaches people'—Javed Akhtar quoting his father Jan Nisar Akhtar's advice to him

Javed Akhtar has often talked about being influenced by a not-so-lofty branch of literature. 'Like many other people, I had a weakness for a good line. I'll say that I was influenced to some extent by the modern American novel. Not great literature, to be honest, but bestsellers, paperbacks. They taught me one thing: precision. One-liners. Saying things in a few words, making an art of understatement.' And this is so well borne out in almost every Salim–Javed film.

Ravi (Amitabh Bachchan) barges into a room where Mr Rai (Madan Puri) is closeted in with his mistress and asks for information. Rai refuses to tell him anything and threatens to call the police for disturbing an honourable man like this.

'*Main ek izzatdaar shaadi shuda aadmi hoon . . .*' he bristles.
Ravi drawls, '*Police ko inform mat kijiye. Varna na aap izzatdaar
rahenge aur naa shaadi shuda . . .*'[lxxx] This line—and indeed the
script of *Majboor*—is in the best traditions of American pulp
fiction where pithy epigrams and sharp comebacks energize
the storyline. Salim–Javed were big fans of the genre and
their voracious reading obviously helped them create dramatic
situations where such lines–flourished.

Writer–director Sriram Raghavan has his own favourite
of this genre. 'And in a film [*Deewaar*] full of memorable
lines, I must mention Vijay's first meeting with Samant, his
first assignment. He sees Samant and his goons entering a
lift. Vijay stops the closing doors of the lift with his foot.
The gang stares suspiciously at him. Moving lift. Suddenly
Vijay stops the lift midway. The goons pull out their guns in
a jiffy. Vijay says relax, I want to talk business with Samant
sahib. Samant says if you want to talk business come to my
office. Vijay says: "*Suna hai lift ke darwazon ke kaan nahin
hote . . .*"[lxxxi] Why don't we hear such dialogue today?' With
this one line, we get a glimpse of Vijay's intelligence and
daredevilry, and realize that the dock worker has neatly fit
into the world of smugglers.

Salim Khan repeatedly uses film-maker Alexander Korda's
quote, 'Film dialogue should be like a poor man's telegram', to
drive home the same point—that lines need not be long and/or
bombastic to be considered good.

Javed Akhtar says, 'Exaggeration is traditionally accepted in
literature. In the theatre and in cinema, we nearly always had
lengthy dialogues that were full of similes, full of metaphors,
an overdose of melodrama. In films, every time the characters
would try to describe his emotions, he'd go into great detail. We
didn't do that. Our dialogue was intense but crisp.'

One of their biggest strengths was writing simple lines that became memorable in context. Salim Khan laughs when he says, 'People are repeating lines like "*Kitnay aadmi thay*" or "*Holi kab hai*" and those have become very famous. But what are they really? They are not great lines!' Javed Akhtar explains this further, using what is probably their best-known and most-repeated dialogue. 'Ravi could have said all sorts of things, for example, "*Aaj mere paas Maa ka pyaar hai, mujhe yeh mil gaya, woh mil gaya*". By contrast, take Vijay, who is providing the platform for this punchline. He has many lines before Ravi makes his mark with his single statement. And it works!'

This felicity in creating short, sharp punchlines was complemented by their equally strong ability to write well-constructed scenes that were either a give-and-take between two people or a long monologue establishing a complex emotion.

The antithesis of *Deewaar*'s '*Mere paas maa hai*' is the mandir scene from the same film, where Vijay confronts God with an angry monologue. The scene builds from Vijay's atheist angst that is evident right from his childhood when he refuses to enter the temple. It is only when his mother is critically ill that he finally walks into the temple and confronts God for the injustice done to his mother.

Another equally famous monologue is Gabbar Singh's first scene in *Sholay*. Starting from the shaming of three hapless cronies to bragging about his notoriety to conducting a totally unpredictable execution, the monologue—written in a curious mix of dialects and unusual words—was like a roller-coaster ride. You never knew where Gabbar was going and that scene set the pace for the villain's crazy unpredictability. And yes, it ended with yet another crisp punchline—'*Jo darr gaya, samjho mar gaya!*'[lxxxii]

While Gabbar's was an iconic scene, even a lesser-known one like the jailer's conversation with Thakur is a great example of how the writers set up two characters to feed off of each other's dialogues and throw some memorable lines (though they got lost in a dialogue fest like *Sholay*).

> — '*Thakur sahib, main yeh to nahin jaanta ki aapko kya kaam hai lekin itna zaroor jaanta hoon ki yeh dono kisi kaam ke nahin.*'
> — '*Agar ek taraf in mein yeh kharabiyaan hain to doosri taraf kuch khoobiyan bhi hain.*'
> — '*Khota sikka to dono hi taraf se khota hota hai.*'
> — '*Sikke aur insaan mein shayad yehi farq hai . . . woh badmaash hain lekin bahadur hain, khatarnaak hain isliye ki ladna jaante hain, bure hain magar insaan hain.*'[lxxxiii]

This ability to construct a longish passage of words that built up a certain mood was something Salim–Javed had right till the very end. In *Shaan*—not considered to be a great script—one line stands out in the scene between Vijay (Amitabh Bachchan) and Sunita (Parveen Babi). Exiting a hotel after stealing a priceless necklace, Vijay compliments Sunita by saying, '*Soch raha hoon aapke gale ki taarif karoon ya aapke haathon ki, aapki awaaz ki taarif karoon ya aapke andaz ki, apni jeet ki baat karoon ya aapke haar ki.*'[lxxxiv] Fantastic! But this was not the only clever line in *Shaan*, which had a surfeit of them. In fact, in this scene itself, Vijay and Sunita carry on a conversation that crackles with chemistry.

If one of *Shaan*'s strengths was the characters' cleverness, it was the film's weakness as well—since all the characters spoke in a similar style. This was a result of the jadedness that had crept in to their later scripts and certainly not how they planned their characters.

Javed Akhtar says, 'When you listen to people, you should notice the particular style they have of speaking, what stress they place on different words. You remember such phrases and expressions, and how a person constructs a sentence. Then you imagine your character speaking as a person who might be a composite of different people you've met.' Different kinds of speech for different characters mean a distinct character graph for each, making even similar characters in different films stand out.

We all remember *Sholay*'s Basanti as the talkative working girl who had a lot to say and did so in her typical brand of chatter. Hema Malini played a somewhat similar role in *Chacha Bhatija*, where she was Mala, a country bar owner. She had a set way of delivering clever lines—'*Tu case karegi to main suitcase . . .*', and '*Tere saare tension ko pension de doongi*'[lxxxv]— that not only distinguished the character from all the others in the same film, but also from the earlier roles they had written for Hema.

In *Immaan Dharam*, Rekha played a Tamilian and had a substantial number of lines in Tamil when she was speaking to other people from her home state. The writers planned this right at the script stage, using Rekha's mother tongue to good effect.

In *Seeta Aur Geeta*, foreign-returned doctor Ravi (Sanjeev Kumar) often starts speaking in English, while the upstart cousin—a shallow college girl—also uses a smattering of English but her words are more basic. Roadside performers Raaka and Geeta use typical tapori lingo; their language has a different tempo and meter from the 'upper-class' characters in the film.

In *Haath Ki Safai*, the use of 'local colour' is taken a step further when Shankar (Vinod Khanna) greets a French smuggler in French.

Another element that the duo did very well was the changing speaking styles for characters as they evolved during the course of a film. In the first scene in *Trishul*, R.K. Gupta (Sanjeev Kumar) is a relatively junior employee in the company and expresses his solution in a somewhat diffident manner—'*Is tarah aaraam se kaam kaise chalega? Aap beshaq dus pandrah aadmi zyada le lijiye lekin kaam waqt par ho jaana chahiye . . .*'[lxxxvi]—though you can sense his impatience. But by the time he becomes a tycoon, his confidence and impatience have both peaked. In his first scene the older R.K. Gupta barks into the phone—'*I don't want any bloody excuses. Just get the work done. Labour double kar do.*'

In a more famous example, Mafia boss *Don* speaks in a clipped style and exudes ruthlessness while street performer Vijay—though identical in appearance—has an accent straight out of eastern UP by the banks of the Ganga. When Vijay impersonates Don, their languages merge but the '*Ganga kinarewala*' language returns later in the film to build a nice story about the character's predicament—explained by a one-liner, '*Jaise dhobi ka kutta, na ghar ka na ghaat ka!*'

In *Kaala Patthar*, the two leading characters—Vijay (Amitabh Bachchan) and Mangal (Shatrughan Sinha)—have two very distinct speaking styles that pit them against each other right from the beginning. Interestingly, there are occasional glimpses of Vijay's hidden past as the disgraced naval captain in his outbursts in English: 'Pain is my destiny and I cannot avoid it.'

And in the mother of all scripts, every set of contrasting characters has very different speaking styles. Thakur's measured tone is countered by Gabbar's slightly insane ramblings; Jai's sardonic one-liners are matched by Viru's garrulous banter; and Basanti's non-stop chatter is a contrast to Radha's silences. Even bit parts like Imam sahib (A.K. Hangal), Jailer (Asrani) and Soorma Bhopali (Jagdeep) have distinctly different speaking styles that make the story more interesting.

The character graphs led to some very memorable '*takiya kalaam*s,' a pet phrase that is usually repeated several times by a character.[39] Asrani's '*Angrezon ke zamane ka jailer*'[lxxxvii] is probably the most famous such phrase that has stuck on despite his character having screen time of just a few minutes. But nevertheless, many of their characters had one such line that served as a quirky reminder of their nature and brought a smile to the lips. In *Haathi Ki Safai*, Raju (Randhir Kapoor) had a cocky '*Kyun, kya khayal hai?*' to go with his every line.

Often, even the villains had a phrase like this. In *Chacha Bhatija*, Laxmidas (Jeevan) accompanies his treacherous behaviour towards his employer with an ironic '*Maine aap ka namak khaya hai*'[lxxxviii] while in *Kranti*, Shambhu Singh (Prem Chopra) underlines his two-faced behaviour with '*Shambhu ka dimaag do dhaari talwar hai.*'[lxxxix]

These are certainly not Salim–Javed's best-known lines but they are an interesting indicator of the thought that went into the creation of memorable characters. As they understood audience psychology really well, the duo packed their scripts with these interludes that were not critical to the plot but nevertheless increased the enjoyment and repeat value of the film.

Due to the nature of many of their stories—families separating, brothers becoming estranged and then dramatically reuniting—Salim–Javed often brought in situations of heightened irony. The audience (and sometimes one participant

---

[39] One of their most repeated lines is from *Don*—'*Don ka intezar to gyarah mulkon ki police kar rahi hai lekin Don ko pakadna mushkil hi nahin, namumkin hai.*' The impact of this line is such that it feels like it was Don's signature line and repeated several times in the film. Actually, it was just said once.

of a conversation) knew of the relationship and the exchange was full of 'loaded statements'.

In *Haath Ki Safai*, the famous line of one-upmanship, '*Bachche, tum jis school mein padhte ho, hum uske headmaster reh chuke hain . . .*' is followed by a smart exchange between the two brothers separated since childhood. Shankar (Vinod Khanna) catches Raju (Randhir Kapoor) in the act of stealing his wallet and says the (now famous) line. He then follows it up with an allusion to the photo in the wallet that will eventually unite the brothers. And Raju ends the scene with yet another loaded statement: '*Ye to apna bhi bada bhai nikla.*'[xc]

The separated brothers are seen coming together once again in *Chacha Bhatija* when Shankar (Dharmendra) bumps into his elder brother Teja (Rehman) at the cinema where he sells tickets in black. When admonished by the elder brother (who does not recognize him), Shankar says '*Chhota hoon isi liye chup hoon, bhaisahab,*' and then returns his wallet, which Teja had accidentally dropped. '*Ye to sirf batua hai, bhaisahab. Aap khud kab, kahan, kitna gir gaye . . .*'[xci]

Probably the most famous such exchange takes place in *Trishul*, when Vijay (Amitabh Bachchan) saves R.K. Gupta's daughter, Babli (Poonam Dhillon), from an accident and is injured while doing so. He comes to R.K. Gupta's home with Babli, where father and son shake hands and R.K. Gupta's hand is smeared with Vijay's blood. Vijay says, '*Theek se saaf kijiyega varna koi dekhne wala samjhega ki aapke haath kisi ke khoon se range hue hain.*' And R.K. Gupta replies, '*Maine jab apne haath pe khoon dekha to ek second ke liye maine samjha mera apna hi khoon hai. Baad mein pata chala tum zakhmi ho.*'[xcii] This too is a masterfully written scene where a regular conversation alludes to Vijay's mother who died bitter and angry after R.K. Gupta abandoned her, and Vijay's own relationship with him—except he doesn't know about it yet.

By all accounts, Salim–Javed brought in a very modern sensibility to their characters and the way they behaved or spoke. Moving away from the exaggerated, theatrical notions that typified all emotions in Hindi cinema, they brought in a more urbane, understated way of dealing with them. Hence, their dialogues—in most cases—were very real, even when conveying something very heroic. In *Deewaar*, for example, a dock worker calmly reminds a millionaire smuggler about an incident from many years ago and then drawls, '*Main aaj bhi phenke hue paise nahin uthata.*'

This and many other such lines elicited a very different kind of audience response, completely unlike the typical exultation or tearfulness. In many of their early films, the characters and their lines were so radically altered from what the audience was used to that cinema halls would be completely silent; the exclamations were more of surprise than anything else (*Sholay* and *Zanjeer*, for example). Their dialogues were sharp, simple and fit their situations perfectly. In a way, Salim–Javed revolutionized Hindi film dialogues—the way they were written and the way the audience expected them to be.

Hindi film buff K.Y. Thomas, who was an avid cine-goer in the 1970s, remembers Salim–Javed's dialogues serving another purpose. He says, 'There used to be radio programmes that played short audio snippets from forthcoming films and invariably Salim–Javed's films had dialogues that peaked our curiosity. I did not know them by name then but now I remember all their lines from radio programmes that made me want to see the films.'

Lines that filled memories; lines that filled seats. What more can you ask from a writer?

God in the Details

'Life is strange. Sometimes if you look back, you feel like editing your life, rewriting it. You want to change Scene 12 which is less pleasant, but the story is so well knit, you realize Scene 32, which is the highlight of the story, will also have to vanish. It is not possible to retain Scene 32 because it has some connection with Scene 12'— Javed Akhtar talking about his childhood

What Javed said about his life is also true for Salim–Javed's scripts. Even in the weakest of their scripts, a Scene 32 would not have been possible without a Scene 12, in which it had its genesis. And it wasn't only the links between scenes—every small character had a name, every location had a landmark (often with directions to get there), every motivation had a backstory.

Aakhri Daao begins in the offices of a safe-manufacturing company. Ravi (Jeetendra) is a consultant with the company who has just managed to open their latest safe in seven minutes. He now advises the company's engineer on how to make the design and actually talks about levers and making some part more compact and so on. These simple details—unlikely to have any connection to a real safe's design—established Ravi's expertise in safe designing, his modest demeanour and hinted at the crux of the film.

Deewaar's Vijay (Amitabh Bachchan) is the proverbial '*lambi race ka ghoda*', christened so by smuggling kingpin, Davar (Iftekhar). The scene in which this epithet is delivered begins with two men—Davar and Jaichand (Sudhir)—buying two race books from a stall before getting their shoes polished. In a crisp bit of conversation, Davar is established as the expert on races, especially on horses that run the first half of the race slowly but leave everyone behind once they pick up speed. Their shoes shined, they toss a coin to the shoesshine boy which falls on the ground. Salim–Javed's script has the boy Vijay (Master Alankar), snap back about the way in which he has been paid and thus get labelled as the '*lambi race ka ghoda*'.

Trishul's characters talked about cement and steel quotas, meetings with lawyers, hobbies of the rich and famous and other such details. Geeta (Rakhee) rattles off file numbers and exact payment details to vendors, all of which add little nuggets of realism to the script. One can argue that much of these 'high finance' conversations are not technically accurate but in the popular format, it was enough to give a very real feel of the corporate world to the common man.

Salim–Javed did not create the lost-and-found formula nor were they its most famous exponents. However, they always managed to insert an innocuous detail in the initial part of the story that would be picked up in the latter part as a vital clue.

In *Haath Ki Safai*, the connecting link between the lost brothers is a photograph (of the two of them as children). But how would two street urchins get a photograph taken? The writers built in a scene where the younger brother Raju (who grows up to be Randhir Kapoor) steals a foreigner's Polaroid camera. When his elder brother Shankar (later played by Vinod

Khanna) finds out, they run back to the station to return the camera. The grateful tourist clicks a picture of the two of them and gives it to Shankar. This small sequence not only creates the 'lost-and-found link' for the film, it also establishes the contrasting characters of the two brothers.

In both *Yaadon Ki Baaraat* and *Haath Ki Safai*, a train separates the brothers. In the former, it is a relatively simple matter of one brother unable to hop on to a departing train. In the latter, the whole drama is elaborately orchestrated with the two brothers getting on to two different bogies of a goods train, which are separated in the night while they are asleep.

Salim–Javed also invested considerable thought into the names of their characters, even the supporting ones. When asked about the sound of a character's name, Javed Akhtar gives an example: 'Take the name Davar. Davar is an Indian name. Because it starts with a "D" and ends with an "R", it has a certain ring of Western sophistication . . . So crisp. It's possible that a villager may be called Davar. But I wouldn't give a villager such a name, neither would I name a paan-eating man Davar.'

When *Sholay*'s Mausi exclaims to a villager, '*Arre kaise haan kar doon, Dinanathji?*'[xciii] you realize the nondescript villager could have only been a Dinanath. Just as Viju Khote—in black clothes and sporting a thick moustache—could only have been a Kaalia!

Not only characters, every place got a name too. *Sholay*, for example, is full of places like Jamalpur, Daulatpur, Belapur, Haripur, Pipri, Naopur, Fatehgarh—places that not only had a name but also a clear direction and were at known distances from other areas. *Deewaar*'s gold landed at Versova[40], which was also the location of Narang's (Kulbhushan Kharbanda)

---

[40] Present-day residents of Mumbai will have to stretch their imagination considerably to visualize Versova as a deserted spot, conducive for receiving smuggled gold!

warehouse in *Shakti*. In *Majboor*, the location for the final rendezvous—involving a lot of money and a murder—is explained in meticulous detail: '*Kasara ghat se pehle . . . chhota sa bridge cross karne ke baad . . . daine haath ko kachcha rastaa . . . nadi kinare ek toota-foota cottage*',[xciv] adding flesh and blood to the skeleton of a story.

Salim Khan often talks about the Mahabharat when highlighting the importance of details. A small detail in Karna's early life (where he lies to his guru) comes back to haunt him in the most crucial battle of his life (when he forgets his learnings).

This has a parallel in many of their films—most important being *Deewaar*, where they encourage the audience to invest emotion into an initially insignificant object by slowly building detail around it. Vijay's dockyard token—'*billa number 786*'— is first featured in a conversation that explains its religious significance. It then manages to save Vijay from a bullet and then again during another attempt on his life. The final time it appears is in a tragic situation, when the billa slips out of Vijay's hands, effectively signalling the end of his run of good luck. The build-up of detail was so effective that the number 786 became a national phenomenon with people asking for the number for their cars or wearing necklaces with the number.

Breaking Up the Films

'Humne ek set of characters liya. Humne ek khaas haalaat dikhaye jo seedhi chalte chalte ek jagah kahin aisi ghoomi ke ab samajh nahin aa sakta ki yeh ab kidhar jayegi . . . woh moment interval ka hona chahiye'—Javed Akhtar

Film critic Shubhra Gupta makes a case for doing away with the interval when she says, 'It forces the storyteller to create a faux climactic moment, at a pitch higher than the rest of it till then, whether the plot allows for it or not. And then to have to resume from where it was left off, sometimes having to repeat the last few scenes for those stragglers who return leisurely from loo breaks and concessionaire stands.' Of course, her point of view is based on the films of 2010s that are increasingly experimenting with form—length, songs (or the lack of them), the traditional problem-resolution structure—to a great extent.

The interval has always been a part of the Hindi film and, rather than challenge the set notions of commercial cinema, Salim–Javed played with it, often using it to heighten the drama of the storyline. Javed Akhtar says, 'In India, we still follow the Victorian script structure because even today we have an interval in the middle of the film. So once you find an interesting interval point, you can weave the story back to the beginning, and then you can develop the second half of the story at a later point.' As is evident, they weren't too happy about the forced break but they invested considerable thought in it and actually made it bigger, thus making the intervals of their films points of tremendous dramatic turmoil.

In *Kaala Patthar*, the interval arrives at the exact moment where Vijay (Amitabh Bachchan) and Mangal (Shatrughan Sinha) have just had a high-voltage fight and are bring separated by Ravi (Shashi Kapoor). The freeze frame happens with the two fighters being held apart by their collars, signifying the moment when Vijay and Mangal will suspend their hostilities as bigger calamities befall them.

In *Deewaar*, the film breaks for the interval just when Vijay has moved into his new mansion with their mother and Ravi rushes in excitedly to announce his induction into the police force. The two brothers have been going down separate paths right from their childhood but this is the moment when the audience realizes their paths will now cross and it will not be pleasant. Again, a moment of heightened emotional suspense.

Sholay probably had the most dramatic interval post the revelation of Gabbar's brutal revenge on Thakur. While the first half establishes Jai and Viru's prowess, they are still hired guns out to make a quick buck by catching a bandit. At the halfway point, their motivation changes with the knowledge of Thakur's misfortune and they too become emotionally invested in the cause. This was again an important signal to the audience, telling them to start expecting an upping of the ante.

The other device Salim–Javed specialized in was the montage sequence. Their tales of lost-and-found siblings and children growing up to take revenge meant there was a fair amount of growing up to be shown—preferably depicting the heroic nature of the main character.

In *Haathi Mere Saathi*, four elephants are shown playing football with a child who kicks the ball in the air. When the ball lands, we see Rajesh Khanna—still as much in love with the elephants as he was as a kid.

In *Yaadon Ki Baaraat*, we have the child Shankar stealing a fruit, running away and stopping to rest on a railway overbridge. As he looks at the passing train, the camera does a 360-degree turn and comes back to Dharmendra.

In *Deewaar*, we leave a defiant little boy at the steps of the mandir and follow a young mother and her younger son inside. As the bells kept pealing, we return to dockyard coolie Vijay and educated unemployed Ravi—just as they embark on their two separate paths.

In *Chacha Bhatija*, a young Shankar starts selling tickets in black for the Dilip Kumar-starrer *Yahudi* (1958). As he keeps muttering '*ek ka do*' under his breath, the camera pans away from the boy, and in the next scene we see the poster of Raj Kapoor's *Bobby* (1973), tickets to which Shankar (Dharmendra) is selling at the rate of '*teen ka chhe*'—probably the best way any film has depicted the passage of fifteen years.

In *Shakti*, child Vijay kicks a can in depression on his way to school. The next person to kick the can is the adult Vijay (Amitabh Bachchan), who is sullenly walking past the romancing couples on Marine Drive, lost in his thoughts.

In most Hindi films, these montages would have been planned at the director's level and executed in the manner best suited to heighten the drama and excitement associated with a hero's first appearance in the film. But given Salim–Javed's penchant for detailed description of scenes (and even shot division in some cases), most of these critical scenes were written by the duo in the script itself.

Masters of creating several emotional highs in every film, Salim–Javed used these two points—the hero's first appearance and the interval—as key moments in the narrative to whip up audience frenzy through carefully choreographed sequences of events. The dramatic tension was palpable whenever they did so.

Part V:

IMPACT AND LEGACY

A Brief History of Hindi Screenwriting

To better understand the impact Salim–Javed had on Hindi cinema, it would be instructive to first briefly consider the screenwriting legends who preceded them and how their legacies shaped the evolving screenwriting conventions in the industry. This will also allow one to assess how much—or how little—has changed in the intervening years.

Salim Khan says his biggest influences are from aeons ago. 'I feel very strongly there has been no screenplay better than Mahabharat and no story better than Ramayan. Apart from the great situations and characters, the stories are full of small things—weaknesses—planted at one point that emerge at the end to become key to the narrative.'

And that is indeed the starting point of most Indian stories. Screenwriter Kamlesh Pandey says, 'We are the oldest storytelling country in the world and perhaps the richest. Our storytelling was originally verbal and there is not much difference between verbal and visual storytelling, which is cinema. Our cinema came from the folk theatre and that's why music plays such an important part. Folk theatre, like the Indian thali, would have a little bit of everything—song and dance, lyrical dialogue, spoken dialogue, comedy, action and so on.'

Starting with *Raja Harishchandra* (1913), and for nearly a decade after, all the films made in India were based on themes drawn from mythology and history. After the talkies began (in 1931), the source material expanded to picking up stage plays and filming them. Some of the earliest screenwriters, thus, were playwrights from popular theatre traditions. Parsi theatre, for example, produced many such writers and its style of rhetorical dialogues became somewhat institutionalized in Hindi cinema. After mythological and historical themes came literary influences. In 1936, *Devdas* (starring K.L. Saigal), with its combination of unrequited love, popular music and a familiar story, became a superhit film. This would be a popular formula (which, some may say, has carried on till this day) for Hindi cinema—a plot that is reasonably familiar, a screenplay that leaves room at regular points in the story for a few hit songs of varying moods. *Devdas*'s script also represented another common feature of Hindi films—a director who wrote the screenplay.

Hindi cinema has always seen directors working with a team of writers, many of whom put to paper the broad vision of the maker. Film critic and writer–director Khalid Mohammad says, 'Most Hindi directors formed long-lasting teams with writers that produced great scripts. Raj Kapoor had V.P. Sathe and K.A. Abbas, Guru Dutt had Abrar Alvi.' Most leading directors of the time (Bimal Roy, Mehboob Khan and the like) had a team of talented writers (many of whom started writing independently or even directed films later on in their careers) which became the starting point of the 'story department' where the writers were mostly anonymous and shared credit. Sriram Raghavan expresses his bemusement over this system: 'The studio system of the 40s and 50s had dissolved into another system where every prominent director/production house had a select group of writers working in an atmosphere of insulation and camaraderie—the story department. I have no idea how they actually functioned. Perhaps they were a group of people who read a lot of books, brainstormed all day and eventually zeroed in on an idea.' Also, they were all on a monthly salary that had no connection to the fortunes of the films they wrote.

The influence of literature on Hindi cinema grew as films based on popular novels or plays became successful. Saratchandra Chattopadhyay's works were a big favourite, with hits like *Devdas*, *Parineeta*, *Biraj Baju* and *Majhli Didi* in the 1950s. Kamlesh Pandey says, 'In the 1950s, a lot of Urdu writers from literature came in to cinema and they enriched our cinema. Manto, Abbas, Krishan Chander, Akhtar Ul Iman and even Prem Chand came for a while. Mukhram Sharma, Kamleshwar, Rahi Masoom Reza were all from literary backgrounds. Lyricists like Sahir and Kaifi were also from the literary world.' Writers with a literary bent— writing in Bengali, Urdu and Hindi—began arriving in the film industry and eventually became forces to contend with.

However, there was also the other end of the spectrum and often that formed the bulk of the industry's output. At that end, film-makers were interested in churning out quickies based on existing stories—either ripped off from successful films or popular novels—for which they did not seek talented writers. They wanted hacks who could write cheaply and quickly, without any intellectual bearing so that they were amenable to changes in the script as per the demands of the market. And such writers were aplenty. Kamlesh Pandey explains, 'The writer became a default option. Someone came to become an actor, could not succeed and he became a writer. And the mediocrity began at that time and still rules in writing. Writing often became the weakest link in a film.'

Writers without any creative conviction were also poorly paid—often not paid at all. Salim Khan says, 'The writer always had to give an excuse to ask for money. My kid's school fees are due. I need to pay the monthly rent. The money was not a right, neither was credit. We have written films where the director or the producer has been given credit for the screenplay even though we wrote it.'

There is another curiosity of Hindi cinema that was brought about by the cultural and linguistic diversity of India. The script was never conceived as a whole, written from start to finish. Typically, the director or producer got the source material— which could be a popular novel or a 'plot' (usually described in a few lines). After that, a writer associated with the makers wrote a detailed screenplay of how the film would unfold. Often, this was 'polished' by the director or a 'senior' writer. Finally, there would be dialogue writer who would create the exact lines that would be spoken in every scene. A large proportion of the early directors (and their associates) were not Hindi-speaking and, therefore, were unable to write the full script, complete with Hindi or Urdu dialogues.

For example, Bimal Roy's *Parineeta* credits Saratchandra Chattopadhyay for the story and the director for the 'scenario'. It names four people as 'scenario assistants': Asit Sen, Nabendu Ghosh, Kamal Chowdhury and Moni Bhattacharjee, and credits Vrajendra Gaur for dialogues. Likewise, K. Asif's *Mughal-e-Azam* credits the screenplay to the director and Aman while Kamal Amrohi, Ehsan Rizvi and Wajahat Mirza are credited with the dialogues. Multiple dialogue writers often meant that different scenes were written by different people, and held together by the common vision of the director.

While the process of writing was rather chaotic and the direction of the story largely resided with the director, this did not mean the quality was poor. The 1950s was a period of idealism and the stories told had great social resonance. Khalid

Mohammad summarizes this: 'I was weaned on cinema of the 1950s, justly described as the glorious era of Hindi-language cinema. There were great stories endowed with humanism, entertainers which were uncontaminated by vulgarity, stories which had credibility and on occasion, a literary source. Hollywood and world cinema did influence Bombay products but not as indiscriminately as they would in the decades to come. The stars and the stories mattered, of course, more than the technicalities of the script. Yet the names did register in one's adolescence, names like Pandit Mukhram Sharma, K.A. Abbas and V.P. Sathe who collaborated with Raj Kapoor, and Sachin Bhowmick whose plots were thoroughly formulaic and yet enjoyable. The scripts of Mehboob Khan, V. Shantaram and Guru Dutt also had an unparalleled resonance which continues to this day and age.'

What the 1960s brought was a fair degree of predictability to the plot though newer technical vistas opened up for film-makers. Colour, better audio equipment, modern cameras and the world as shooting location turned Hindi cinema into more of a spectacle than a pure story. Charismatic stars were born and they came with their own ideas of how they should be presented on-screen and what constituted entertainment.

While there were some great writers and director–writers in the 1960s as well, it was also the time when the clichés of Bollywood—the formulaic dialogues, the predictable scenes, the repetitive characters—took firm shape. Each leading and supporting character had a set role, which they strictly adhered to. The 1960s was the golden age of Hindi film music and while films became memorable because of their soundtrack alone, the stories remained steadfastly similar to each other.

For example, in nearly all of Shammi Kapoor's hit films of the 1960s—*Janwar, Kashmir Ki Kali, Professor, Junglee, Dil*

Tera Diwana, Rajkumar—one finds parental (or step-parental) opposition to romance, a gag around mistaken identities, an excellent soundtrack and a happy ending where the haughty rich come to a fall before the righteous poor. All the leading heroes of the day were different kinds of romantic—suave (Dev Anand), wild (Shammi Kapoor), passive (Rajendra Kumar) or tragic (Dilip Kumar)—and that brought another level of 'sameness' to Hindi cinema. Until, that is, Rajesh Khanna arrived on the scene and started doing pretty much all the aspects of romance.

Writer–directors like Vijay Anand and Manoj Kumar brought some difference as they were associated with distinct themes—suspense and patriotism respectively.

The only writer who was a star was Gulzar, but his talent was multifaceted; he was also a lyricist and was becoming very well known for the offbeat films he directed.

Film critic Bhawana Somaaya writes, 'The writer was more often than not treated like a munshiji by the production houses. Two versatile writers who could not be patronized and who stood their ground all through their careers were Inder Raj Anand and Pt. Mukhram Sharma. Inder Raj Anand was a very knowledgeable man and Mukhram Sharma was apparently the most dependable and systematic writer of all times.' Javed Akhtar echoes her assessment of Pt. Sharma. He says, 'We weren't the first [writers whose names appeared on posters]. Pandit Mukhram Sharma's name figured on film posters . . . *Dhool Ka Phool* was produced by BR Films, a very big banner, and the publicity material read, "Pandit Mukhram Sharma's Dhool Ka Phool".'

Going by the names mentioned thus far, there was certainly no dearth of good writers before Salim–Javed joined the industry. Be it established authors or poets or writers who began their careers with films, there were some excellent screenwriters who operated in the industry right from its inception.

What was missing then was *formal* training in writing for films. Kamlesh Pandey says, 'There were a lot of good writers but after they died or retired, no new talent came in or we did not have facilities or institutes to train writers. Even the successful writers did not have time to teach. Whereas in Hollywood, there are books on screenwriting, every university has a film course and almost every city has a film school.'

Even during Salim–Javed's time, and after, there were powerful and successful writers. Sachin Bhowmick continued well into the 2000s, writing for Subhash Ghai (*Karz*, *Karma*, *Saudagar* among others) and Rakesh Roshan (*Karan Arjun*, *Koyla*, *Koi Mil Gaya*, *Krrish*) among the latter-day makers. Kader Khan, dialogue writer par excellence, started off with Manmohan Desai. Interestingly, Desai wanted someone who would write in colloquial language and not the high-flying Urdu most writers favoured. When Kader Khan first wrote for Desai in *Roti*, the director was so happy that he asked Khan how much he got for writing a script. When Kader Khan said, 'Twenty-five thousand rupees,' Desai told him, 'From now on, your price is one lakh rupees.'

Other popular writers of the 1970s included Rahi Masoom Reza (known for dialogues that cover the entire gamut from *Mili* to *Rocky*, *Gol Maal* to *Karz*), Vijay Tendulkar (the iconic playwright who adapted his plays and wrote original material for the screen) and, of course, Gulzar.

The 1980s and 1990s were not the best of times for Hindi cinema. There was a fair bit of rehashing of the action–revenge–melodrama formula and flogging to death of the Angry Young Man character. With very few writers of note, several young film-makers—scions of film families—like Sooraj Barjatya and Mansoor Khan entered the industry towards the end of the 1980s and started writing their own scripts with some help from their companies/families. This became a popular trend in Bollywood of the 2000s as well, where, as Sukanya Verma says, 'The only screenwriters we truly acknowledge and adore right now happen to be some of the best film-makers in the country.'

As a screenwriter, probably the biggest success in recent times has been Rajat Aroraa, who has done both understated, urban humour in *Bluffmaster!* as well as bombastic 70s-style dialoguebaazi in *Once Upon a Time in Mumbaai* and *The Dirty Picture*.

Although not as a writer of film scripts, but as a source material for successful films, Chetan Bhagat deserves a mention because three of his books have been turned into extremely successful films (*3 Idiots*, *Kai Po Che* and *2 States*) while two more are in the pipeline.[41] Bhagat went through an acrimonious war of words with Vinod Chopra Films over the credit accorded to him in *3 Idiots* (where he was relegated to the rolling credits at the end of the film). While the producers were contractually bound to give only a 'rolling credit', the consensus among writers was that the author on whose book the film was based deserved a more prominent mention.

With the entry of international production houses, certain professional standards in screenwriting have been adopted. Scriptwriting software, for starters, has made the writing process much more standardized and locking scripts before shooting the film has also become the norm.

Kamlesh Pandey, in his capacity as the secretary of the FWA, sounds a message of hope. 'Now there is a lot of interest

---

[41] Only one film—*Hello*—based on his book has failed. The film based on his latest book (*Half Girlfriend*) was announced by the A-list team of Mohit Suri and Ekta Kapoor even before the book had hit the stands.

in screenwriting. I get about 200 new members for FWA every month. This has increased in the last few years and screenwriting has become fashionable. People come from small towns and distant places to write scripts. When I take my workshops, most of the students are from engineering or IT who have left well-paying jobs because there is a fascination for storytelling. This is a big leap because people are consciously training to become writers instead of becoming one by accident.'

Coupled with this training is a stronger assertion of writers' rights, led by FWA and members of the film industry. Implementing a 'model contract' for film and television writers is something that is likely to go a long way in securing the rights and remuneration for a writer. The Copyright Amendment Act of 2012 mandates the writers' rights to royalty, a share of the earnings from language rights and other media, though the quantum of the royalty is obviously subject to negotiation.

What is still missing is the spontaneous appreciation and awareness of the writer. When researching for this book, I realized that *Ghayal* (dialogue), *Damini*, *Mohra* (dialogue), *Andaz Apna Apna* (dialogue), *Dabangg*, *Dabangg 2* and *Jai Ho* have all been written by the same person—Dilip Shukla. For more than two decades, he has produced some of Hindi cinema's most memorable dialogues and successful films, though very few people even know his name. While music composers and lyricists are fairly well known, writers of even extremely popular films don't get due recognition. Film critic Sukanya Verma says, 'Honestly, it's not the viewer but the industry that doesn't respect the film writer. If only producers started valuing writers, promoting them in trailers/posters and paid them on time and handsomely, their lot would prosper and it would begin to rain terrific films every Friday.'

It would be appropriate to end this chapter with the final scene of *Happy Ending*, a film about a novelist who becomes a screenwriter. In the scene, the novelist-turned-screenwriter's script is being filmed. The hero of the script belts out a few lines of 'kick-ass' dialogues, which is followed by a behind-the-scenes conversation.

- *Writer: 'Excuse me, sir . . . maine toh nahin likkha hai yeh dialogue. What is he saying?'* [xcv]
- *Director: 'First time, huh?'*

The story of Salim–Javed is yet to reach its happy ending.

Larger than Life

In 1975, a massive flood affected large numbers of people in Bihar, Assam, Orissa and Gujarat. The film industry took out a massive procession (on 26 September) as a drive to collect funds for the victims. Pretty much every major star joined in this procession, urging the common man to donate small sums of money. Before this mass mobilization, all the stars had also contributed substantial sums of money to the relief fund and a list of the donors was published in the next issue of *Trade Guide*. The list had names like Rajesh Khanna and the Kapoor family at the top (contributing Rs 2,00,001 and Rs 2,00,000 respectively)[42] followed by Dilip Kumar (Rs 1,00,000). Several top stars and producers made the list as well—G.P. Sippy, Shakti Samanta, Gulshan Rai, Hema Malini, Amitabh Bachchan and Parveen Babi had all contributed Rs 51,000 each. There was one more name in this group (of people who had donated Rs 51,000)—Salim–Javed.

In September 1975, Salim–Javed were at their peak, having just delivered *Deewaar* (in January) and *Sholay* (in August)

---

[42] Those familiar with the one-upmanship prevalent in the Hindi film industry would understand the significance of the additional one rupee in Rajesh Khanna's donation.

but their earnings (then) were much lower compared to top producers and even top technicians (like composers R.D. Burman and Laxmikant–Pyarelal, who had contributed lesser amounts). Nevertheless, they made a strong statement with this huge donation, which literally catapulted them into the industry's A-list; this gimmick was something of a typical move on their part, showcasing their ability to attract attention.

In a telling piece of statistic, the FWA collectively donated Rs 1000 to the fund.

Salim–Javed were the only writers who were advertised in trade magazines. Producers of huge films like *Zanjeer*, *Deewaar*, *Sholay* and *Don* took out ads that highlighted only them. Even for a film like *Sholay*—which had nearly all the major stars of the time—Salim–Javed's story got a separate ad.

Also, they were the only writers who advertised in trade magazines. The ad they placed for *Sholay* is—of course—legendary for they went against industry pundits and took out an ad in *Trade Guide*, predicting record-breaking business for the film, which was then reeling under the weight of expectations and had made a slow start. Again for *Immaan Dharam*—their next release after *Sholay*—they took out an ad challenging their critics and positioning the film as their 'answer to all criticism'. With a first-time director like Desh Mukerji and comparatively smaller producer like Premji at the helm, the film was considered Salim–Javed's baby as they were the biggest names associated with it. From the back room, where writers were usually relegated, Salim–Javed had elbowed their way right up front. And they were not hesitant in taking either credit or blame for the success and failures of their films.

Salim–Javed always saw their equals in A-list stars like Amitabh Bachchan (even benchmarking their fees to his for a major part of their careers) and hobnobbed with top producers, directors and stars with confidence. In fact, they gave interviews in which they proclaimed how stars depended on them to deliver hits. Regarding their less-than-cordial relationship with Rajesh Khanna, they said, 'Rajesh Khanna is a shrewd professional. He realized that not only was he not getting good scripts, but that good scripts were going to his rivals. So he made the first move [to make up with us].'

They did not mince words about the quality of directors either. 'Here the films are either writers' films or actors' films. Even films made by the so-called giants like B.R. Chopra were basically writers' films. As a director, Chopra's contributions weren't much . . . Directors have never had confidence in themselves. It used to be a hit-and-miss affair with them. Now that they have realized a good script makes a good film, they are all looking for good scripts.'

As a duo, they broke away from the coterie of behind-the-scene technicians and participated actively in the film-making process. They were regulars at film premieres, sharing print space with directors, producers and leading actors. Front-page pictures in trade magazines—a space always reserved for high-profile mahurats and premieres—routinely featured Salim–Javed.

Salim Khan's residence for many years—Galaxy Apartments—was the scene of many high-powered meetings between actors, directors, producers and financiers who were brought together by Salim–Javed. Casting flip-flops, financing crises, fee negotiations, post-mortems of stories and a mind-bogglingly large number of incidents of assorted wheeling-and-dealing seemed to take place in their presence.

In his autobiography, Naseeruddin Shah narrates an incident where he was summoned to the 'plush seaside residence . . . it didn't take me long to figure that I was dealing with very big brass here'. He was called to replace a very big star with a 'prima-donna attitude' and he was asked to make himself available from the very next week. When he replied that he was in the midst of shooting a film, it was met with an incredulous guffaw. 'What film, yaar? Who is going to see it?'

He looks back at this incident with a fair bit of anger at the team's audacity in asking him to abandon a film midway but the fact remains that the writer duo had enough clout to push through unusual casting decisions for their films. And of course, they were arrogant enough to believe that nothing was as important as the films they wrote themselves.

An integral component of Salim–Javed's success was their ability to market themselves. They often talked themselves into high-profile assignments. This is best demonstrated in the way they got their first job with Sippy Films. They weren't a team then and had just written one film (*Adhikar*) together, more for the quick money it offered than with any plans to become a team. When they met G.P. Sippy and his son Ramesh for the first time, they projected themselves as two people who would change the way films are written in the industry. '*Yeh to kuch nahin hai* . . . the kind of screenplays we write, nobody can do it in the industry,' they bragged. Ramesh Sippy agreed to hear their ideas more out of amusement than anything else because he had not seen such confident writers, ever.

This continued well into their careers, and success certainly did not bring humility. In the February 1975 issue of *Trade Guide* (just after the release of *Deewaar*), the writer of a column called 'Movieman's Diary' wrote: 'The highest marks for the success of the movie should go to its writers Salim Javed. Recently at some functions and also in interviews published in film periodicals, they have been trying to outbeat Shatrughan Sinha. But after seeing their work in this film, I must admit that they have done a fine work and I want to forgive them for their bad dialogues outside and instead compliment them for a good screenplay and very good dialogue in Deewaar. Very good job indeed.'

This had been the case with Ramesh Sippy also. He agreed to meet them without really believing that they could be as good as they claimed but they turned out to be exactly that—and more. Everybody knows good marketing works only when it has a great product and Salim–Javed mastered the art of backing a good product with good marketing. Right from their days as the newbie writers of *Zanjeer* (when they released ads in trade magazines to announce their past hits) to their stardom in *Don* (when they used their own box-office clout to increase the selling price of the film), marketing was something they did almost as well as they wrote.

And they did so by demonstrating an almost fanatical pride in their work and protecting the script—resisting changes— fiercely. Salim Khan says, 'Earlier when writers put together a script, it had contributions from the novelist from whom the story was taken, the director who would make the film, the actor who would act in it. When we started working together, we said we will give you the complete script. You will neither interfere in the writing, nor change the finished script.' By doing so, they created for themselves some amount of notoriety because the industry was geared toward extreme flexibility (to put it kindly) and unplanned chaos (to put it not so kindly). They had a reputation of not agreeing to ad-hoc changes and insisted on rewriting scenes themselves, if there was a genuine reason. Director of *Don*, Chandra Barot, remembers asking them to make certain changes—necessitated by Zeenat Aman not being available for a schedule—to which they agreed. But at the same time, they opposed writing in a scene that allowed Amitabh Bachchan to change costumes in the second half of the film. Even getting them to agree to insert songs in *Deewaar* took a lot of convincing by director Yash Chopra and producer Gulshan Rai.

Salim Khan says, 'If we don't protect our work, who will? We were the first writers who started putting forward our views and defending things we believed in. Initially people resisted but we kept at it. After our films started becoming successful and our scripts got appreciation, people started accepting that we have put considerable thought into the writing process.'

They also did something quite unprecedented to protect their scripts: if it was changed without their consent, they told producers not to credit them. This happened with at least three big films—*Sauda* (starring Vinod Khanna), *Bhola Bhala* and *Humshakal* (both starring Rajesh Khanna). They said, 'Big stars here are used to being pampered by writers. We are different. Rajesh Khanna tried tampering in *Humshakal* and we withdrew from the film. Rajesh has done it again in *Bhola Bhala* and we have written to the producers not to credit the script to us.'

After years of writers toiling and not getting their due, here were two who refused to take credit because their work was tampered with. The line between pride and arrogance is very thin but Salim–Javed made it their own!

In the Hindi film industry of the 1970s, Salim–Javed were known to be excessively arrogant. They defend this by citing the position of writers then. 'When we entered, writers had no authority. There was no tradition of a writer putting his foot down or talking like an equal. If a downtrodden speaks to you like an equal, it sounds arrogant. We were seeking that equality, which sounded like arrogance.' In retrospect, they feel, 'We were very young—in our twenties and thirties—then. Now we feel it is important to make one's success palatable for others but we did not do that. Maybe it was a mistake. Maybe it wasn't.

Maybe it was the need of the hour. If we had been gentle, they could have trampled us.'

Success also allowed them to charge astronomical prices unheard of for writers in the industry. They reached a sort of milestone with *Dostana* when their fees overtook even Amitabh Bachchan's—who was also a huge star when he signed the film. But Salim–Javed's fees went up even after that.

Salim Khan explains, 'In today's films, there are additional expenses of Rs 3-4 crore due to changes in scripts/dialogues that require reshooting. With writers contributing a strong, well-thought-out script right at the beginning, this can be saved. When we started asking for the price we did, we gave these as reasons.'

He recounts a negotiation with producer Ramesh Behl, who called them to write a film (which was eventually not made).[43] Film rights are sold for six territories in India. They asked him how much he hoped to make per territory with the stars he had finalized and he quoted a price of Rs 18 lakh. They then told him, 'Ask your distributors how much are they willing to pay for the film if the script was by Salim–Javed.' Behl found out that the price would go up by 3–4 lakh per territory. Salim Khan recalls telling him, 'Six territories sold at an additional Rs 4 lakh would give you Rs 24 lakhs. This is the money you are making from our name, which is what we are asking from you. We are not taking any money for the script.'

They were paid Rs 10,000 for their first film, and even after all this time Salim remembers the fees they were paid for their first four films. 'Rs 10,000 for *Haathi Mere Saathi*, Rs 55,000 for *Zanjeer*, Rs 25,000 for *Yaadon Ki Baaraat*, Rs 50,000 for *Haath Ki Safai* . . . after the success of *Zanjeer*, we decided to

---

[43] The film was supposed to be made with Amitabh Bachchan, Shashi Kapoor and Parveen Babi.

increase our price to Rs 2 lakh and did not manage to sell a script for nine months,' he sighs.

Javed recounts a story of them going to a producer to narrate a script. 'We told him right at the beginning to hear our price before the script. We wanted to do so because we didn't want him to feel we had increased our prices after he liked it. So we told him two lakh. He remained silent for a while and then rang the bell for his peon. He then told his peon to get his partner urgently. All this while, we were sitting there silently. When his partner came, he said, "Hey, tell him what you just told me!"' This reaction is a good indicator of the general response to Salim–Javed's attitude in the 1970s film industry. People found it unbelievable!

And they did manage to sell a script for Rs 2 lakh (*Majboor*) and another for an amount very close to that (*Sholay* for Rs 1.5 lakh), not to mention that their prices went up further after the success of *Deewaar* and *Sholay*. Yash Chopra's assistant director Ramesh Talwar remembers them charging the producer a lot less than their market price for *Kaala Patthar*, and he estimates that amount to be around Rs 7.5 lakh. This kept on increasing till their asking price reached the astronomical Rs 21 lakh for their last couple of films. And of course, as described, they had a reason for that price.

This clarity in commercial matters helped them right from the beginning and they never changed. Javed Akhtar says, 'Producers and distributors are not bothered about content and the script is always lowest on the list of their priorities. The only way we can change that is by convincing them that there is great money in our scripts. The buyer should be impressed. After all, we are not dealing with saints but businessmen.'

And with the equity they had in the trade—distributors, financiers—they built their price, their swagger and their difference from other writers. How much were the other writers getting when you were asking for Rs 21 lakh, I asked. '*Ek lakh ke upar mil jaye toh celebration hota tha writers mein*,' Salim Khan grins.

They changed the fulcrum of the Hindi film rivalry. Their success and brash attitude brought them many rivals—many of whom were waiting for them to fail—and industry camps suddenly had two heavyweight writers weighing in. Their success meant they had several actors in their camps, who were keen to work on films based on their scripts, considered to be sure-fire hits. All of this contributed to their becoming a much bigger force than what is indicated by the number of films they worked on.

In the eleven-odd years they worked together, Salim–Javed wrote twenty-one films (of which nineteen released within this period and two released later). In the same period (1971–82), another top writer, Sachin Bhowmick, wrote twenty-eight films including some very successful ones (*Caravan, Hum Kisise Kum Nahin, Gol Maal, Karz, Bemisal*). Kader Khan started writing in 1974 and in his first decade, he wrote dialogues for nearly fifty films (including blockbuster successes like *Amar Akbar Anthony, Parvarish, Muqaddar Ka Sikandar, Naseeb, Laawaris, Satte Pe Satta, Himmatwala, Coolie*). Inder Raj Anand wrote twenty-plus films in the 1970s and early 1980s (which included hits like *Safar, Julie, Jaani Dushman, Ek Duuje Ke Liye, Kaalia*), many of which had hugely popular dialogues. Yet none of them managed the clout or the larger-than-life impression that Salim–Javed commanded (or command even now). The only writer who comes close to their aura is Gulzar, though his reputation is as much as a lyricist and director as a screenwriter.

No other screenwriter can claim to have influenced such a large number of films as Salim–Javed did in the 1970s and

1980s. Their Angry Young Man and the action-revenge-thriller format ruled for nearly two decades and spawned a multitude of imitators.

But apart from their influence, what completely distinguished Salim–Javed from other writers is the confidence with which they backed their craft. Their unwavering belief that a film is nothing but a blank page before a writer gets involved, that it is the writer who makes or breaks a film, is what drove them to become the most impactful screenwriters of Hindi cinema, if not the finest. Their passion and dedication to the screenplay are what has made them as big they are.

As Salim Khan says, 'Films should be made for only one reason. I have a script on which I will bet my last shirt.'

Strengths and Weaknesses

Writer–director Sriram Raghavan—a self-confessed Salim–Javed fan—says, 'Looking back at the movies I love and watch repeatedly, I think it's not the stories but how they were told that finally grabs the viewer. As writers, Salim–Javed never forgot the viewer within themselves. And critically, Salim–Javed didn't think their audience was dumb! In fact, any film-maker who considers the audience dumb is actually saying he's dumb himself because in a sense, he's the film's first viewer. I don't think Salim–Javed ever said to each other the audience won't accept this, that they will not understand this.'

Both Salim and Javed were avid movie-watchers and continued to do so in theatres even after they became stars. They remember watching their own films along with the audience to gauge their reaction, to see what had worked and—more importantly—what hadn't.

Salim gives an interesting perspective on how to keep the audience engaged. 'The audience must be allowed to guess some of the things. It is like playing football with a child. If you don't let him kick the ball at all, he will lose interest and walk away from the game. You need to keep him chasing after the ball and the audience chasing after the plot. *Dekhna, ab aise hoga* is something the audience keeps on saying . . . you need to build the screenplay to build in these guessing nodes.'

It is with this thought in mind that they constructed their scripts as one living, breathing whole. Director Ramesh Talwar, who assisted Yash Chopra during the making of all three of his Salim–Javed films, says, 'Salim–Javed's scripts did not have "buffer scenes". Their scenes had links or continuations from previous scenes, so that one scene flowed into another. Even props were thoughtfully used and were part of the story.'

Writer Kamlesh Pandey adds to this when he says, 'When we saw *Zanjeer* or *Deewaar*, we—as young boys— used to discuss the script and not Amitabh Bachchan. They were the first team who wrote logical screenplays where something happened because of something else in an earlier scene. Before them, nobody had done so and we really enjoyed that.'

Sriram Raghavan echoes this thought, 'I think they managed to get the dramaturgy exactly correct to make it exciting and taut, with the dramatic transitions perfect. The earlier films did not have this. As a director, I would find my transitions from one scene to another. But in Salim–Javed's films, you can see the writer has written the transition there. *Deewaar* is full of these things.'

However, that completeness of vision was backed by a grand imagination coupled with an eye for detail. Film critic Sukanya Verma calls this a perfect balance. 'Their biggest strength is balance. Salim Khan's explosive, intense impulses perfectly complemented Javed Akhtar's wit and idealism. One's ideas, another's depth, together they created stories and characters we cared about, rooted for, connected with or wanted to become.'

While Salim–Javed never officially divulged who did what in the partnership[44], it can be inferred that Salim's sense of plotting and screenplay was a perfect match for Javed's sense of detail and dialogue.

Javed says of the partnership, 'We were a really great team! We really complemented each other. He had everything that I didn't have, and I had everything he didn't have. As a writer, he had the courage and I had the intricacy. He would introduce in our work the broad and bold strokes of drama and I had the detail and the finesse. How do I define this? Well, the power in drama, boldness in developing the story, bringing something extraneous to the script, thinking of something new . . . something that would shock.'

Along with this grandness of story plotting, as film-maker and film critic Khalid Mohammad finds, their dialogue perfectly suited the situations. He says, 'The dialogue penned by Salim–Javed has been brilliant, packing in punchlines even in straight colloquial lines. They introduced effective, quotable lines of dialogue, erasing the theatrical and ornate language used earlier by most dialogue writers.'

Kamlesh Pandey continues, 'Salim–Javed introduced to us the modern Indian screenplay. Our films did not have that before them. The vocabulary and the attitude of the characters were very contemporary.'

While several of their inspirations were from other classic Hindi or Hollywood films, the situations and the manners in which they played out were completely attuned to the times. *Mother India*'s mother, who became the mother of *Deewaar*, was no longer fighting dacoits in villages. She had to contend with urban problems like unemployment and crimes like

---

[44] Their standard answer to this question has been, 'He used to write the nouns and I, the verbs.'

smuggling. The mercenaries of *Sholay* were not honourable samurais but small-time thieves who had no qualms in stealing from their employer. The lost brothers of *Waqt* returned in a rock-'n'-roll avatar in *Yaadon Ki Baaraat*. All their set pieces, their lines, their milieu were deeply rooted in the times they lived in and that drew the audience to theatres like nothing else.

However, all these strengths would have come to nought if not for that one winning quality of theirs, borne out of their formidable intelligence and an anti-feudal mindset. Coming from the backgrounds they did, they challenged the 'caste system' of the Hindi film industry and managed to actually turn it around. In the film industry, actors were the brand names on which films were sold and the audience's love for music meant the composer/lyricist/singers were the only other group who were celebrated. Not even directors—except for a few very accomplished ones—were stars in the truest sense. In this situation, Salim–Javed's conviction in the scripts they wrote and the confidence that writers—not actors or composers—made or unmade films was their true strength. Salim Khan says, 'A lyricist writes five songs, which means just five scenes, but he is mentioned on the film's banners. How can a writer who writes sixty–seventy scenes of the same film not get mentioned on the posters?'

Holding on to their scripts and their vision, Salim–Javed were in a position to discuss which actors could play certain roles and how the films would be mounted. One of the reasons they never ventured into direction is that their complete vision was visible on-screen anyway. Of course, preserving this vision meant convincing legendary producers (like Gulshan Rai) to drop superstars (like Rajesh Khanna) even though the advance had been paid, because the actor did not suit the role (in *Deewaar*) and talking another superstar (Shashi Kapoor) into playing a supporting role (in *Deewaar*) that was a very strong one as well.

Ramesh Talwar remembers Salim–Javed's script-reading sessions to be one of complete unity. 'They used to fight amongst themselves while writing the script but sorted out their differences before narration and presented one common vision to the producer–director. Then, they used to insist that the scene and dialogues remain unchanged.'

In the film industry of those days, where scripts changed on a producer's whim, songs were inserted on a distributor's insistence and dialogues changed because the actor said so, their ability to say 'no' because they didn't believe in something was their biggest strength. Salim Khan sums it up, 'You should know the worth of your product and you should be sure of its success. *Phir aap ko naa bolne ke bhi paise milte hai.*'

When I asked popular screenwriter Rajat Aroraa what he thought Salim–Javed's weaknesses were, he just laughed and couldn't come up with anything. Anything you dislike, I prodded? He said, 'What I don't like about them is that they broke up . . . they probably had many more great films left to do.' This is an apt summation of what Salim–Javed's strengths were and their impact on later writers.

However, what has often been counted as a weakness of Salim–Javed is their lack of originality. Kamlesh Pandey says, 'There is no doubt about the fact that Salim and Javed were both incredibly wonderful writers. But most of their works were derivative. If there was no *Mother India* or *Gunga Jumna*, there would have been no *Deewaar*. And *Shakti*, in one way, was *Deewaar* in reverse. I only wish that they had done something that was really their own.' It is indeed true that Salim–Javed worked on scripts that Javed jokingly calls 'totally original [but] have come before'. Khalid Mohammad puts it differently, 'What I miss from the scripts of Salim–Javed is an experiential quality. Their stories have been derivative of western films and books.'

Salim Khan doesn't dismiss this completely when he says, 'Originality is the art of concealing the source'[45] and adds that there has been no original story after Ramayan and Mahabharat. He says everything is derived or inspired from something that has 'come before'. With this mindset, they have been absolutely open about their sources—going so far as to mention some of the more obscure films from which they had picked up even minor parts of films. Salim attributes *Sholay*'s coin toss to determine course of action to a film called *Garden of Evil* but the scene wasn't an exact replica. It was a pack of cards that decided which cowboy would stay back while the other tried to escape with the lady.[46] Salim also attributes the dockyard setting of *Deewaar* to *On the Waterfront*. There was hardly any other similarity between *Deewaar* and the Elia Kazan classic but again, it was openly called out. Salim says, 'A lot of people who are not aware of these influences say Salim–Javed are geniuses. But the genius is placing the right thing at the right place after changing it to suit the new situation perfectly.' It is rather obvious that they never blindly lifted material but brought a new touch that made their creation bigger or more memorable than the original.

Sriram Raghavan feels that they are certainly not un-original. 'The journey of a four-line idea to a full-fledged screenplay is an

---

[45] In a supreme bit of irony, it is really difficult to ascertain the person who said this. The Internet attributes it to Benjamin Franklin, journalist Franklin P. Jones and even Albert Einstein. *QuoteInvestigator.com* believes this aphorism began with a statement by one C.E.M. Joad in 1926 and kept on evolving.

[46] Another film to which the double-sided coin is attributed is *One-Eyed Jacks*, starring Marlon Brando, but even that does not have a coin. The film has a situation where one guy (Brando) rigs a draw of lots to let his partner/mentor escape.

arduous and fantastic process, where the writer has to draw from within and from outside. The world of Salim–Javed was full of as many outside influences as it was of their own lives, their own struggles coupled with their imagination, ambition and intent. One can detect influences ranging from James Hadley Chase and Harold Robbins to Conrad's *Lord Jim*, from our own films, literature, poetry, culture and mythologies.' What he correctly notices is a rich tapestry of threads that were not groundbreaking but they were certainly innovative—in their own way. Kamlesh Pandey adds, 'Taking plot points from different sources—American novels, Hollywood Westerns—and then weaving them into something so Indian was not easy. They had perfected that skill and that's why we, modern scriptwriters, owe everything to them. We are whatever we are today because of Salim and Javed.'

Or as film-maker Jean-Luc Godard said, 'It's not where you take things from. It's where you take them to.'

Salim–Javed's lack of originality has also been seen in a different way, where they stopped experimenting with form and content after a point. While their earlier films had a lot of material—characters, plot devices—that was new to Hindi cinema, their later films were often repeats of their previous ones. And some even had exact repetitions of scenes or dialogues. Two of their last films together—*Kranti* and *Shakti*—had the same subplot of father putting his duty above his son's life. In *Shakti*, the police officer father (Dilip Kumar) refuses to give in to the demands of the smuggler who has kidnapped his son, even telling the smuggler to execute his son. In *Kranti* (which came earlier), we have Sanga (again Dilip Kumar) who orders the execution of Shakti Singh (Shashi Kapoor), a traitor to his cause, despite knowing their relationship. After *Sholay*, they wrote *Shaan* for Ramesh Sippy—it turned out to be an exact replica of the former. Obviously under a lot of pressure to repeat the success of the earlier film, they attempted to do so by writing pretty much the same script in a modern, James Bond-style setting. Even *Shakti*—though still considered to be a classic—was the story of *Deewaar*, retold with a father and a son as protagonists.

Javed Akhtar explains, 'You lose that hunger. You start feeling secure within the formula. You think this is what is expected of you, and you think this is what works because it's always worked.' Sukanya Verma is an unabashed Salim–Javed fan and she puts this repetition somewhat differently. 'I don't know if it's a weakness but it would have been nice to see them do more outside the blockbuster realm, the Angry Young Man imagery. I think it overpowered their intelligence to create something more subtle or sensitive, like they accomplished in Ramesh Sippy's *Andaz* and one saw flashes of in several other movies.'

Salim–Javed's sense of humour, different approach to romance, keen social antennae and razor-sharp intelligence indicate that they would have been a success in any genre. A host of very interesting film-makers, especially in the art-house and middle-of-the-road genres, were appearing on the scene in the late 1970s and in hindsight, one feels that many of them could have been collaborators for a different brand of Salim–Javed scripts. Govind Nihalani—whose *Ardh Satya* has been called 'arthouse *Zanjeer*'—and his activist film-making could have been the perfect fit for Salim–Javed's brand of socialism, seen in so many of their earlier films. In fact, writing for this kind of film they could have brought their muscle to such films' marketability and may well have given parallel cinema a boost. Salim–Javed has accepted that a certain fatigue had crept into their later films and a new kind of challenge may well have brought intellectual stimulation to their work and thus extended their partnership. This is obviously speculation stemming from the basic question about Salim–Javed not being experimental enough with their scripts.

Despite these few weaknesses, Salim–Javed remain Hindi cinema's most impactful screenwriters—a position that is almost reverential to many writers today. And they reached this position on the strength of their skills. To quote Sriram Raghavan yet again, 'As sheer craftsmen, their strong points were economy, pace, dialogue, visual language of storytelling, sharp characterization and clever transitions.' In one breathless sentence, he has packed in so many different qualities that would be pretty much impossible to find consistently in any screenwriter—Indian or international!

The Salim–Javed Ripple Effect

Trade Guide, a popular industry magazine of the 1970s, used to print a page full of the titles registered by producers for their forthcoming films. Then, it helped the industry keep a track of the titles (and by extension, subjects) coming in, and now, it serves as an interesting barometer of the times as indicated by the type of titles (and by extension, subjects). While researching for this book, one name stood out. On 8 August 1975, someone had registered the title 'Salim Javed'. This—in one sentence (or thereabouts)—was the impact the writer duo had on the film industry of the 1970s.

There are many urban legends about their run-ins with producers, asking for money and credits. They were regulars at mahurat functions and filmi parties. Their children were best friends with star kids. Distributors and financiers used to say, 'Take as much money you want if the script is by Salim–Javed.' But nothing exemplifies their influence better than someone deciding to name a film after the two writers.

And it went far beyond the period they worked in.

In 2005, Indian diplomat Vikas Swarup wrote a novel—*Q&A*—about a street urchin winning a billion rupees in a *Kaun Banega Crorepati*-style game show. The bestselling novel featured the hero learning the answers to the show's questions through his life's experiences. The novel featured the hero's best friend in a peripheral role (among other characters). In 2008, the novel was turned into a film— *Slumdog Millionaire*—by award-winning director Danny Boyle.

In a major departure, the focus of the film changed completely. The book was about the quiz questions and the hero's adversarial relationship with the game-show host. The film, on the other hand, revolved entirely around the conflict between a good brother and a bad brother, the difference in their outlooks towards life and their contrasting ends. While writing the film's screenplay, writer Simon Beaufoy 'studied Salim–Javed's kind of cinema minutely'. Separately, director Danny Boyle described *Deewaar* as being 'absolutely key to Indian cinema'. In fact, the film's script resembled *Deewaar* to a large extent—being about two brothers who take different paths to find success. Both Beaufoy and Boyle spent significant amounts of time in India while researching for the film and it is absolutely conceivable that they watched and were inspired by *Deewaar*. Salim–Javed were inspired by *Gunga Jumna* and *Mother India* when they wrote the script of *Deewaar*. It is, therefore, only fitting that the film that went on to showcase a distinctive brand of Bollywood to the entire world was based on their film. In a way, their stories defined Indian cinema, and *Slumdog Millionaire* demonstrates that perfectly.

Salim–Javed's films, their characters, their situations, their lines have permeated our lives, our conversations, our reflexes.

When WhatsApp was acquired by Facebook for an unprecedented $19 billion, the founder of the messaging app—Jan Koum—walked a couple of blocks to a welfare kitchen to sign the documents that made him a billionaire. This was the place where he had collected free food vouchers as a kid. Abhishek Asthana (who is extremely popular on Twitter as @gabbbarsingh) tweeted, 'Jan Koum is 1970s Amitabh Bachchan', alluding to the 'proportional justice' Salim–Javed were famous for.

In 2014, graphic novel author Saurav Mohapatra wrote *Mumbai Confidential*—a series of noir crime stories set in the Mumbai underworld. He says, 'If you read *Mumbai Confidential*, you'd realize it's basically Salim–Javed meets James Ellroy,' referring to the author of *LA Confidential* (who was known for his staccato dialogues and pithy one-liners).

Salim–Javed's influences have been found in the most diverse of situations, primarily because they have been absolutely spot-on in understanding audience psychology. Many youngsters (born mid-1980s onwards) I spoke to while writing this book came up with '*Mere paas maa hai*' when asked for an iconic Hindi film line even though most of them hadn't heard of Salim–Javed or watched *Deewaar* in its entirety.

The duo's lines and characters have been the subjects of endless spoofs, parodies, advertising spots, tributes and homages. Sujoy Ghosh's debut feature, *Jhankaar Beats*, was essentially a film-length homage to *Sholay* and R.D. Burman. Two modern-day yuppies traded dialogues with and quizzed each other on *Sholay* when they were not singing RD's songs. *Sholay* is a different ball game altogether, given the number of inspirations it has evoked. To some extent, *Dilwale Dulhania Le Jayenge* has also seen similar styles of tributes though the numbers are not yet comparable. What sets Salim–Javed apart is the number of their films that have become sources for future derivatives.

Film critic Sukanya Verma says, 'Salim–Javed are Salim–Javed. They represent an era, a style of film-making that's evolved as they too did from what prevailed before them. Has their relevance faded with time? No, rather it's become a point of reference and something Anurag Kashyap notably celebrated in *Gangs of Wasseypur* and Atul Sabharwal to a lesser-acknowledged extent in *Aurangzeb*.'

Apart from the official/unofficial remakes, Salim–Javed's set pieces have permanently influenced the way some things always happen in Hindi cinema. There had been films with lost-and-found stories before but with *Yaadon Ki Baaraat*, *Haath Ki Safai* and *Chacha Bhatija*, they laid down the norm for how long-lost family members meet each other unknowingly before finally coming together in the climax. The combating brothers, the hired guns who take on a larger-than-life adversary or the son rebelling against the father are all elements Bollywood has recycled endlessly from Salim–Javed's stock tropes. One of Salim–Javed's weaknesses was that they repeated their formula far too often but those repeated plots also became guard rails for future writers and directors.

Unlike some who are very possessive of their work, Salim–Javed are quite open to remakes of their scripts. Salim says, 'A lot of people oppose remakes but I don't. I feel it shows that our thirty-year-old work is still relevant and that is a compliment. [When I heard about the remake of *Sholay*] I told Ramesh Sippy that it is a win-win situation for you. If he makes a very good and successful film, people will compliment you for the source material. If he makes a bad film, people will say nobody could make it like Ramesh Sippy. Whatever happens to the remake, you win!'

Three of Salim–Javed's scripts have been officially remade though two of them have had a rough ride.

Farhan Akhtar's *Don* brought an intelligent twist in the tale that managed to interest the modern film audience and successfully bring a fresh bunch of people to join the cult of *Don*. Film writer Jai Arjun Singh says, 'Akhtar inverted the mood and tone of the original film, which progressed from darkness to light, evil to good. (Remember that the real Don, the one genuine bad guy Amitabh played during his superstar phase, is killed off just forty minutes into the film.) The new *Don* heads in precisely the opposite direction and it's one of the most cheerfully, unapologetically cynical films I've seen from mainstream Hindi cinema. Nearly *everyone*, it turns out, is corrupt, there's no one to root for (except for Arjun Rampal's character and his son), there's a lot of messing about with people's sentiments (including those of a child) and this is basically a story about Evil vs Evil. The winner isn't the guy who's nicer, it's the guy who has more style, more sangfroid. And that's perfectly all right, because that's really what this film is about: being stylish.'

The other two remakes—*Zanjeer* and *Ram Gopal Verma Ki Aag*—were so bad that they routinely feature in discussions on the Worst Hindi Films of All Times. How could a winning script go so wrong when remade? What needs to be understood here is that a story works only in a context. When *Zanjeer* was originally written, the police officer taking up arms against a smuggling ring and winning was a satisfying mixture of the real and the unreal. Everyone knew smuggling and black-market dealings were common but no lasting action was seen to be taken. Inspector Vijay Khanna brought that action and, however unreal he was, his heroism was what the country was waiting for. When the new *Zanjeer* was released in 2013, the audience had become far too cynical and far less tolerant of vigilantes in khaki. In fact, one of the most popular films of 2012 was *Dabangg 2*, which had a police officer who was corrupt but used his ill-gotten gains for noble causes. An honest, snarling officer was something Bollywood had left behind in the 1990s.

It only goes to show what Salim–Javed have always said—you need a fair bit of intelligence to copy well!

As far as Indian cinema is concerned, Salim–Javed's films have influenced nearly two decades of themes and character archetypes.

In the 1950s, Hindi cinema was largely about social causes and subdued romance that often ended in tragedy. This gave way to more flamboyance in the 1960s as songs, costumes and locales aiding the romance became flashier. Sriram Raghavan says, 'The late 60s and early 70s saw the bulk of Hindi cinema dominated by the romantic social drama. The style of working then was to broadly select a story, think of song situations, a basic scenario to embellish the song situations, add some comedy moments and to ensure that there was an action climax. Oh yes. Whatever the genre of the film, the climax had to have action.' Barring the occasional dacoit film, action as a genre was largely restricted to the B-grade 'talwaarbaazi' films (made famous by Dara Singh). It was only in 1973 that Salim–Javed brought in the 'action hero' to mainstream Hindi cinema (with *Zanjeer*, though you could see shades of that character in *Yaadon Ki Baaraat*'s Dharmendra).

Even after they split in 1982, the character did not stop. Sunny Deol in *Ghayal*, *Damini* and countless other films was an extension of Salim–Javed's action hero. Mithun Chakraborty, Anil Kapoor, Sanjay Dutt, Akshay Kumar, Ajay Devgn, Sunil Shetty and several other less successful actors kept on playing various versions of the Angry Young Man throughout the 1980s and 1990s. They were almost always an avenging angel, exacting revenge for their father's death or mother's dishonour or both.

There was the occasional twist in the tale. *Aatish* was the story of two brothers, where the older one (Sanjay Dutt) joins a crime syndicate to pay for his younger brother's education that ends with him becoming a police officer (Atul Agnihotri). The story was straight out of *Deewaar* but the twist was that the mother (Tanuja) supports the criminal brother. Many other twists or changes necessitated by technology could be found but the basic character remained unchanged.

It is important to note the strength of their template because the 1990s' romantic hero (think Shah Rukh Khan or Aamir Khan) was radically different from the 1960s' one (Rajesh Khanna) but the 1990s' action hero was largely in the same mould as the 1970s' one.

This influence was not only confined to Hindi cinema. Salim–Javed became the first writers whose scripts were regularly remade in the south. Salim Khan says, 'South Indian rights were usually sold after a film was declared a hit, a few months after the Hindi release. The producer sold it off, without any share to the writers. We argued that when a film's rights are sold, it is the script that gets sold. You don't sell actors, the shooting style or the production values. If you are remaking *Zanjeer*, you are actually remaking the same story. With this logic, we convinced them to give us money from the rights.' They first made money from southern remake rights by selling *Zanjeer* for Rs 1.5 lakh, which was nearly three times of what they made from selling the Hindi script.

Seeta Aur Geeta, *Zanjeer*, *Haath Ki Safai*, *Deewaar*, *Don* and *Trishul* are some of the films that were remade in different south Indian languages and went on to become massive hits there also. In fact, Rajinikanth starred in several remakes of Salim–Javed scripts and these films—full of Salim–Javed's distinctive brand of heroism—were important stepping stones towards Rajinikanth's superstardom and, ultimately, divinity. Rajinikanth had opted out of films for a brief while but was coaxed into a comeback by his well-wishers; he returned with *Billa* (1980), a superhit remake of *Don*. After that, came *Thee* (1981) based on *Deewaar* and *Mr Bharath* (1986) based on *Trishul*—all huge hits that were scene-by-scene remakes of the Hindi films.

In 2014, Bollywood's top-grossing films like *Kick*, *Singham Returns*, *Holiday* and *Jai Ho* were remakes of south Indian films[47]; the tide has well and truly turned.

Gulzar says, 'We must be grateful to writers like Salim Khan and Javed Akhtar who fought hard to get a fair price for screenwriters. They did a great deal to improve things.' Khalid Mohammad puts it all together when he says, 'I would salute Salim–Javed for giving writers the credit they deserve. Their names were mentioned on posters and hoardings, and they asked for and received the kind of fees no other writer could have imagined before them.' And that was a great thing, for the writers to come into the foreground for a change. Salim Khan says, 'When we asked for big money, other writers also increased their fees. From a time when producers used to decide their fees and give them no credit, other writers could also demand more.'

Some of the changes were seen through articles in trade magazines of the times. The *Screen* issue of 28 November 1975 carried a report of a meeting between film writers and information and broadcasting minister, V.C. Shukla. The report went on to say, 'It cannot be denied that film writers in this country have not been accorded the status they deserve. Monetarily also, many of them are in bad shape . . . The fact that

---

[47] Of the top ten box-office hits of 2014, six were remakes (official or unofficial) of previously made films. Apart from the four films mentioned above, *Bang Bang* (official: *Knight and Day*) and *Ek Villain* (unofficial: *I Saw the Villain*) were also 'inspired'.

the Minister met a cross-section of the writers' fraternity and sought its help in nation building activities is proof that there is a new awareness on the role of writers.' It could be a coincidence that this meeting came within three months of *Sholay* hitting screens and *Deewaar* completing its silver jubilee. Or maybe it wasn't.[48]

What can indeed be noticed is some writers also getting prominence in Salim–Javed-style celebratory ads. Writer K.A. Narayanan, for example, got top billing with *Do Jasoos* (1975) and it was called 'Super Script by the Emperor of Stories' in an advertisement in *Trade Guide*. He also took out a full-page ad that called him 'Emperor of Stories' and listed all his hit films (and that was quite impressive). Clearly, here was another writer who was trying to get noticed.

But while the lot of writers improved directionally, it still never reached a point where writers were considered a natural part of the group of people who make a film. What Salim–Javed achieved through their grit and talent was surprisingly short-lived and to a great extent, restricted to them only.

It would be interesting to note this transition of the writer through the films of one maker.

The story of Salim–Javed's obsession to get credit for Prakash Mehra's *Zanjeer* is legendary and has already been talked about. In both *Zanjeer* (1973) and *Haath Ki Safai* (1974), Salim–Javed were named in the opening credits of the film, though the posters and publicity material did not have their names. When Prakash Mehra launched *Hera Pheri* (1976), the first advertisement had no mention of the writers though the film's credits featured them.

---

[48] One of the objectives of this meeting was to seek land for building cooperative housing for writers and a loan from the Film Finance Corporation to make a film, proceeds of which the writers would use for the construction of the building. However, Salim–Javed weren't present for the meeting.

For his biggest hit—*Muqaddar Ka Sikandar*, a film known for its memorable dialogue—Prakash Mehra had no space for writers in the opening credits. (They appeared for about five seconds in the closing frame.) And *Namak Halaal* too had no mention of any writer either in the film's credits or the posters. Many film fans still remember Amitabh Bachchan's famous '*Engliss is a phunny language*' monologue from the movie but there is no official record of the writers.

It is shocking but true that films have released in India with no credit to the writers. It happened to Salim–Javed at the beginning of their careers, and it haunted other writers long after their reign ended. Sukanya Verma says, 'For better or worse, Hindi film industry is completely star-driven. And it's an effective visual medium. We tend to remember Amitabh Bachchan saying, "*Tumhara naam kya hai, Basanti?*" in *Sholay*. We never think of Salim or Javed sitting on their desk and scribbling some iconic line. Having said that, when the writing is exceptional, the writer does make the audience want to look up the credits to check who wrote that line. Every now and then the dialogues are so full of "entertainment, entertainment, entertainment", a Rajat Aroraa is bound to get his due.'

With recent changes in the Copyright Act, the FWA has made it mandatory for writers to receive a percentage of the film's profits. While the exact percentage is open to negotiation, this is nevertheless an important step that secures royalty from a film's earnings for the writer. Interestingly, one film production house had started sharing profits with their writers much before the FWA stipulated it. This production house is Excel Entertainment Limited, owned by one Ritesh Sidhwani and one Farhan Akhtar.

The Dynasties of Salim–Javed

Salim's Family

Salman Khan was born in 1965, when Salim was still a struggling actor and had just made the decision to take up writing. To pursue this career choice, he had cut down on his acting assignments, which affected his earnings. In fact, all his children were born before any of Salim–Javed's successes released and their initial years were not easy. Despite their initial hardships, the family has always had a streak of altruism that has recently come into the limelight with Salman's charity, Being Human, but really has been there right from the beginning. Salman was always the boy who brought home hungry friends and supported many people unconditionally. In fact, rumours suggest that Salim Khan's youngest daughter Arpita was adopted after she was left destitute when her mother died on the roadside and the family brought her home.

Salman entered showbiz without his father's backing and started off as a model in his early twenties. He appeared in a few advertisements for brands like Limca and Smash T-shirts (both very popular in the 1980s).

There is a hilarious story about how Salim Khan's son inherited his father's confidence and swagger—much before he became a superstar. Salman Khan remembers meeting Govinda when the latter had just started to make a mark in films (and Salman hadn't even begun acting, having only done some modelling assignments). As Govinda passed him in a studio, Salman gave a thumbs up and drawled, 'Hey man, doing good work!' Govinda, still with a struggler's mindset, did a grateful namaste and mumbled thanks many times. Salman says this incident gave him a lesson in humility.

He became friendly with Kumar Gaurav and Sanjay Dutt (who were working in films written by his father) and often recounts stories of their generosity that helped him a lot in his early days. He says he tries to pay it forward with today's youngsters.

He debuted with a small role in *Biwi Ho To Aisi* starring Rekha. However, his very next film—*Maine Pyar Kiya*—was a career-defining one that established him as a major star and a youngster with promise. His career meandered in the late 1990s and early 2000s but his recent decade as a star has been phenomenal because he has become that darling of the masses whose on-screen antics cannot go wrong. In 2009, he acted in *Wanted*—a typical over-the-top remake of a south Indian film—and he entered a record-breaking zone where he has had only two flops (*Veer*[49] and *Main Aurr Mrs Khanna*) while most of his films did mind-boggling business.

Incidentally, Salman also wrote the story for *Veer*. He had come up with the idea nearly twenty years earlier, though it was not a particularly novel plot. If the plot was indeed written in the early 1990s, it would coincide with two other films—*Baaghi*

---

[49] *Veer*, despite being a flop, grossed nearly Rs 60 crore worldwide and was among the top-ten grossers of 2010 but the production costs were reportedly much higher.

(1990) and *Chandramukhi* (1993)—for whose 'story idea' Salman received credit. This seems to have been a particularly fertile period for Salman, coinciding with the time when Salim Khan was also writing.

However, Salman's personal life was fraught with major romantic issues (including some acrimonious and high-profile break-ups) as well as legal tangles. He has been indicted in one case of killing protected animals near Jodhpur (during the shooting of *Hum Saath Saath Hain*) and in another case of alleged drunk driving where his SUV ran over and killed a person and injured others (in September 2002).

Arbaaz and Sohail's acting careers have not been particularly flourishing. They have often co-starred with Salman in hit films and have also done roles without him or with external producers, with varying degrees of success. Arbaaz has done relatively well as the handsome but ruthless villain (*Daraar*, *Qayamat*, *Kuch Naa Kaho*, *Fashion*) while Sohail has often been seen in roles that portray him as a lovable goon (*I Proud to Be an Indian*, *Fight Club*, *Salaam-e-Ishq*, *Heroes*).

The brothers have now branched into production, with Sohail co-producing many of Salman's films since 1998 (he started with *Pyaar Kiya To Darna Kya*, starring both his brothers). He has produced and starred in smaller films without Salman as well (*Fight Club*, *I Proud To Be An Indian* etc). Sohail has also directed many Salman-starrers that he produced—breezy love stories (*Pyaar Kiya To Darna Kya*, *Hello Brother*) as well as action thrillers (*Auzaar*, *Jai Ho*).

Arbaaz became a producer with *Dabangg* and became a director–producer with *Dabangg 2*. He is now trying out his hand at films that star no members of his family but seem to be a good commercial proposition, well produced and well promoted.

While Salman has been an exceedingly successful star, and both Arbaaz and Sohail have found success in production, they still seem to be quite in awe of their father—maybe even a bit scared. The three brothers have often claimed that they involuntarily stand up when they receive a call from him. Salim Khan, on the other hand, says that his advice is often lost on his sons. 'I used to be a voracious reader and always advise people to do so. But with my sons, I see that even the newspapers don't get picked up from their doorsteps for days on end,' he sighs exaggeratedly.

Salim has always been the true patriarch, keeping his flock together and united. Salman Khan, despite being India's top star, still lives in a flat above his father's in Galaxy Apartments—which has been their family home ever since they moved in in October 1973 (on the day of Dussehra). Salim claims to be an advisor to his three sons, while feigning a bit of exasperation because all their calls seem to come at 11 p.m. He is an informal script advisor though he refuses to take any official credit and dismisses all questions saying it is up to the director to decide if his suggestions have any value.

Salim's second marriage to Helen, the legendary dancer of Hindi cinema, was conducted with a dignity that managed to control the gossip and acrimony that is the usual fallout. Salim and Helen adopted a daughter—Arpita—and the two families have now coexisted quite happily for three decades now and routinely get together for family functions.

Javed's Family

One movie connection Zoya Akhtar obviously cherishes and has mentioned in several of her interviews is that she was born in the same year the *Godfather* was released (1972). She remembers seeing it first when she was about nine or ten years old; the film was projected on the wall of their Juhu flat. Her mother Honey Irani had a movie projector and used to get prints from theatre owners (many of whom she knew very well) to watch them on a 'big screen' at home. Zoya says that she didn't understand it very well the first time and remembers shielding her eyes in some scenes that she found very violent.

Born in October 1972, Zoya has lived in Mumbai—studying in Maneckji Cooper school and St Xavier's College—her entire life, except for a brief stint in New York University Film School to study film-making. She says, 'The writer in me is very strong. I feel whether I direct my next film or not, that will not majorly affect my life. But no matter where I am, I can't stop writing. In school, I would always score the highest on essays. Since school, I was told that I can write.' Her mother Honey joined FTII Pune for a course when Zoya was still in school and many of her weekends were spent there, in an environment steeped in cinema.

Like most star kids, Zoya also started off in supporting roles—both behind and in front of the camera. Zoya recalls, 'I did a lot of jobs as an AD [assistant director] and as a PA [production assistant]. As a casting director, I cast extras. As an AD, you work with extras a lot. I was an executive producer. I've done a lot of jobs and I think each one helps you get closer to what you want as a director. It also helps you—when you work with different film-makers—to absorb, to adapt, to know what to watch out for, to know pitfalls.' One of her most unusual roles was in Mira Nair's *Kama Sutra* (a film she was casting junior artistes in), where she played one of the girls being trained by Rekha in the fine art of seduction. She was the first AD in brother Farhan's first two films, which happened before she got a chance to direct.

She cut her cinematic teeth in these assignments before she started pitching her first script for financing. Called *Kismet Talkies*, it was to star Hrithik Roshan and Kareena Kapoor but it never got made, which was attributed to a variety of factors ranging from non-availability of the actors' dates to acceptance of the script by producers. Eventually, Zoya made her debut with *Luck by Chance*, which was produced by brother Farhan's company—Excel Entertainment. While *Kismet Talkies* was also written around the film industry, *Luck by Chance* was a completely different script and turned out to be an incredibly nuanced and balanced take on the crazy world of Hindi cinema.

She sealed her spot as a top writer-director with her second feature film, *Zindagi Na Milegi Dobara* (*ZNMD*) as well as a short segment in *Bombay Talkies*. Her latest film, *Dil Dhadakne Do*, did well commercially and critically and further cemented Zoya's position in the industry.

As children, while Zoya was the more balanced sibling, Farhan—by all accounts—ran into all sorts of trouble. But if there was one thing that distinguished him from other children his age, it was his 'vivid imagination'. 'Or lies, as they were called then,' he laughs. He specifically remembers an instance where he convinced his schoolmates that he would be coming to school in a helicopter, while sitting in the school bus with all of them. 'It was the first time I realized people are easy to fool and there were many instances like this one,' he says, though he's not sure if that helped him become a writer.

He was a bit of a drifter because he dropped out of college in his second year—something his father did not approve of as Javed considered graduation an important milestone in one's life. Farhan was crazy about cinema too and watched films by the dozen, to the point that his mother threatened to throw him out of the house. When he considered getting a job, he chose the field of photography and film-making, things he was most interested in. He borrowed cameras and lenses from well-known cinematographer Baba Azmi (Shabana Azmi's brother) and went around shooting, using his friends as models. He also worked as an assistant to cameramen in films like *Lamhe* (which his mother wrote) and *Himalay Putra* (which was the debut vehicle of Akshaye Khanna). This was a fairly long period of drifting (nearly all of the 1990s) when he was trying to get a foothold in the industry. He says that he had no clear idea of what he wanted to become but after observing all aspects of film-making, he decided that the director's role was something worth pursuing.

Finally, he ended up writing the script of *Dil Chahta Hai* and asked his childhood friend Ritesh Sidhwani to read it, primarily because the film had many aspects of friendship they were both familiar with. Ritesh—whose family was in the kitchen appliances business—was keen to try out something different. 'That script sealed my decision in terms of what I wanted to do next in life,' Ritesh says. They pitched the script to Aamir Khan, though Farhan initially wanted him to do the role Akshaye Khanna eventually played. Aamir Khan was impressed enough with the script, the associated detailing of the characters' looks and motivations and the director's vision to say yes, and Excel Entertainments got off to a blockbuster opening.

Farhan has borrowed quite heavily from his own life for his films, at least in the first two. He recalls being emotionally dependent on his friends after his parents' divorce and formed very strong bonds with them, some of whom have become fodder for his films. The characters of *Dil Chahta Hai* were a combination of three or four such friends and bits of himself. His own lack of focus about careers and a profession was something that he depicted in the first part of *Lakshya*.

Farhan calls himself a 'director who can act' though his huge popularity as an actor[50] has put the brakes on his directing career. While his production house continues to churn out films—on all of which he has a say—he has directed just four films till now. The second one, *Lakshya*, was written by Javed Akhtar while the next (*Don*) was a remake of a Salim–Javed script and his fourth film (*Don 2*) was a sequel to the third.

While Javed Akhtar's influence on both his children is obvious, it would be apt to look at Honey Irani's career as well. She started off as a child actor and later graduated to small supporting roles as an adult. She stopped acting after she married in 1972 (and became a mother soon after). While married, she enrolled in a course with FTII and was an assistant director to Ramesh Talwar in films like *Duniya* and *Sawaal* (both in the early 1980s).

She says that she always wanted to write and tried her hand at short stories but was shy of sharing them because she thought her works would be dismissed as Javed's writing. After her divorce came through in 1984 (though they separated in 1978), she got over her diffidence and briefly outlined a story idea to Pamela Chopra (Yash Chopra's wife) for what she thought would be a TV serial. That script went on to become *Aaina* (starring Jackie Shroff, Juhi Chawla and Amrita Singh), which Yash Chopra loved. But before *Aaina* was completed, she wrote the film that would make her a writing star—*Lamhe*. While the

---

[50] Farhan Akhtar became a heart-throb after his performance in *Rock On!* and gained a lot of critical acclaim after *Karthik Calling Karthik* and even more so after *Bhaag Milkha Bhaag*. Strangely, his first acting role (which convinced Zoya to cast him in *Luck by Chance*) was in a film that never released in India— *The Fakir of Venice*. In the limited release the film had in USA, the *Hollywood Reporter* praised his performance by saying, 'Akhtar, making his film debut here as an actor, is talented and handsome enough—and with looks that could translate into any number of ethnicities—to have a huge career ahead of him.'

movie was a commercial disaster, it became a cult classic for its very unusual plot and Honey Irani went on to write several blockbusters like *Darr*, *Kaho Naa Pyaar Hai* and *Koi Mil Gaya*. In-between, she had a somewhat acrimonious separation with Yash Chopra's house because of a controversy around *Dilwale Dulhania Le Jayenge* where she claimed that she had been denied credit for the story and screenplay of the film. While her maiden directorial venture—*Armaan*—did not do well, Honey Irani continues to write, having co-written screenplays for *Krrish* and *Krrish 3* in recent times.

As a single mother who took the break-up of her marriage with grace and dignity, Honey Irani's influence on her children has been substantial.

Javed's second marriage to Shabana Azmi has been cordial for all concerned. Shabana calls Javed a friend first and says their friendship is so strong that even a marriage could not ruin it. She has also been supportive of Javed's relationship with his children, both of who spent significant periods with their father while they were growing up.

Common Threads

There are some interesting similarities between the ways in which the film careers of Salim–Javed's children began.

For starters, none of them had the benefit of their fathers' contacts and recommendations. Turning away from the sifarish that they so often ridiculed in their films, both Salim and Javed ensured that their children charted their own course. Apparently, in order to pitch his first script, Farhan Akhtar sought an appointment with Aamir Khan without using his father's name, which impressed Aamir a lot. Though the lyrics for *Dil Chahta Hai* were written by Javed Akhtar, the script was written completely by Farhan and in a manner and sensibility that was far removed from his father's. His second film was based on a script written by Javed Akhtar, though—again—the mood and milieu were very modern. Likewise, Salman tried his luck and hit jackpot with his second film—*Maine Pyar Kiya*. One of his earlier films—*Patthar Ke Phool*—was based on a Salim Khan script but by then, Salman had established himself as one of the leading new-age romantic heroes. In fact, Salim Khan attributes his retirement timing at least partially to Salman being in films. 'When I pitched scripts to producers when my sons were working, I felt they would be wondering why is he not making the film with his son if it is so good?' he says. 'There is a big problem if I write scripts for Salman. The film becomes his if it is a hit and daddy's, if it is a flop.'

Both Salim and Javed have played an advisory role in their children's careers and films, without interfering beyond a point. This restraint is commendable because—in a way—the children are working in an industry in which their fathers were masters, and yet Salim and Javed supported their efforts only by way of offering help in technical capacities and in credited departments alone.

The script of *Luck by Chance* was written by Zoya and Javed wrote the dialogue. Zoya says, 'I wrote the English draft and my father wrote the Hindi dialogue. There are certain scenes he's translated. But there are certain scenes he has taken and twisted and translated and moved it to another level. A lot of [the scenes with] Rishi Kapoor and the entire acting class. That was all him. He knows these people . . . I don't have a one-on-one experience with them. He does. He just layered that [scene] perfectly for me.'

Javed Akhtar has written lyrics for all the films Farhan has produced, including *Rock On!* which, as film critic

Mayank Shekhar puts it, means 'the Urdu-Awadhi poet, quite uncharacteristically one would imagine, [would have] managed to pen the words "Mary Jane ka ek packet", referring to marijuana joints in the track "Pichle saat dino mein"'. Javed later told Mayank that the expression was Farhan's idea.

Film dynasties have, by and large, been associated with grand old surnames like Chopra (B.R. and Yash), Kapoor (Prithviraj) and, more recently, Bachchan. Salim–Javed's families are not one dynasty and yet they have managed to churn out an unbelievably diverse range of films. Salman Khan has obviously been the commercial giant, with an incredible number of films in the top grossers of Bollywood. Farhan and Zoya, on the other hand, have gained a lot of critical acclaim built on the base of commercial success and not art-house recognition. They have won Filmfare Awards for writing (Farhan for *Dil Chahta Hai*'s screenplay and *ZNMD*'s dialogues), direction (Zoya for *ZNMD*), acting (Farhan for *Bhaag Milkha Bhaag*) and producing (*ZNMD* again). If we add the prizes Javed and Honey have won—five for lyrics and two for story/screenplay respectively[51]—then we have a creative powerhouse that is also commercially successful (*Don 2* is among India's top-grossing films.)

Salim–Javed came to Bombay with certain ambitions but ended up becoming writers, something they had not envisaged. Not only did they reach the pinnacle of success, their dynasties have now become as influential as they were in their prime and are looking good for a lot more.

---

[51] Honey Irani has won two Filmfare Awards for best story (*Lamhe* and *Kya Kehna*) while Salim–Javed have won only one (*Deewaar*). She has also won a best screenplay prize for *Kaho Naa Pyaar Hai*.

As Mayank Shekhar wrote, 'Javed had entered movies to become a director. His son fulfilled that ambition. Having done 25 films as an actor, Salim couldn't quite make it as a successful leading man. His son Salman Khan became a superstar. The circle was complete.'

The circle is complete but the journey is not.

Epilogue:
Will They Meet Again?

'Dad has never spoken about what the issues were. Salman, Arbaaz and Sohail tell me that neither has Salim uncle. They used to be such close friends. It would be great if they could be friends again'—Farhan Akhtar

When the new *Zanjeer* was announced, the first person to call Javed Akhtar was Salim Khan. During the initial negotiations (which seemed to head towards an amicable settlement) and the court hearings (when the negotiations broke down), the duo was back as a team. They used their considerable clout with film-makers, stars and industry bodies to swing public opinion in their favour. Major stars—reacting to the controversy—advocated the payment of dues to the writers, despite being friends with the makers of the new films. The rights of a creative person were back in the news. Their combined efforts and star power led to a far greater buzz around this story than what is usually seen around other writers' cases for credit or compensation. The court case was a blessing in disguise because they had to spend considerable time together—four to five hours at a stretch at times—in courtrooms, attending the hearings.

During the mid-to-late 1980s, gossip columns were abuzz with news of their rivalry and how they revelled in each other's failures. While gossip columns are meant to be taken with a pinch of salt, their rivalry definitely existed. In subsequent years—when both had given up writing scripts—they studiously avoided each other at public functions.

When they split in the early 1980s, they both told their families that it was a business decision and all personal relations should continue. While the relations were not entirely normal, the children too remained cordial with each other and deferential towards the two writers. In fact, Farhan Akhtar personally met Salim Khan to take his permission to remake *Don* before he purchased the rights. Salim Khan, on his part, was gracious enough to endorse the film heartily.

While the thawing of the relationship was not rapid, it has definitely eased out in the recent past and the two have become more open to appearing together.

In 2013, they first talked about their differences being resolved. This was probably a direct result of the conversations they had during the court battle and a realization that the two of them were very similar after all.

Salim Khan said, 'We worked together for fifteen years and despite our different personalities, complemented each other professionally. I don't rule out the prospect of us coming together again. We are more mature now and can look beyond petty issues. There is no block between Javed and me today. We have a few ideas, but they are still half-baked. If we can pen a script together, I don't think there will be any dearth of producers.' Echoing his view, Javed Akhtar added, 'We have resolved our differences. There is no animosity between us now and we are open to working together.'

In January 2014, they appeared on a television show together and talked about their joint career with humour and intelligence. In the interview (to Rajeev Masand of CNN-IBN), Salim Khan emotionally said that as the elder member of the team, he was responsible for the split. 'I should have shown the maturity of reaching out and solving our differences,' he said. Javed Akhtar affectionately held his hand while he spoke and reminded him that both team members are always equally responsible.

For fans, it was an emotional moment.

Old warhorses coming together for (often impossible) projects has always been a big favourite theme of Hollywood movies. Maybe we will see it once in real life also . . .

Acknowledgements

Salim Khan and Javed Akhtar have been much more than the subject of a book that I worked on for the better part of two years. Ever since I started watching films, they have given me endless smiles, guffaws, sighs, tears, exhilarations, heartbreaks, dreams and memories.

This book is an insignificant way of thanking them for all that.

For this book, I interviewed several writers and directors of Hindi cinema, who were extremely generous with their time and thoughts. In alphabetical order, they are Dileep Shukla, Kamlesh Pandey, Khalid Mohammad, Loveleen Tandan, Mansoor Khan, Rajat Aroraa, Ramesh Talwar, Sriram Raghavan and Vinay Shukla.

I also spoke to some excellent writers and passionate films fans, whose thoughts gave heft to some of my theories: Anita Padhye, Carla Miriam Levy, Jai Arjun Singh, Kaushik Bhaumik, K.Y. Thomas, Rachel Dwyer and Sukanya Verma.

The archive departments of the *Hindustan Times* and *Indian Express* were extremely helpful in locating scans of old issues of newspapers and magazines.

The Library at the National Film Archives of India is like a temple for movie buffs. I spent many happy hours researching less and browsing more through their treasures.

Dhirendra Ukarde translated long Marathi passages into English, often adding his own valuable opinions as a film fan.

Manisha Lakhe helped a lot with her contacts in the film industry.

At Penguin, Ambar Sahil Chatterjee shepherded the book from the rambling-incoherence stage to its final form.

Shatarupa Ghoshal extricated a readable book from the mess of my awkward sentences and wonky grammar.

Udayan Mitra has to be thanked specifically for kicking off this book and generally for being that sort of guy who knows Salim-Javed's only flop.

Udayan Chakrabarti was the first reader of the book, who then advised me to rewrite pretty much the whole thing.

Nimilita Chatterjee was a dream host, providing me a luxurious room (with free breakfast and Wi-Fi) during my research visits to Mumbai.

Debapriya Chaudhuri planted the seed of this book with a casual comment while Rita Chaudhuri ensured I never took my movie-watching casually.

Trishna Chaudhuri slept soundly through the nightly clacking of the keyboard and kept her sighs at inaudible levels when I replayed *Trishul* for the seventeenth time. It couldn't have been easy.

And finally, this book is dedicated to the Dynamic Duo of my life—Dyujoy–Drishti—wishing that they write blockbuster lives for themselves.

Translations of Dialogues

i.   'I still don't pick up money thrown at me.'

ii.   'These elephants shall be your companions.'

iii.   'Come down from your perch, little one.' 'You join me here, fat one.'

iv.   'We are your uncle and aunt.' 'Look more like hangers-on.'

v.   'Where had you gone off, my girl?' 'Had zipped off to Mahabaleshwar, my pachyderm!'

vi.   'I always look fetching in borrowed clothes.'

vii.   'Till I wipe away your tears, till I make you happy, till I make this home peaceful again, I will not leave.'

viii.   'The day this three-kilo beast of a hand knocks you, you'll be as flat as a movie poster on a brick wall.'

ix.   'Unless I tell you otherwise, keep bloody standing. This isn't your bloody living room. It's a bloody police station.'

x.   'Sher Khan has met a lion for the first time in his life today.'

xi.   'Kabir was just telling me that a police officer needs some money.'

xii.   'Fifty thousand rupees to kill a mere inspector? Seems like a really honest guy.'

xiii.   'We will put up some really nice curtains in our home and I will never even try to find out what's going on beyond them.'

xiv.   A typically hyperbolic line, characteristic of breathless radio promotions: 'A glowing ember of revenge wrapped in the chains of memory.'

xv.   'Boy, I was the headmaster of the school you are trying to graduate from.'

xvi.   'I give lessons to the headmaster of the school where you are learning these tricks.'

xvii.   'Well, what do you think?'

xviii.   'Acting is in my blood. Several generations of my family have been at it.'

xix.   'Whether it's Chandramukhi or Paaro, what difference does it make, friends?'

xx.   'I have always heard of honour among thieves.' 'You heard right . . . it is only thieves who have honour.'

xxi.   'My father is a thief.'

xxii.   'But I have Mother.' Admittedly, this translation is somewhat futile because there is hardly anyone remotely interested in Indian cinema who doesn't know the import of this line.

xxiii.   'If my voice is reaching the owners of our mine . . .' 'What is Anand babu's particular weakness?' 'One day this boy will become someone [important].'

xxiv.   'May your hand remain steady when you fire.'

xxv.   'You do not know this area.' 'You do not know me.'

xxvi.   'If this is a coincidence, it is a very interesting coincidence.'

xxvii.   'You'd do well to remember that I can be as hot-blooded as you are.'

xxviii. 'I won't let you rest till you become like steel in a furnace. You have to become your mother's true son and earn the mother's milk.'

xxix.   'I will forget this gold, Raj Singh, but not you.'

xxx.   'I don't like his shoes.'

xxxi.   'There are just two kinds of girls I don't like. One, who take too long to be wooed. Two, who get wooed too easily.'

xxxii.   'Sonia, Don is wanted in eleven countries but get this straight . . . it is not just difficult to catch Don, it is impossible.'

xxxiii. 'It's suffocating to pass through the terrible atmosphere of this area.'

xxxiv.   'The men who die like flies in mines every day, their wives buy bangles only to take them off [when they become widows].'

xxxv.   'This mine is like a hungry python which swallows hundreds of miners every day, sucks every drop of their life blood and then spits them out as the living dead.'

xxxvi.   'There's no place on earth which can hold Mangal back.'

xxxvii. 'Oh my fifty-third card of the pack, I am the third ace of the flush.'

xxxviii. 'People find me terribly attractive, especially my eyes.'

xxxix. 'Anger has turned these lovely pink flowers red.'

xl.   'Shaakaal has as many aces up his sleeve as he has in his hands.'

xli.   'Our family tradition'

xlii.   'My father has been married twice . . . I am his first wife's son and his second wife's son is the law he upholds, which is just like my stepbrother.'

xliii. 'I have not become so weak that I cannot bear the weight of my husband's honesty.'

xliv.   'Please tell him to find witnesses and evidence against me.'

xlv.   'Let this burden of principles be borne by the man who considers it to be his hobby.'

xlvi.   'Mogambo is pleased.'

xlvii. 'Where on earth are you floating around?'

xlviii. 'A full fifty thousand.'

xlix.   'The job has been given to someone else.'

l.   'Teja, I have arrived.'

li.   'The entire city knows me by the name of "Loin".'

lii.   'You son of a pig!'

liii.   'How many men were there?'

liv.   'Now what will happen to you, Kaalia?'

lv.   'The way he riled me in the court . . .'

lvi.   'Get this clear baby . . . if you play coy any longer, I will scrape this fair skin of yours right off your body.'

lvii.   'You want me to run away as well?'

lviii. 'When you see your mother die a little every single day for twenty-five years, you are no longer scared of death.'

lix.   'Another daylight robbery? This government can't go on.'

lx.   'People who have nothing to do often perform miracles. I am a miracleworker these days.'

lxi.   'Looking for a job itself is a very difficult job.'

lxii.   'If a man doesn't get his first job, how will he gain experience? Believe me, I can do this job.'

lxiii. 'You don't know [how tough] this task [is].' 'You don't know me [how tough I am].'

lxiv.   'Should the millions of starving Indians start stealing to feed themselves?'

lxv.   'As the money in your [rich people's] accounts grows, so does the hunger and helplessness among the common people of this country.'

lxvi.   'I see that the greed in the hearts of the rich and the adulteration in the food of the poor is steadily increasing.'

lxvii.   'Today's India will no longer tolerate black maketeers, smugglers and hoarders.'

lxviii.   'Friends, if my voice is reaching the owners of our mine, then I would like to assure them that we are not concerned about the overflowing flower vases in their drawing rooms. We are only concerned with the empty tins in our kitchens. We are not at all worried that these mines are giving them pots of gold. We are only worried about the ashes and dust that are coming our way.'

lxix.   'Here to collect the ashes from our burnt homes, is it? And use it to shine your boss' silverware?'

lxx.   'Saxena, you seem to have no sense of simple arithmetic. Don't you know four hundred is way lower than forty lakhs?'

lxxi.   'A really useful miner is one who is always half-dead and has just enough energy to keep his head down and dig.'

lxxii.   'The dawn would have truly arrived when everyone will have an income and a home, not having to spend their lives on the pavement.'

lxxiii.   'Unfortunately, small talk is completely beyond me.'

lxxiv.   'Here, have some tea.' 'I will but you do know what kind of dirty thoughts come to my mind after I drink tea, don't you?' 'Do you ever think of anything else?'

lxxv.   'If Dhanno, a mare, can pull the tonga, why can't Basanti the girl drive it?'

lxxvi.   'Even women should take some responsibility. If you are in the streets wearing clothese like these, what do you expect? That these roadside Romeos will chant hymns instead of whistling?' 'What's wrong with these clothes?' 'They're barely there.'

lxxvii.   'And, fortunately, she is my mother.'

lxxviii.   'Whatever he did was to protect us, to let us live.'

lxxix.   'A horse meant for long races'

lxxx.   'I am a respectable, married man.' 'If you call the police, you'll remain neither respectable nor married.'

lxxxi.   'Apparently, lift walls don't have ears.'

lxxxii.   'If you are scared, you're dead.'

lxxxiii. 'Thakur sahib, I don't know what use you have for these guys but I think they are completely useless.' 'Not really. Along with their faults, they also have some strengths.' 'But isn't a bad apple all bad?' 'That's how people are different . . . they are gangsters, but brave ones. Dangerous because they know how to fight. They are bad men but human beings, after all.'

lxxxiv. 'Don't know if I am more impressed by your dulcet voice or your deft fingers. Don't know if your delightful victory impresses me more or your wonderful necklace.' (The writers are punning on the word 'haar' that means both 'necklace' and 'loss'.)

lxxxv. 'If you file a suit, I'll pack a suitcase . . .' 'I will retire your tensions with a pension.'

lxxxvi. 'We can't afford such a slow pace. You should consider putting a few more people on the job but we have to finish on time.'

lxxxvii. 'A jailor from the British era'

lxxxviii. Literally, 'I have eaten your salt,' but the idea is of being loyal to one's employer.

lxxxix. 'Shambhu's mind is a double-edged sword.'

xc. 'He turned out to be my big brother.'

xci. 'Brother, I am keeping quiet because I am the younger one.' 'It is not only your wallet that has fallen out, sir. You yourself have fallen so much.'

xcii. 'Do wash your hands off this, or people might think there is someone's blood on your hands.' 'When I saw the blood on my hands—for a second—I thought it was my own blood. Then I realized it is you who is hurt.'

xciii. 'How can I agree, Dinanathji?'

xciv. 'Just before Kasara ghat, you will cross a narrow bridge . . . rough track on the right . . . a ramshackle cottage next to a river . . .'

xcv. 'Excuse me, sir, I did not write this dialogue . . .'

Filmography of Salim–Javed

Andaz

Release Date: 30 April 30 1971
Director: Ramesh Sippy
Other writing credits: Sachin Bhowmick (Story & Screenplay), Gulzar (Dialogue), Satish Bhatnagar, Sippy Films Story Department (Additional Script Work)
Cast: Shammi Kapoor (Ravi), Hema Malini (Sheetal), Rajesh Khanna (Raj, in a guest appearance), Roopesh Kumar (Badal), Aruna Irani (Mahua), Achala Sachdev (Ravi's mother), Simi Garewal (Mona, Ravi's wife), Ajit (Raj's father)
Music: Shankar–Jaikishan
Lyrics: Hasrat Jaipuri

Haathi Mere Saathi

Release Date: 15 May 1971
Director: M.A. Thirumugham
Other writing credits: M.M.A. Chinappa Thevar a.k.a Devar (Story), Inder Raj Anand (Dialogue)
Cast: Rajesh Khanna (Raju), Tanuja (Tanu), K.N. Singh (Saawan Kumar), Madan Puri (Seth Ratanlal, Tanuja's father), Junior Mehmood (Chhote, Raju's sidekick)
Music: Laxmikant–Pyarelal
Lyrics: Anand Bakshi

Seeta Aur Geeta

Release Date: 3 November 1972
Director: Ramesh Sippy
Other writing credits: Satish Bhatnagar (Story), Sippy Films Story Department (Screenplay)
Cast: Hema Malini (Seeta and Geeta), Dharmendra (Raaka), Sanjeev Kumar (Ravi), Manorama (Chachi), Satyendra Kappu (Chacha), Roopesh Kumar (Ranjeet), Honey Irani (Sheila)
Music: R.D. Burman
Lyrics: Anand Bakshi

Zanjeer

Release Date: 11 May 11 1973
Director: Prakash Mehra
Cast: Amitabh Bachchan (Ravi Khanna), Jaya Bhaduri (Mala), Pran (Sher Khan), Ajit (Dharam Dayal Teja), Bindu (Mona), Om Prakash (informant D'Silva)
Music: Kalyanji–Anandji
Lyrics: Gulshan Bawra

Yaadon Ki Baaraat

Release Date: 16 November 1973
Director: Nasir Husain
Other writing credits: Nasir Husain (Dialogue)
Cast: Dharmendra (Shankar), Vijay Arora (Vijay), Zeenat Aman (Sunita), Tariq (Ratan/Monto), Ajit (Shaakaal), Satyen Kappu (Jack), Imtiaz Khan (Roopesh)
Music: R.D. Burman
Lyrics: Majrooh Sultanpuri

Haath Ki Safai

Release Date: 30 August 1974
Director: Prakash Mehra
Cast: Vinod Khanna (Shankar), Randhir Kapoor (Raju Tardeo), Hema Malini (Kamini), Simi Garewal (Roma), Satyendra Kappu (Usmanbhai), Ranjeet (Ranjeet)

Music: Kalyanji–Anandji
Lyrics: Gulshan Bawra

Majboor

Release Date: 6 December 1974
Director: Ravi Tandon
Cast: Amitabh Bachchan (Ravi Khanna), Parveen Babi (Neelu), Pran (Michael D'Souza), Satyen Kappu (Narendra Sinha), Rehman (Surendra Sinha), Iftekhar (Inspector Khurana), Farida Jalal (Renu Khanna, Ravi's sister), Madan Puri (Mahipat Rai)
Music: Laxmikant–Pyarelal
Lyrics: Anand Bakshi

Deewaar

Release Date: 24 January 1975
Director: Yash Chopra
Cast: Amitabh Bachchan (Vijay Verma), Shashi Kapoor (Ravi Verma), Nirupa Roy (Sumitra Verma, Vijay and Ravi's mother), Parveen Babi (Anita), Neetu Singh (Veera), Davar (Iftekhar), Satyen Kappu (Anand Verma, Vijay and Ravi's father), Manmohan Krishna, A.K. Hangal
Music: R.D. Burman
Lyrics: Sahir Ludhianvi

Aakhri Daao

Release Date: 8 August 1975
Director: A. Salam
Cast: Jeetendra (Ravi), Saira Banu (Reena), Danny Denzongpa (Saawan), Padma Khanna (Julie), Satyen Kappu (Kaul sahib), Iftekhar (Inspector Khurana), Ramesh Deo (Inspector Verma)
Music: Laxmikant–Pyarelal
Lyrics: Hasrat Jaipuri

Sholay

Release Date: 15 August 1975

Director: Ramesh Sippy

Cast: Sanjeev Kumar (Thakur Baldev Singh), Dharmendra (Viru), Amitabh Bachchan (Jai), Hema Malini (Basanti), Jaya Bhaduri (Radha), Amjad Khan (Gabbar Singh), Satyen Kappu (Ramlal), A.K. Hangal (Imam sahib), Sachin (Ahmed), Jagdeep (Soorma Bhopali), Asrani (Jailor), Leela Mishra (Basanti's Mausi), Kaalia (Viju Khote), Sambha (Macmohan)

Music: R.D. Burman

Lyrics: Anand Bakshi

Immaan Dharam

Release Date: 14 January 1977

Director: Desh Mukherji

Cast: Amitabh Bachchan (Ahmed), Shashi Kapoor (Mohan), Sanjeev Kumar (Kabir), Rekha (Durga), Aparna Sen (Shyamlee), Helen (Jenny), Prem Chopra (Ranjeet), Om Shivpuri (Seth Jamuna Das, Kabir's father), Utpal Dutt (Balbir Singh), A.K. Hangal (Masterji, Shyamlee's father)

Music: Laxmikant–Pyarelal

Lyrics: Anand Bakshi

Chacha Bhatija

Release Date: 1 April 1977

Director: Manmohan Desai

Cast: Dharmendra (Shankar), Hema Malini (Mala), Randhir Kapoor (Sunder), Yogita Bali (Pinky), Rehman (Teja Seth), Jeevan (Lakshmidas), Roopesh Kumar (Kiran), Indrani Mukherjee (Sita), Sonia Sahni (Sonia)

Music: Laxmikant–Pyarelal

Lyrics: Anand Bakshi

Trishul

Release Date: 5 May 1978

Director: Yash Chopra

Cast: Amitabh Bachchan (Vijay Kumar), Shashi Kapoor (Shekhar Gupta), Sanjeev Kumar (R.K. Gupta), Hema Malini (Sheetal Verma), Rakhee (Geeta), Waheeda Rehman (Shanti), Prem Chopra (Balwant Rai), Yunus Parvez (Bhandari), Poonam Dhillon (Babli), Sachin (Ravi), Shetty (Madho Singh)

Music: Khayyam
Lyrics: Sahir Ludhianvi

Don

Release Date: 12 May 1978
Director: Chandra Barot
Cast: Amitabh Bachchan (Don/Vijay), Zeenat Aman (Roma), Pran (Jasjit), DSP De Silva (Iftekhar), Om Shivpuri (Interpol officer Malik/Vardhan), Kamal Kapoor (Narang), Satyen Kappu (Inspector Verma), Shetty (Shaakaal), Helen (Kamini)
Music: Kalyanji–Anandji
Lyrics: Anjaan, Indivar

Kaala Patthar

Release Date: 1 August 1979
Director: Yash Chopra
Cast: Amitabh Bachchan (Vijay Pal Singh), Shashi Kapoor (Ravi Malhotra), Shatrughan Sinha (Mangal), Rakhee (Dr Sudha), Parveen Babi (Anita), Neetu Singh (Channo), Prem Chopra (Dhanraj Puri), Manmohan Krishna (Dhaba owner), Parikshit Sahni (Jagga), Macmohan (Rana the card shark)
Music: Rajesh Roshan
Lyrics: Sahir Ludhianvi

Dostana

Release Date: 17 October 1980
Director: Raj Khosla
Cast: Amitabh Bachchan (Vijay Verma), Shatrughan Sinha (Ravi Kapoor), Zeenat Aman (Sheetal Sahni), Pran (Tony), Prem Chopra (Daaga), Amrish Puri (Balwant), Helen (Sylvia),
Music: Laxmikant–Pyarelal
Lyrics: Anand Bakshi

Kranti

Release Date: 20 February 1981

Director: Manoj Kumar
Other writing credits: Manoj Kumar (Dialogue)
Cast: Dilip Kumar (Sanga / Kranti), Manoj Kumar (Bharat / Kranti), Shashi Kapoor (Shakti), Shatrughan Sinha (Karim Khan), Hema Malini (Meenakshi), Parveen Babi (Surili), Sarika (Sheetal), Prem Chopra (Shambhu Singh), Madan Puri (Sher Singh)
Music: Laxmikant–Pyarelal
Lyrics: Manoj Kumar, Santosh Anand

Shakti

Release Date: 1 October 1982
Director: Ramesh Sippy
Cast: Dilip Kumar (DCP Ashwini Kumar), Amitabh Bachchan (Vijay Kumar), Rakhee (Sheetal), Smita Patil (Roma), Kulbhushan Kharbanda (K.D. Narang), Amrish Puri (J.K.)
Music: R.D. Burman
Lyrics: Anand Bakshi

Zamana

Release Date: 22 February 1985
Director: Ramesh Talwar
Cast: Rajesh Khanna (Inspector Vinod Kumar), Rishi Kapoor (Ravi Kumar), Poonam Dhillon (Sheetal), Ranjeeta (Geeta), Girish Karnad (Satish Kumar, Vinod and Ravi's father), Kulbhushan Kharbanda (J.D.), Om Puri (Shyamlal)
Music: Usha Khanna
Lyrics: Majrooh Sultanpuri

Mr India

Release Date: 25 May 1987
Director: Shekhar Kapur
Cast: Anil Kapoor (Arun Verma/Mr India), Sridevi (Seema Soni), Amrish Puri (Mogambo), Satish Kaushik (Calendar), Annu Kapoor (Editor Gaitonde, Seema's boss), Sharat Saxena (Daaga), Ajit Vachani (Teja), Bob Christo

(Mr Walcott), Yunus Parvez (Maniklal), Harish Patel (Roopchand), Ashok Kumar (Professor Sinha)
Music: Laxmikant–Pyarelal
Lyrics: Javed Akhtar

Sources

Books

- *40 Retakes: Bollywood Classics You May Have Missed* (Avijit Ghosh, Tranquebar, 2013)
- *Amitabh Bachchan* [Bengali] (Soumya Bandyopadhyay, Anand Publishers, 1995)
- *...And Pran: A Biography* (Bunny Reuben, Harper Collins, 2011)
- *And Then One Day: A Memoir* (Naseeruddin Shah, Penguin India, 2014)
- *Bollywood: A History* (Mihir Bose, Tempus Publishing, 2006)
- *Dongri to Dubai: Six Decades of the Mumbai Mafia* (S. Hussain Zaidi, Roli Books, 2012)
- *Half a Rupee Stories* (Gulzar, Penguin India, 2013) for the short story 'Sahir and Jaadu'
- *In the Company of a Poet: Gulzar in Conversation with Nasreen Munni Kabir* (Rainlight/Rupa, 2012)
- *India After Gandhi: The History of the World's Largest Democracy* (Ramachandra Guha, Picador, 2008)
- *Mumbai Fables: A History of an Enchanted City* (Gyan Prakash, Princeton University Press, 2011)
- *On Cinema* (Utpal Dutt, Seagull Books, 2009)
- *Rachanasamagra* [Bengali] (Sachin Bhowmik, Dey's Publishing, 2011)
- *Rajesh Khanna: The Untold Story of India's First Superstar* (Yasser Usman, Penguin India, 2014)

- *RD Burman: The Man, The Music* (Anirudha Bhattacharjee & Balaji Vittal, Harper Collins India, 2011)
- *Satyajit Ray: The Inner Eye* (Andrew Robinson, IB Taurius, revised edition in 2004)
- *Sholay: Gabbar* (Saurav Mohapatra / Sascha Sippy / Sharad Devarajan / Ashwin Pande, Westland / Graphic India, 2014)
- *Sholay: The Graphic Novel* (Sascha Sippy / Sharad Devarajan, Westland / Graphic India, 2014)
- *Sholay: The Making of a Classic* (Anupama Chopra, Penguin India, 2000)
- *Talking Films: Conversations on Hindi Cinema with Javed Akhtar* (Nasreen Munni Kabir, Oxford University Press, 2000)
- *The Making of* Don (Krishna Gopalan, Rupa Publications, 2013)
- *To Be Or Not To Be Amitabh Bachchan* (Khalid Mohamed, Saraswati Creations, 2002)
- *Yahi Hai Rang Roop* [Marathi] (Anita Padhye, Shabd Prakashan)
- *Yash Chopra: Fifty Years in Indian Cinema* (Rachel Dwyer, Roli Books, 2002)

Magazines/Newspapers/Offline Resources

- Article on Salim-Javed by Sriram Raghavan, written for GraFTII (alumni association of FTII Pune)
- Seminar speech by Vinay Shukla on Reflections on the Popular Indian Cinema, delivered at Jawaharlal Nehru University
- Review of *Zanjeer* in *Times of India*, 13 May 1973
- Interview with Salim-Javed in *Filmfare*, 13 December 1974
- Movieman's Diary column (written by Shabd Kumar), *Film Industry*, February 1975
- Interview with Chinnappa Devar in *Filmfare*, 21 February 1975
- Review of *Sholay* in *Filmfare* dated 5 September 1975
- Coverage in *Trade Guide* (Page1), 3–9 October 1975
- Review of *Sholay* in *Hindustan Times*, 5 October 1975
- Interview of Manoj Kumar (by Promilla Kalhan) in *Hindustan Times*, 12 March 1977
- Review of *Amar Akbar Anthony* in *Hindustan Times*, 6 May 1977
- 'Manmohan Desai's Trilogy: A Celebration of the Inane' (by Haimanti Banerjee), *Times of India*, 21 May 1978

- Review of *Shaan* from *Trade Guide*, 13 December 1980
- Answer to a reader's question by Salim Khan in *Stardust*, October 1981
- Interview of Javed Akhtar in *Stardust*, November 1981
- Interview of Salim Khan in *Stardust*, February 1982
- From the gossip column 'Without Makeup' in *Hindustan Times*, 8 March 1987
- Interview with Nasir Husain in *Screen* magazine, 22 March 2002
- Profile of Farhan Akhtar in *Caravan Style & Living* magazine (by Mayank Shekhar), March 2013

Online Resources – Video

- Farhan Akhtar on The Boss Dialogues https://www.youtube.com/watch?v=-xQ-UMtrIiE
- Farhan Akhtar on Salim Khan https://www.youtube.com/watch?v=1NfvPvPKVRM
- Helen on *Movie Mahal* (made for Britain's Channel 4) https://www.youtube.com/watch?v=bXwiixqa2Hs
- Javed Akhtar on *Galaxzee* https://www.youtube.com/watch?v=LYsFVB_r124
- Javed Akhtar on *Guftagu* (Rajya Sabha TV) https://www.youtube.com/watch?v=aXMfu5yMy2A
- Javed Akhtar on Teacher's Achievement Awards present Achievers' Club with Vir Sanghvi https://www.youtube.com/watch?v=XqZlw0VozJc
- Javed Akhtar delivering the 5th BD Pande Memorial Lecture at Almora https://www.youtube.com/watch?v=quuXrx-KDAI
- Javed Akhtar (and Shabana Azmi) on *Koffee with Karan*, Season 2, Episode 23
- Javed Akhtar (and Shabana Azmi) on *Rendezvous with Simi Garewal* (2000) https://www.youtube.com/watch?v=4nSAa1eujbI
- Salim Khan on *Cinema and Me* (Tehelka TV) https://www.youtube.com/watch?v=MaW2vJ2xe2k
- Salim Khan on *Guftagu* (Rajya Sabha TV) https://www.youtube.com/watch?v=A_M1wV28Ano
- Salim Khan with Komal Nahta (ETC Networks) https://www.youtube.com/watch?v=YuHEe0DxqW8
- Salim Khan on The Boss Dialogues https://www.youtube.com/watch?v=h3mxTWGxSKM

- Salim Khan and Javed Akhtar interviewed by Rajeev Masand (CNN IBN) https://www.youtube.com/watch?v=oTBM45Ek1t4
- Salman Khan (and Salim Khan) on *Koffee with Karan*, Season 4, Episode 1
- Zoya Akhtar on *Cinema & Me* (Tehelka TV) https://www.youtube.com/watch?v=IbcABY5c6vw

Online Resources – Text

- Amitabh Bachchan interview in *Man's World* http://www.mansworldindia.com/cover-stars/being-amitabh-bachchan/
- Angry Young Men Wikipedia entry http://en.wikipedia.org/wiki/Angry_young_men
- Anil Kapoor interview http://www.rediff.com/movies/2007/jul/27anil.htm
- Arjun re-appraisal by Sukanya Verma http://www.sukanyaverma.com/2014/09/revisiting-the-angst-and-fury-of-sunny-deols-arjun/
- Bhawana Somaaya column on writers of Hindi cinema http://bhawanasomaaya.com/blog/2010/08/02/day-52-mere-paas-kalam-hai/
- Chandra Barot interview in *The Hindu Cinema Plus* http://www.thehindu.com/features/cinema/my-first-break-chandra-barot/article3631520.ece
- Chasnala Mine Disaster summary http://www.history.com/this-day-in-history/coal-mine-explodes-in-india
- *Deewaar* fun facts http://movies.ndtv.com/bollywood/indian-cinema-100-12-fun-facts-about-deewar-633015
- *Deewaar* re-appraisal by Jai Arjun Singh http://jaiarjun.blogspot.com/2005/04/revisiting-deewar.html
- *Don* (1978) facts around its making http://www.imdb.com/title/tt0077451/trivia
- *Don* (2006) appraisal on Jai Arjun Singh's blog http://jaiarjun.blogspot.in/2006/11/not-review-but.html
- Excel Entertainment's profile in *DNA* (10th June, 2012) http://www.highbeam.com/doc/1P3-2682371851.html
- Farhan Akhtar profile as part of a review of *The Fakir of Venice* in *Hollywood Reporter* http://www1.hollywoodreporter.com/hr/film-reviews/the-fakir-of-venice-film-review-1003966552.story

- Gabbar Singh's origins, as imagined by Soumik Sen http://ibnlive. in.com/news/how-gabbar-singh-became-a-feared-renegade-director-soumik-sen-blogs/443077-8-66.html
- *Haathi Mere Saathi* re-appraisal by Rajiv Vijayakar http://www. bollywoodhungama.com/movies/features/type/view/id/3718/
- Honey Irani interview on iDiva.com http://idiva.com/news-entertainment/honey-irani-on-divorce-survival-shabana-azmi/13218
- Javed Akhtar internet chat with fans (organised by Rediff) http://www. rediff.com/chat/0408chat.htm
- Javed Akhtar's reminisces on his website http://javedakhtar.com/Apne-Baare-Mein.php
- Javed Akhtar speech by at Indian Screenwriters' Conference (organized by Film Writers' Association), February 2013. Notes taken by an attendee: http://moifightclub.com/2013/02/26/notes-from-fwa-indian-screenwriters-conference-day-1/
- Javed Akhtar on *Walk the Talk with Shekhar Gupta* http://archive. indianexpress.com/news/creating-the-angry-young-man-was-not-a-conscious-decision/1120627/0
- Javed Akhtar and Farhan Akhtar interview on Rediff.com http://www. rediff.com/movies/2006/oct/17farhan.htm
- Kaala Patthar review on movie blog Post Punk Cinema Club http://p-pcc.blogspot.in/2007/09/kaala-patthar-1979.html
- Kader Khan interview http://www.haham.net/kader_khan_interview. htm
- Kitne Ad The ... (Ads inspired by Sholay) http://articles.economictimes. indiatimes.com/2005-10-19/news/42809522_1_sholay-gabbar-singh-ramesh-sippy
- *Lakshya* review by Mayank Shekhar http://thew14.com/movie/mayank-shekhars-review-lakshya/
- Loveleen Tandon interview on IBNLive.com http://ibnlive.in.com/ news/slumdogs--codirector-speaks-up/82472-8.html
- 'Mogambo Khush Hua' on Shekhar Kapur's blog http://shekharkapur. com/blog/2010/06/mr-india-mogambo-khush-hua-the-creating-of-mogambo/
- 'Movie Star as Auteur' by Jai Arjun Singh http://jaiarjun.blogspot. in/2012/02/movie-star-as-auteur.html

- Mumtaz interview: http://www.bollywoodlife.com/news-gossip/mumtaz-many-big-heroes-refused-to-work-with-me/
- Prakash Mehra interview on the making of *Zanjeer* http://www.rediff.com/entertai/1998/may/19zan.htm
- Pran's biography http://www.imdb.com/name/nm0695199/bio
- Rajesh Khanna article by Malavika Sangghvi http://www.business-standard.com/article/beyond-business/original-superstar-112063000003_1.html
- Ramesh Sippy interview by Baradwaj Rangan http://www.thehindu.com/todays-paper/tp-features/tp-metroplus/the-man-behind-gabbar/article5207822.ece
- Ramesh Sippy interview by Baradwaj Rangan https://baradwajrangan.wordpress.com/2013/10/06/those-days-we-could-afford-to-launch-a-film-without-a-script/
- Ramesh Sippy interview in *The Hindu* http://www.thehindu.com/features/friday-review/still-got-the-fire/article5120201.ece
- Ritesh Sidhwani (and Farhan Akhtar) interview in *India Today* http://indiatoday.intoday.in/story/india-today-38-anniversary-actor-farhan-akhtar-producer-ritesh-sidhwani/1/331204.html
- Salim Khan interview in *The Hindu* http://www.thehindu.com/todays-paper/tp-features/tp-fridayreview/my-first-break-salim-khan/article789674.ece
- Salim Khan interview in *Hindustan Times* http://www.hindustantimes.com/television/salim-khan-behind-mahabharata/article1-1115883.aspx
- Salim Khan interview in *HT Brunch* http://www.hindustantimes.com/brunch-stories/i-ve-never-written-a-scene-or-dialogue-that-you-can-t-watch-with-your-family-salim-khan/article1-1296019.aspx
- Salim Khan's first person account of *Sholay* in *Open* magazine http://www.openthemagazine.com/article/arts-letters/sholay-the-beginning
- Salim Khan interview in *Open* magazine http://www.openthemagazine.com/article/living/salman-khans-father-on-his-superstar-son
- Salim Khan interviewed in *Telegraph* http://www.telegraphindia.com/1101114/jsp/7days/story_13173933.jsp
- Salim-Javed patching up, news item in the *Times of India* http://timesofindia.indiatimes.com/entertainment/hindi/bollywood/news/Salim-KhanJaved-AkhtarZanjeer-Salim-Javed/articleshow/25355690.cms

- Salim-Javed reunion possibilities, news item in the *Telegraph* http://www.telegraphindia.com/1111228/jsp/entertainment/story_14933643.jsp#.VSrBJfmUcgQ
- Satyajit Ray interviewed in *India Today* http://indiatoday.intoday.in/gallery/satyajit-ray-91st-brithday/10/7060.html
- *Seeta Aur Geeta* re-appraisal on Carla Miriam Levy's blog http://www.filmigeek.com/2006/10/seeta_aur_geeta.html
- *Seeta Aur Geeta* review by Dinesh Raheja http://m.rediff.com/%0Amovies/2003/may/28dinesh.htm
- Shabana Azmi interview on *Firstpost* http://www.firstpost.com/bollywood/theres-not-a-single-romantic-bone-in-javeds-body-shabana-472175.html
- *Shakti* re-appraisal by Sukanya Verma http://www.sukanyaverma.com/2013/08/shakti-dilip-kumar-big-bs-ultimate-face-off-in-ramesh-sippys-1982-drama/
- Shatrughan Sinha interview in the *Times of India* http://timesofindia.indiatimes.com/entertainment/hindi/bollywood/news/Amitabh-hit-me-and-cried-Shatrughan-Sinha/articleshow/11385622.cms
- Slumdog Millionaire*'s Bollywood Ancestors* by Amitava Kumar http://www.vanityfair.com/hollywood/2008/12/slumdog-millionaires-bollywood-ancestors
- 'We Don't Need No Intermission', column by Shubhra Gupta in the *Indian Express* http://indianexpress.com/article/entertainment/bollywood/we-dont-need-no-intermission/
- *Zanjeer* (1973) turning 40, news item in *Hindustan Times* http://www.hindustantimes.com/bollywood/amitabh-bachchan-s-zanjeer-turns-40/article1-1063080.aspx
- *Zanjeer* (2013) news item http://businessofcinema.com/bollywood_news/salim-javed-finally-win-in-the-zanjeer-remake-case/100008
- *Zanjeer* (2013) news item in *DNA* http://www.dnaindia.com/entertainment/report-salim-javed-settle-with-producers-over-copyright-of-zanjeer-1884382
- *Zanjeer* (2013) news item in the *Times of India* http://timesofindia.indiatimes.com/entertainment/bollywood/news-interviews/Salim-Javed-are-the-rightful-owners-of-Zanjeer-script-observes-DSC/articleshow/19146930.cms

* *Zanjeer* (2013) sequence of events by Subhash K. Jha on Bhaskar.com http://daily.bhaskar.com/article/ENT-salman-khan-fails-to-rescue-neo--zanjeer-4231541-NOR.html
* Zoya Akhtar interview in *Mid-Day* http://www.mid-day.com/articles/writer-in-me-very-strong-says-zoya-akhtar/189921
* Zoya Akhtar interview on Rediff.com http://www.rediff.com/movies/slide-show/slide-show-1-interview-with-zoya-akhtar/20090907.htm

Interviews by Author

* Carla Miriam Levy (http://www.filmigeek.com), January 2015 (Online chat)
* Kamlesh Pandey, Mumbai, 22 March 2014
* Kaushik Bhaumik (http://www.jnu.ac.in/Faculty/kbhaumik/), Delhi, 3 April, 2014
* Khalid Mohamed, June 2014 (Email)
* K.Y. Thomas, January 2015 (Skype)
* Mansoor Khan, March 2014 (Telephonic)
* Rajat Aroraa, Mumbai, 6 November 2014
* Ramesh Talwar, Mumbai, 5 December 2013
* Salim Khan, Mumbai, 21 March 2014
* Saurav Mohapatra, December 2014 (Email)
* Sriram Raghavan, Mumbai, 23 August 2013
* Sukanya Verma (http://sukanyaverma.com), September 2014 (Email)
* Vinay Shukla, Mumbai, 23 August 2013

Copyright Acknowledgements

Grateful acknowledgement is made to the following for permission to reprint copyright material:

Magna Publishing Co Ltd for the Salim Khan interview and the later photograph of Salim–Javed

Kumar Gaurav for the poster of *Naam*

Jagdish Aurangabadkar for Salim–Javed's earlier picture taken by the Late Shyam Aurangabadkar

Screen magazine for the picture of Salim–Javed popping champagne and the group photo from the *Deewaar* premiere

Index